Cambridge Studies in Ethnomusicology

General Editor: John Blacking

Polish folk music

A study of Polish folk music is especially enlightening as it both reveals the history and practice of a musical tradition and offers an illuminating view of a culture and its social activities. Within her study, Anna Czekanowska analyses the vocal and instrumental traditions of Polish folk music, tracing the background history, the influences of geography and politics, and the practice, often within contemporary society, of such social events as the harvest, the solstice, and weddings. The function of folk culture within contemporary life, for both Polish and non-Polish inhabitants of the country, is examined, and Czekanowska also discusses the birth of Polish ethnomusicology as a discipline and details some methodological aspects for research. This study contributes to a greater understanding and appreciation of Polish music and, in a wider aspect, of Slavonic culture.

The book contains numerous illustrations of instruments and cultural events, music examples, maps, a discography, and a bibliography.

Cambridge Studies in Ethnomusicology

General Editor: John Blacking

Ethnomusicological research has shown that there are many different ingredients in musical systems. The core of this series will therefore be studies of the logics of different musics, analysed in the contexts of the societies in which they were composed and performed. The books will address specific problems related to potential musical ability and practice, such as how music is integrated with dance, theatre and the visual arts, how children develop musical perception and skills in different cultures and how musical activities affect the acquisition of other skills. Musical transcriptions will be included, sometimes introducing indigenous systems of notation. Cassettes will accompany most books.

Already published:
Bonnie C. Wade, *Khyāl: Creativity within North India's Classical Music Tradition*
Regula Burckhardt Qureshi, *Sufi Music of India and Pakistan: Sound, Context and Meaning in Qawwali*
Peter Cooke, *The Fiddle Tradition of the Shetland Isles*
Anthony Seeger, *Why Suyá Sing: A Musical Anthropology of an Amazonian People*
James Kippen, *The Tabla of Lucknow: A Cultural Analysis of a Musical Tradition*
John Baily, *Music of Afghanistan: Professional Musicians in the City of Herat*
Bell Yung, *Cantonese Opera: Performance as Creative Process*
Hormoz Farhat, *The* Dastgāh *Concept in Persian Music*

Polish folk music

Slavonic heritage – Polish tradition –
contemporary trends

Anna Czekanowska

Director of the Institute of Musicology
University of Warsaw

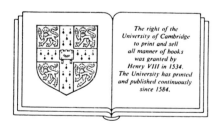

The right of the
University of Cambridge
to print and sell
all manner of books
was granted by
Henry VIII in 1534.
The University has printed
and published continuously
since 1584.

Cambridge University Press
Cambridge
New York   Port Chester
Melbourne   Sydney

CAMBRIDGE UNIVERSITY PRESS
Cambridge, New York, Melbourne, Madrid, Cape Town, Singapore, São Paulo

Cambridge University Press
The Edinburgh Building, Cambridge CB2 2RU, UK

Published in the United States of America by Cambridge University Press, New York

www.cambridge.org
Information on this title: www.cambridge.org/9780521300902

First published 1990
This digitally printed first paperback version 2006

A catalogue record for this publication is available from the British Library

Library of Congress Cataloguing in Publication data
Czekanowska-Kulinska, Anna.
  Polish folk music: Slavonic heritage, Polish tradition,
contemporary trends / Anna Czekanowska.
        p.   cm. – (Cambridge studies in ethnomusicology)
  Bibliography.
  ISBN 0 521 30090 8
  1. Folk music – Poland – History and criticism.   I. Title.
II. Series.
ML3677.C9   1990
781.62′9185 – dc20   89–17250 CIP

ISBN-13 978-0-521-30090-2 hardback
ISBN-10 0-521-30090-8 hardback

ISBN-13 978-0-521-02797-7 paperback
ISBN-10 0-521-02797-7 paperback

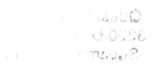

Contents

Illustrations and maps

ILLUSTRATIONS

MAPS

Preface

A study of Polish folk music involves reflection on the complexity of cultural phenomena which have been created and developed in this transitional territory. It is a study of historical processes which resulted in the creation of a culture against a differentiated background of west and east European components. It is also a study of the cultural reality that has developed in the area between northern and southern Europe and which is evident in both the geographical and the historical sense. Finally, it is a study of a culture very differentiated in its social structure, clearly hierarchic and conservative, but at the same time open to innovations, as well as absorbing and assimilating many influences and migrations of people from other parts of Europe and Asia.

The complex and transformed culture of contemporary Poland is characterized by a strong integrating power articulating characteristic national features and concentrating on the basic necessity to preserve the continuity of traditional patterns and national uniqueness during times of global transformation and change.

Thus, this interpretation of Polish folk music should be seen as an attempt to approach the underlying transformational processes as comprehensively as possible, i.e., by applying a number of different methods.

So there are the consequences of World War II and mass emigration, as well as the distortions of traditional social structure which have transformed Polish culture in recent years. No less important are the consequences of the modern technological revolution, as well as recent changes in institutions and in the system itself which here contributed to the transformation of contemporary culture. Naturally enough, the accumulated results of progressive changes and the fresh impact of the recent diversity of trends have transformed traditional culture to a greater extent than ever before.

The transformation of Polish culture can be seen today not only in cultural artifacts, but even more in the consciousness of the people, in their habits, ways of thinking and styles of life. These recent changes have, however, also stimulated a re-evaluation of traditional resources.

This analysis of Polish folk music points to the specific nature of musical phenomena and to the intrinsic value of music in the processes of communication. The directness of musical messages and their integrational power are especially significant in the social mobilization and psychological stabilization of contemporary humanity. It is precisely this value that enhances the position of music in contemporary Polish society and makes music so much demanded and needed. It leads to the discovery of the traditional legacy and to the essence of the transformation processes that are taking place today. In evaluating the social function of folk music and its significance as communication, it is also necessary to take account of its aesthetic qualities, which transform the basic media of transmission into works of art.

The main objective of this study is to present a vision of Polish folk music as it has developed often along different streams in which past and present coexist side by side. It is also a vision of culture that has been created against a background of varied historical, social and religious traditions while being integrated and transformed into a unique quality which must be identified as being clearly Polish.

1 *Introduction*

1.1 Basic concepts and notions

Polish culture is one of the most homogeneous cultures in eastern and central Europe, but it is also one with a very diverse background. The heterogeneous aspects of Polish culture will be discussed here in their ethno-historical, geographical and psychological senses, with related factors of space and time, demography and social structure all taken into consideration. Historical data are obviously of fundamental importance, though other factors must not be overlooked. Geographical and social factors are of basic significance, not least for certain psychologically motivated aspects of artistic activity and perceptual attitudes. These components can be clearly discerned in performance situations. The character of these situational responses and patterns of communication, especially non-verbal and musical, make vital contributions to the creation of a national character and style. One can assume that psychological factors, above others, express and confirm the concept of self-identity in both the individual and social senses.

This introduction will consider some basic notions that are of central significance in an examination of Polish folk music: the concepts of *ethnicity* and *nationality*, *folk* and *region*, and finally the concept of *style*.

The concept of ethnicity will be understood in this study basically as a phenomenon of social homogeneity motivated by a recognized common heritage linked to a notion of genetic legacy. This kind of homogeneity will be seen to have its roots in the deepest strata of common prehistory. At the same time, however, we should like to stress the significance of social recognition in the acts of ethnic identification, pointing out the rôle of 'the underlying motivation that leads human beings to seek solidarity with those whom they recognize as being "of the same people" or as "sharing descent"' (Keyes 1981: 6), i.e., accepting that 'Man is an "incomplete animal" who completes himself through culture he himself has created and, moreover, not through culture in general but through highly particular forms of it' (Geertz, 1973: 49; cf. Francis 1978 and Berghe 1978). The concept of nationality, however, will be interpreted in more specific and recent historical terms and understood more as a dynamic aspect than as a product of migration and other historical processes. Such an understanding of nationality is far more dependent upon the social and political consciousness of a society.

The precise differentiation between the concepts of nation and folk will also be of great importance for this study. I shall suggest limiting the concept of folk to Béla Bartók's definition (Bartók 1925: 1. English translation 1931: 1–2). By contrast, the concept of nationality we understand in more functional terms. Thus, the concept of nationality will be applied to the nature of the historical and political structures which were developing in Europe in modern times, between the sixteenth and twentieth centuries. Some authors, however, believe that this concept also applied to the societies of mediaeval Europe (Zientara 1985: 330–60). Nevertheless, it is obvious that the concept of nationality hardly applies to tribes and peoples that were still very dispersed and without any clear tendency to identify themselves as homogeneous societies. Similarly, we cannot easily apply this concept for the complex and transformed structures of our own time, i.e., to the multi-national and multi-ethnic systems controlled by political power alone. Still, it should be stressed that the idea of ethnic or national identity remains a vital psychological factor. This idea developed basically in Europe during the last century, at first in the strongest and most homogeneous political structures. Then after spreading to other groups it was transformed and now frequently acts as a factor of social unification and of opposition to dominating upper classes and nations. Ethnic and national identity became especially important with the decline of monarchy, and have been growing with developing democracy. In many cases this has resulted in a shift in emphasis from ethnic to social identity.

It is interesting to note that in Poland's case the loss of state sovereignty coincided with the age of general national enlightenment, and the birth of national consciousness in Europe. While discussing the concept of folk and nation in more detailed terms, one should be aware of the dependence of these concepts not only upon the data of empirical material, but also upon the assumptions and traditions of individual scholarship. For example, Bartók's approach to folk music and his attempt to define it as peasants' music, consists of two parts, the second of which is frequently overlooked. This second part stresses the functional aspect of the process of assimilation and acceptance (Czekanowska 1981: 51). The limitation to peasant society, however, is still evident in Bartók's approach. One can apply this approach, with its obvious limitations, to the traditional rural societies of parts of eastern Europe. Russian and Soviet scholarship, however, have emphasized a much broader understanding of the concept of folk, clearly opposed to the limitations of this approach. Soviet scholarship relies more heavily upon ideological than empirical thought. Nevertheless, one should stress again common aspects of the Russian and French traditions. In both French and Russian 'revolutionary' traditions, the tendency is ideologically motivated and emphasizes the significance of the *populus* understood in the widest sense of the term, being clearly opposed to the concept of the *vulgus* that is limited to the lower strata of class society (cf. *populaire, narodraya*) (Czekanowska 1978a: 553–4; Danckert 1939b: 35).

Finally, it should be stressed that the concept of region should not be limited to the products of historical and geographical processes. In recent years, regional and spatial studies have shown region to be a dynamically changing structure. There have been several attempts to identify region in relation to an empirical reality. In the present study we shall consider simultaneously very different and sometimes contradictory factors. Therefore, the concept of region will be used as an analytical tool, and will be examined as it relates to the empirical data (Wróbel 1965; Pokshishevsky 1975) and as it functions in connection with the different ideological programmes of so-called regionalism.

In conclusion we should like to emphasize the concept of region as being understood in a much broader sense than ethnicity, i.e., as a state of relative equilibrium, in which the balance is the product of interactions between the different systems (historical, geographical, social). The latter and their relations may be classified as supersystems or subsystems, dependent on the situation. It must also be added that, according to more recent approaches employed by social scientists, the significance of psychological involvement is evidently growing. This particularly concerns the psychologically motivated recognition of bound-aries. The latter dominates the recent concept of region – especially its spatial recognition (Strassoldo 1987).

Finally, the concept of a style[1] has to be re-examined. We suggest formulating it once again as the concept of a certain balance attained in a given period and in a concrete context, i.e., as the unification of individual as well as historical and social factors, both being to a great extent determined by the functions which the cultural phenomena under study have to fulfil (Shapiro 1956).

1.2   Poland's diverse background

1.2.1 Ethnohistorical factors

Records show that the Polish state was established in the latter half of the tenth century, basically from the five most important Slavonic tribes.[2] According to H. Ross (1974: 638), the state covered an area of approximately 96,500 square miles and was populated by 250,000 people (see Map 1). These tribes were dominated by the largest and strongest tribe, known as the Polans. Ross continues, 'The Polish heartland crossed by the River Warta, was domi-nated by the Polanie – open country dwellers after whom the Polish nation was later named.' The four other important tribes were the Vistulans, Silesians, Mazovians and Pomeranians. At that time the tribal organization of the western Slavs was quite well developed, and this good organization enabled them to dominate a large territory. It should be stressed that 'these Polish tribes shared a fundamentally common culture and language and were considerably more closely related to one another than were the Germanic tribes who founded the Franconian or German Kingdom between 800 and 1024 AD' (ibid.).

Certain geographical data should also be taken into consideration as having contributed to the establishment of the ethnic and regional structure. Geographical factors are especially important in the development of communication and transportation systems. Geographical and even mineralogical maps are very helpful in a geo-historical interpretation. For example, a river-system is obviously the most important factor in illuminating the processes of interaction that occurred in primaeval times, as well as in explaining the isolation of peoples. A knowledge of geological and geographical structures may also contribute to a better understanding of the cultural creativity and social activities of the people.

To appreciate the historical perspective of Polish regional diversity, four facts are of vital importance. First, the roots of Poland's regional setting lie in the 'pre-state' tribal diversity. Secondly, the so-called 'Provincial Dispersion' (1138–1314)[3] was extremely important for regional differences. Thirdly, the network of the administrative division of the Polish Commonwealth in the period between the fifteenth and eighteenth centuries (see Map 2a) was

---

[1]   See Lippmann 1965: 'eine Sache der Stimmigkeit, der gegenseitigen Entsprechung von Form, Material, Inhalt und Funktion: aber tiefer erfasst, ist es ein Abbild des menschlichen Strebens, das hinter dem musikalischen Werke steht'. Also Pascall 1980: 'manner of discourse ... mode of expression ... surface of appearance ... shape of detail'.

[2]   Chronicles and geographical descriptions of Carolingian, Saxon, Arabian and Byzantine origin.

[3]   Prince Bolesław III, the Wry-Mouthed, divided Poland among his sons in AD 1138. The Polish Kingdom was restored after the period of 'Provincial Dispersion' in 1295, when Prince Przemysław was crowned king.

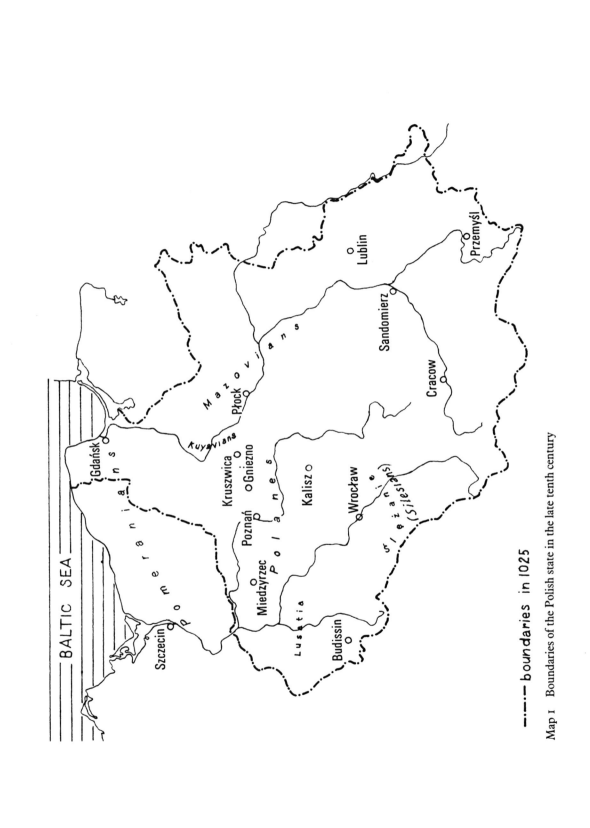

BALTIC SEA

Szczecin

Gdańsk

P o m e r a n i a n s

Kuyavians

Mazovians

Płock

Kruszwica

Poznań o Gniezno

Miedzyrzec

P o l a n e s

Kalisz o

L u s a t i a

Budissin

Wrocław

S l e z a n i e
(Silesians)

Lublin

Sandomierz

Cracow

Przemyśl

–·–·– boundaries in 1025

Map 1   Boundaries of the Polish state in the late tenth century

very influential. Finally, at the end of the eighteenth century the Partition of Poland, between Russia, Prussia and Austria (see Map 2b), determined basic aspects of the development of modern Poland.[4]

Certain regional phenomena can be explained by these four facts. For example, the visible contrast and difference between Great Poland on the one hand and Mazovia, Silesia, Pomerania and Little Poland on the other can be understood as a relic of tribal diversity, the result of which was the opposition of the Polanie's heritage to the other Slavs' legacy. Similarly, as evidence of the so-called 'Provincial Dispersion', one witnesses the emergence of the partition of Little Poland into northern and southern, with the southern capital in Cracow, and the northern capital in Sandomierz, as well as the partition of Silesia into upper and lower parts with capitals in Smogorzów and Opole. The importance of the network of voivodships, which remained in power until the first partition of Poland in 1772, has been demonstrated by Oskar Kolberg, one of the leading experts on folk culture. The regional division based on the network of 'pre-partition' voivodships formed the basis of Kolberg's great monograph (Kolberg 1857–1907, new ed. 1961).

The partition of Poland at the end of the eighteenth century was of lesser importance for the diversification of folk culture, but should be considered nonetheless. There were obvious differences in the levels of civilization of Russia, Prussia and Austria, especially in their economic and social structures. For example, the development of transport and communication systems in the western part of Poland, the expansion of industrial centres in the central parts of Poland, and the flourishing cultural life in the cities of southern Poland can be explained by the influence of the partitioning powers. However, the loss of political sovereignty at a time of social and economic advancement in the nineteenth century had tragic consequences for Poland's national fate, despite some progress and growth that took place during that time. The lack of political independence halted national development and severed natural ties in the social and economic infrastructure for over a century. Poland did not exist in the political sense for an extended period of time during which other countries developed modern civilizations. Political partition also preserved regional diversity.

1.2.2. Geographical factors

To a certain extent geographical factors were of greater importance in Poland's regional diversity than were historical events. In this case, there is less evidence, because there are no direct records. A map reveals the essential evidence of Poland's post-glacial heritage. This is especially obvious in the northern part of Poland, which boasts a great number of lakes, marshes, and post-glacial forests, as well as a relatively sparse population. Conversely, the southern part of Poland has been very densely settled since the earliest times. The clear morphological contrast between the lowlands in the northern and central parts of the country and the highlands and mountains in the south and south-west is also of considerable significance. The oldest mountain formation, the Świętokrzyskie, cuts across the middle of the country and divides north from south. Actually, this old tectonic formation halted the progress of the glacier centuries ago. The geological structure described above shaped the

---

[4] The partitions of Poland took place in 1772, 1793 and 1795. Poland was restored as a sovereign state in 1918.

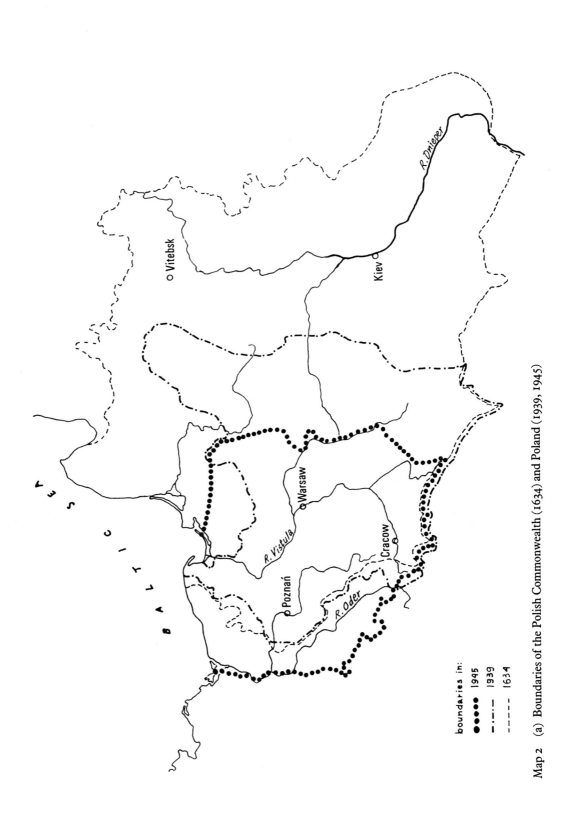

Map 2 (a) Boundaries of the Polish Commonwealth (1634) and Poland (1939, 1945)

boundaries in:
•••• 1945
—·—·— 1939
————— 1634

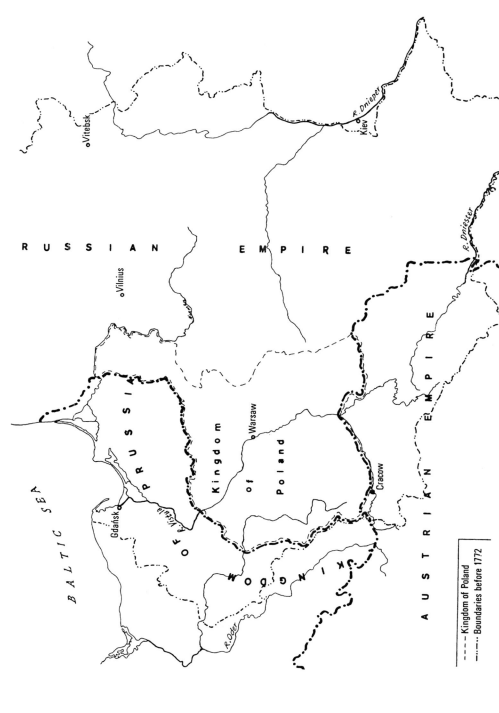

RUSSIAN EMPIRE

BALTIC SEA

oVitebsk

oVilnius

oWarsaw

Gdańsk

Cracow

Kiev

R. Dnieper

R. Dniester

KINGDOM OF PRUSSIA

Kingdom of Poland

AUSTRIAN EMPIRE

R. Vistula

R. Oder

--- Kingdom of Poland
···· Boundaries before 1772

(b) The partitions of the Polish Commonwealth

river-system, and all rivers flow north. From the geographical point of view Poland should be considered as a country located on the border between northern and central Europe. However, from a historical point of view, the differences between the west and the east, that is between central Europe and eastern Europe, are of much greater importance.

There is no doubt that the geographical structure of Poland influenced many different human activities, economically, psychologically and sociologically. The people from the open country of the lowlands communicated and behaved differently from the forest-, marsh- or mountain-dwellers. One can detect at least four kinds of economy in the past. The economy of the north of Poland was based on hunting, fishing, gathering natural products and bee-keeping, whereas agriculture and sheep-farming prevailed in the central and southern parts of the country. Arable farming and cattle-breeding developed in the lowlands and highlands of the centrally located areas, as well as in the countryside of the former steppes in the south-eastern regions. Sheep- and cattle-farming flourished in the mountains, particularly in the Carpathian area. Geographical conditions had a very important effect upon transport and communications and also influenced population density, and the shaping of the landscape. Moreover, people from isolated enclaves and scattered settlements displayed a mentality and sensitivity different from that of the inhabitants of crowded villages. The people from the open steppes, the mountains and the forest were long accustomed to greater space, in all aspects of their lives, and they seem to have felt a greater need for freedom.

The social structure of many ethnic groups was clearly conditioned by geographical factors. The vast forests provided game for hunting, and for a long time the forests were under the control of the ruling authorities. Almost without exception these territories belonged to kings or princes, and so the forest-dwellers preserved a great amount of freedom since there were no governors to intervene between them and the king or prince. This kind of personal freedom greatly influenced the development of Polish folk culture in certain areas.[5]

Geographical factors also influenced natural routes of transport. Rivers and mountains not only shaped the natural borders but also helped to establish inter-group contact. For centuries rivers were the natural means of transport and migration. People travelled north and south along the River Vistula and its tributaries. The Carpathian Mountains were also a landmark for migrations. People migrated toward both north and south across the mountains and from east to west. The southerly migrations across the Carpathians involved wandering cattle-breeders, whereas the goat and sheep nomads travelled in the opposite direction.

Toponymic material supplies us with ample data, basically concerning environmental, historical and sociological phenomena. There exists, for instance, much information concerning the quality of soils taken from Polish toponymic resources. The adjectives red, white and black convey a general impression of the landscape. They most probably describe areas of red moss (red), sand (white) or marsh (black).[6] All the data mentioned above illuminate

---

[5] This concerns the concept of the so-called 'Royal territories' (Królewszczyzna) covering, for example, the forests of Kurpie (Puszcza Kurpiowska), of Sandomierz, of Radom and of Podhale. See Potkański 1922 and 1924.

[6] In place-names we find a predominance of certain adjectives, for example the adjectives red, white and black. In the borderland of Mazovia the popularity of the adjective *biały* (white) is evident in the names Byelsk, Byała, Byałoruś; the adjectives *czerwony* or *krasny* (red) prevail in the names of the south-eastern border lands (Czerwonogród, Krasnobród, Krasno, Krasnystaw); and the adjective *czarny* (black) dominates on the Polish–Lithuanian border or in Polesye (Czarna Ruś, Czernobyl). Black can also be interpreted as related to the deep forest.

Polish environmental conditions in the past[7] and contribute to a better understanding of social and historical phenomena.[8]

1.2.3 Social and political factors

Polish social structure belongs to one of the typical traditional European systems. Nevertheless, it has certain peculiarities. A developed bourgeoisie and city community did not play a significant rôle in the evolution of the traditional Polish system. However, recent research has shown that cultural interaction and exchange occurred as early as the fifteenth century between the city population and other sections of the populace, including the peasant class. The Polish gentry dominated and replaced certain other middle social strata. With time, the gentry separated into upper, middle and lower strata. In a sense, the development of the middle and lower classes of gentry replaced the urban middle class, which was so important in classic European society. Polish cities began to develop in the thirteenth century, but the growth of an urban population and bourgeoisie was very slow until the twentieth century. Foreign residents made a greater impact on the economic and cultural life of the cities than did the native Poles, with both Germans and Jews strongly supporting Polish trade and commerce.

The domination of Polish society by the nobility since the fourteenth century had significant political and social consequences, and the rise of the minor gentry was still the most important factor in the development of Polish social structure between the Middle Ages and modern times. This class developed a large population in territory along the borders as a consequence of several wars with neighbours to the east. The cultural interchange between this 'new' class of nobility and traditional peasant society was rather limited, despite their common rural background. The 'new' nobility represented a 'new' mentality and had a specific attitude towards tradition – which was understood more in national than in ethnic terms. Many song texts contribute data enriching our knowledge of the social consciousness of these people, i.e., the geographical orientation and education of the minor gentry. Representatives of this 'new' class, despite their modest economic means, developed various contacts with the outside world. For example, owing to their political and military activities they travelled widely. The psychological features of this social group were very important in the creation of the Polish national mentality, in both positive and negative senses.[9] In an attempt at comparison, we may assume that the emergence of the minor gentry was a partial substitute for the middle classes of other European societies. The urban population of foreign descent remained relatively isolated, particularly in the seventeenth and eighteenth centuries, though the process of Polonization was constantly on the increase, so that sometimes only personal names and religious affiliation betrayed their foreign descent.

In the nineteenth century fundamental changes in Polish social structure took place as a

---

[7] It concerns the names of trees and bushes. For example the maple (*jawor*) is the basis of several names – Jaworów, Jaworki, Jaworzno; the linden tree (*lipa*) is seen in the names Lipno, Lipnica, Lipowo; the oak (*dąb*) is seen in the names Dębno, Dębica, Dąbrowa, and the guelder-rose (*kalina*) in the name of Kalinowszczyzna, etc.

[8] The names of *Wola* or *Sloboda* mean freedom, and were given to the places populated by free peasantry.

[9] There are records documenting many social conflicts between the peasant and minor gentry classes. The peasant songs stress the economic inefficiency of the gentry, their unreasonable pride and poor hygiene.

direct consequence of industrialization. Only since the second part of the nineteenth century can one speak of the emergence of the urban working classes, and of the interaction between peasant and proletarian cultures. The peasants became 'truly free' people in the Russian part of Poland as late as 1864. The 'free' peasantry finally achieved the opportunity to travel and to emigrate to the new industrial centres both in Poland and abroad. The contacts and links with the outside world were no longer a privilege of the upper and middle classes alone; but, at the same time, the rapid development of a capitalistic system differentiated the social structure in the economic sense more deeply than ever before. These two facts – the development of social consciousness and poor economic conditions – created the background for bitter social conflicts, mass movements, emigrations and revolutions.

The Polish social structure of the nineteenth century had its own peculiar features, among the most important being the emergence of a new class of 'peasant-workers' (Kolberg vol. 20, 1887b: 641; *Slownik Geograficzny* vol. IV, 1883: 355), who exist to this day. While owning land in the country, these people travel every day to work in factories. The life-style of this new class changed the pattern of traditional peasant culture. However, the surviving contacts with their traditional background enabled the preservation of remnants of peasant customs, still relevant in the new environment.

The development of the educational system is another important factor in the creation of modern Polish society. The Polish educational system was organized in the thirteenth century by the church administration and then secularized. Unfortunately, the final partition of Poland in 1795 limited the number of lay schools. Consequently, a large percentage of Polish people remained illiterate until the end of the nineteenth century. According to contemporary research, the illiteracy of Polish folk was far greater in the nineteenth century than in the sixteenth century. The restoration of Polish sovereignty after World War I eradicated illiteracy in Poland. Thus, the three factors described above, the personal freedom of the peasantry, the new possibility of travel and the development of education, transformed Poland's traditional folk culture at the turn of the twentieth century (see map 2a). But even in a transformed state the folk tradition remained an important component of social consciousness, and it inspired people both psychologically and artistically.

The power of the Roman Catholic church has long been of prime importance in Polish social and political structure. Since the Middle Ages it has been the foundation of Polish culture. However, church activity greatly diminished and in some instances wiped out traces of the 'Old' Slavonic background. One of the church's aims was the eradication of Slavonic paganism. As a consequence Gregorian chant and its musical system partially replaced the old musical structure, influencing even the rudiments of Polish folk song. The area dominated by the Roman Catholic religion generally covers the area of 'de-Slavonicized' music, whereas the oldest strata of Slavonic music are to be found in the territory where the 'eastern' Christian religions were practised.[10] The Roman Catholic population became culturally westernized, while the followers of the Greek Rite and the Russian Orthodox church retained the 'Old' Slavonic traditions.

The relics of the old diocesan structure are still visible in the structure of the folk culture. Historical records confirm this fact. We see, for example, that the influence of the old archbishopric of Gniezno played an important part in the Polish culture of Silesia until the

---

[10] I.e., the Greek Catholic Rite and the Russian Orthodox Church in eastern Polish territories.

final years of the nineteenth century, whereas under German domination the rôle of the other Polish centres in Silesia disappeared.

In conclusion, the Roman Catholic church can be seen as a factor in the westernization of Poland, both politically and culturally; it strengthened Poland's relations with western European cultures, especially with the culture of Italy. However, the impact of western civilization in Poland was always balanced by Poland's indigenous culture. This is evident, for instance, in the Polish national dances which were created against the background of folk, court and city dances. It is difficult to judge to what extent the old church polyphony from the thirteenth century was influenced by elements of native and folk tradition. Nevertheless, it is worth stressing that this kind of polyphony is documented only in the southern part of Poland, where the tendency to use folk harmonies in folk songs occurs.

The Roman Catholic church in Poland was also a factor in stabilization and conservatism. By law, in pre-partition Poland the primate replaced the king during an interregnum period. The political weakness of Poland, especially during the partitions, was partially redressed by the power of the Roman Catholic church. At the same time, this power created problems of assimilation for the non-Catholic citizens of Poland. For the peasantry and its folk culture, the Roman Catholic church played an integrating rôle, not only within the country itself but also towards émigré groups.

An understanding of the pre-Christian systems of belief that created differences in Polish social life and art will contribute to a better interpretation of the country's ethnic diversity. Traces of the 'Old' Slavonic background are still to be seen in rituals and social activities, as, for example, in the Polish wedding. The differences between 'Old' Slavonic and central European folk music traditions are obvious in their general atmosphere, their symbols, their herb vocabulary and tunes. The differences are especially clear in the fertility cult and in the ceremonies surrounding the climactic points of the wedding.

2 *Topics and trends*

2.1 The Slavonic world

2.1.1 Preliminary remarks

The basic aim of interdisciplinary Slavonic studies is the reconstruction of a vision of Slavonic culture. Linguists, anthropologists, archaeologists, historians and musicologists are involved also in interpretations of the ethnogenesis of the Slavonic people (J. Czekanowski 1957; Labuda 1969). There are various theories, some of them controversial, of the origins of the Slavonic people. However, most scholars would agree that the 'Old' Slavonic territory of the second half of the first millennium AD lay between the Baltic Sea in the north, the Carpathian Mountains in the south, the River Elbe in the west and probably the River Dnieper in the east.

As is well known, after AD 455 the Slavonic people expanded their territory towards the south, north and east. The southerly migration took place in the seventh century AD, and followed two different routes. The first crossed the famous Moravian Gate skirting the Carpathian Mountains in the west, while the other followed the Rivers Seret and Prut, bypassing the Carpathian Mountains in the east. The migration toward the east was the most recent, reaching Siberia and the Pacific as late as the seventeenth century. In the north, the Slavonic newcomers progressively Slavonicized the Baltic and Finno-Ugric people.

The explosive nature of Slavonic expansion resulted in an intensive absorption of local cultures. These were very often on a much higher level than the culture of the Slavonic newcomers. The strong impact of Mediterranean culture in the Balkan peninsula was particularly important for cultural development in this area. It is still evident in music, in certain customs, and in several magical symbols as well as in agricultural and horticultural traditions.

The diversity of the pre-Slavonic background may be said to comprise four basic components: Mediterranean, Middle Eastern (with a strong Iranian element), Baltic and Celtic. This diversity helps to explain the dispersion and decentralization of Slavonic religious systems. The Iranian, Baltic and Celtic pantheons clearly co-exist in the Slavonic religious tradition. For example, certain Slavonic deities would appear to be of Baltic origin (*Perun*), whereas *Yleli* is undoubtedly derived from the Iranian tradition. According to some authors the pan-Slavonic *Lada*, evidently connected with the cult of fertility, has a mysterious Celtic origin.

Folklore and song texts which contain supporting material for studies of 'Old' Slavonic beliefs and religion can still be found. The documented invocations associated with the names of *Yleli*, *Lada*,[11] and *Lelum-Polelum* are of peculiar significance. Philological analysis of song

[11] For example: quoted in the refrain 'Yleli, Yassa, Lado', see Dlugossi 1964; see also Brückner 1895: 326.

texts reveals additionally the remnants of these names that are now altered and barely recognizable, and that have onomatopoeic functions, e.g., *Leli, Luli, Lutki, Dinga, Ganga.*

Invocations to magic herbs together with the mention of trees or bushes also contribute data for Slavonic studies. The variety of herbs displayed in ritual songs is important because in this kind of material several strata of Slavonic traditions can be identified, showing the differentiation between the spheres of east and west Slavonic elements. For example, invocations to the hop are closely connected with west Slavonic songs; whereas the symbols of the yew, the periwinkle and the guelder rose prevail in east Slavonic songs. The Slavonic cults and their surviving mythology are nonetheless characterized by much fragmentation which thwarts current attempts at their reconstruction. Despite the scarcity of documentation and its diverse nature, some hypotheses and conclusions can be drawn.

It is recognized that evidence of the 'Old' Slavonic culture cannot be easily detected in so vast a territory as that populated by today's Slavonic-speaking people. In an analysis of this extensive territory the cultures of the south Slavonic ethnic groups of western Bulgaria, some Serbian and Croatian peoples in the south, and the Polesyan groups in the north are regarded as the oldest in the Slavonic world. As for Polish cultural material, the 'Old' Slavonic or Balto-Slavonic strata on the eastern borders are of the earliest origin. There are several reasons, historical as well as geographical, for the cultural antiquity of the groups mentioned above. The fact that links exist between these widely dispersed cultural groups sheds light on the hypothesis about their common descent in early times (Moszyński 1939, vol. II: 1,230; 1957). The connections between the Balkan and Polesyan cultures have been discussed in detail by anthropologists and musicologists (K. Moszyński, N. Kaufmann, A. Czekanowska) and recent research has clarified the structure of these relations, contributing towards a more precise chronology of the documented relics of these cultures (Czekanowska 1978b).

The culture of Carpathian ethnic groups and their cross-cultural contacts constitutes the next crucial problem in the discussion of Slavonic ethnogenesis. Some of the cultural links between the Carpathian regions and other early enclaves are of special interest (Moszyński 1957). These are to be found between Carpathian and Polesyan groups on the one hand, and between Carpathian and Balkan groups on the other.

The grounds for reconstructing the 'Old' Slavonic culture are limited mainly to the set of phenomena found in the folk culture of the nineteenth and twentieth centuries. The relation of the Slavonic calendar to the solar-lunar cult and to the lunar cycle in particular is well documented. Wedding and harvest rituals, being based on a concern for fertility, also have links with these cosmological concepts, and the solar rhythm governed the spring (Example 1) and solstice festivities (Examples 2 and 3) and their associated customs. Later, these basic rhythms which were deeply rooted in the religious systems of oriental antiquity were adopted and modified by the Christian calendar. The so-called *Pentacontade* rhythm of Middle

Example 1   *Smiercicha*, Sobieska and Sobierajski 1972, p. 174

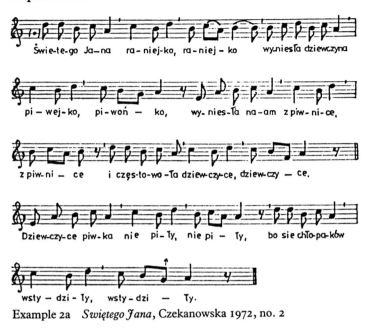

Example 2a *Świętego Jana*, Czekanowska 1972, no. 2

Example 2b *Pocóześ tu przyszed*, Czekanowska 1956, no. 18

Example 2c *Świętego Jana*, J. Stęszewski 1955a, no. 20, p. 31

Example 3   *Kupala*, Kolberg 1968, no. 80, p. 128

Eastern origin formed the basis for the calendar of the Slavonic people. It would seem to be quite probable that the Slavonic annual cycles correspond to Middle Eastern cult cycles (Czekanowska 1975b: 246).

More detailed analysis of harvest rituals emphasizes the rôle played by animals – the goat, the wolf, the rooster, the quail – and human personification – old women, old men (Bystroń 1916: 28, 80, 95). The relation of these rituals to the sun is evident in the use of the symbol of the wheel which is important in the oldest harvest ceremonies. The symbol of the egg was also adopted and could indicate links between these customs and beliefs in the deity of rye and its magical power. According to some 'Old' Slavonic beliefs, the deity of rye escapes during harvest time into the last unharvested ears of wheat and attempts to survive there until the following year (Bystroń 1916). This is why the remaining ears of wheat are preserved by the magic power of an egg that is broken over them. The custom of watering should be interpreted not only as a general concern for a good crop but specifically as a request for sufficient rain.

As far as 'Old' Slavonic family customs are concerned, the Slavs consider the wedding ceremony to be of prime importance, but birth, funeral and other family rites are also of significance. The 'Old' Slavonic culture was recognized as exogenous and organized according to sibs (blood relations) (Gasparini 1974: 875) and marriage did not cancel membership of the clan of one's birth. The importance of women in society and traces of matriarchy are also evident. Ceremonies connected with the celebration of the elevation from one social status to the next played a central part in 'Old' Slavonic family life. Recent analysis of the main episodes of a Slavonic wedding explains this phenomenon in ritual terms. The best documentation of Slavonic symbols and of the cult of fertility in particular is found in the *korovai* ceremony (Figure 1)[12] and in the poetic texts of the songs accompanying it. It is, however, the spiritual and social culture and the artistic activity surrounding the old customs and rites that prove to be the most interesting. There are still some concepts and culturally significant complexes or relations which remain unclear, such as the relation between the festivities dedicated to the summer solstice night and those associated with the cult of fertility. This may be the result of several ritual strata coexisting side by side.

Concern for rain was clearly related to the rituals devoted to the most important Slavonic god, *Perun*, who is to be found only amongst the east and south Slavonic people. Although there is no evidence in Polish material, it is possible that rituals connected with rain had

[12] *Krova* or *korova* means 'cow' in Slavonic languages. The horns of the cow could be interpreted as the symbols connected with the cult of fertility; the pine cones were much the same symbols. They were decorative motifs, often used on wedding cakes. The cap of the bride, after marriage, was fixed on a wheel made of the horns of a cow. This kind of fastening was called *hamełka*. The traces of this custom and the songs connected with it were still to be found in fairly recent times in many Slavonic countries, including the eastern parts of Poland.

Figure 1   *Korovai*, ritual cake, District of Lublin

existed earlier in the eastern border territory of Poland. These rituals accompanied the custom of ploughing the river-bed during drought. The demons responsible for stopping the rain, drying up the cows' milk and decreasing the fertility of women were regarded as the most dangerous and malevolent. There were many practices and rituals protecting the populace from the actions of different kinds of demons.

Intensive Christianization diminished, if not liquidated, the oldest strata of Slavonic beliefs in Poland. The homiletic texts are the best documents of this process of de-Slavicization. In the homiletic sources the names of former gods and deities, magical refrains, rituals and dances are depicted and banned. Descriptions of libidinous and demonic dances are encountered from the Middle Ages[13] to the end of the eighteenth century. The development of the educational system in the thirteenth century by the church administration, together with the second political integration of the Polish state in the fourteenth century after its 'Provincial Dispersion', contributed to the progressive reduction of 'Old' Slavonic strata. De-Slavicization also increased as a result of the political destruction of the neighbouring Slavonic countries, i.e., the Ruthenian states of Galicia and Volhynia (*Ready Reference Index to Encyclopaedia Britannica*, 1984: X: 387, 486–7), and as a result of the limitation of cultural influences from these border Slavonic areas. The cultures of Galicia and Volhynia which

[13] The oldest record is to be found in the chronicle of Gallus Anonimus (AD 1113).

flourished so richly in the Middle Ages became isolated after the fifteenth century. In these cases one can speak of cultural encapsulation.

2.1.2 Methods and dimensions

'Old' Slavonic culture, and its music in particular, can be interpreted as a phenomenon of the time that preceded the emergence of national musical cultures and styles. By 'Old' Slavonic music we mean the remnants of a tradition that developed between the end of the first millennium AD and the fifteenth century at the latest, i.e., the legacy of the first centuries of the Polish state and its Christian identity. This, then, was an age and culture which, at least in folk tradition, may have preserved some strata of the preceding, proto-Polish period.

The paucity of direct documentation limits our knowledge of the earliest Slavonic culture and music, so that studies of extant folkloristic materials in related cultures are significant. The oldest and probably the most authentic Slavonic stratum is that of the culture within the orbit of the Greek Catholic church traditions of eastern Europe. Enclaves of this culture are still to be found in eastern Poland. Identification of the 'old' strata of the western Slavs is still more indirect and involves more complex methods.

Nevertheless, the existence of west Slavonic strata and their possible links with a Celtic background (Czekanowska 1964: 97–101) are a significant point in theories which have attracted the attention of scholars over many years.

From the research completed to date, one can establish sets of east and west Slavonic songs that accompany the many Slavonic customs. Nevertheless, despite certain general similarities, it is difficult to speak of a Pan-Slavonic cultural and musical tradition. 'Old' Slavonic music, like the Slavonic religion, adopted many heterogeneous elements which often existed side by side and were not incorporated into a homogeneous whole.

According to the scant written documentation currently available, 'Old' Slavonic music was principally connected with customs and rituals. Among the best-documented music are the festivities associated with annual feasts, especially with those held on Mount Sobótka in Silesia and on Mount Łysa Góra in the Świętokrzyskie Mountains during the summer solstice night.[14] However, an important methodological question arises if one attempts to correlate surviving songs with data recorded for the most part in the fourteenth and fifteenth centuries.

The identification and dating of folkloristic material poses still more methodological problems. The procedures traditionally involve basic cross-regional studies and distribution maps, which show the spatial representation of the phenomena under study (see Map 3; Stęszewski 1965). Recent comparative studies were simultaneously verified by means of quantitative methods and source examination and were complemented by psychosociologically orientated interviews that explored the awareness of modern interviewees.

Historical verification is based primarily upon an examination of information about particular features and circumstances of performance, although the musical structure of the songs usually remains unknown. In contrast, the statistical method enables one to detect basic regularities in material gathered recently, looking at its morphological-stylistic and

---

[14] See *Thietmar's Chronicle*, VII, cap. 59: 555, quoted in Łowmiański, 1979: 211. These festivities are confirmed in several homiletic texts and in sermons of the fourteenth and fifteenth centuries in particular.

Map 3   Distribution of western and eastern versions of the Polish wedding ceremony and its music

functional features (Czekanowska 1977: 108–17; 1986: 94–110). The traditional comparative method basically supports an interpretation in ethnohistorical terms revealing the cross-Slavonic references, which not only contribute to a better understanding of previous contacts but also shed light on the distribution of Slavonic culture in the past (Czekanowska 1978).

According to the results of cross-regional comparisons, three kinds of data appear to have ethnohistorical significance: first, the relations between east Slavonic Polesye and south Slavonic Bulgaria; secondly, the relations between Volhynia, Byelorussia and west Russia (compare Examples 5a, 6 and 10); and finally, the relations between west Poland and the Slovak and Moravian lands. The first kind of relation can be regarded as a documentation of Slavonic migration to the south across the basins of the Rivers Seret and Prut, bypassing the Carpathian Mountains in the east. The second type sheds light upon Slavonic migration to the north-east (probably the migration of the Krywicze tribe). The last type again documents Slavonic migration towards the south but in this case along the western track, through the Moravian Gate. All of these migrations directly or indirectly concern the Polish material under study. These interrelationships merit special consideration since they concern the oldest strata of preserved Slavonic tradition, which seem to be of greatest importance for Polish culture, especially that of Volhynia and Galicia.

In considering the whole spectrum of ethnohistorical problems, two other points should be noted. The first is the question of the relation of Slavonic culture to its pre-Slavonic or proto-Slavonic strata. The second is the problem of its relation to later influences emanating from the main cultural centres of Rome, Mount Athos and Constantinople. In its final shape, the spatial structure of Slavonic studies also demands the inclusion of Slavonic material found in non-Slavonic countries, particularly in the non-Slavonic border territories. This applies to relations with countries both on the southern side of Poland (Hungary, Romania), and on the northern side (Lithuania).

Comparative studies based on cross-regional examinations are complemented today by cross-textual comparisons and by analyses of cultural context. Thanks to these studies, we have learned, for example, of the existence of a ritual calendar which determined the rhythm of annual songs, and of various basic cycles and periodicity which were of crucial importance to family life. The cross-textual examination includes the analysis of different modes of transmission (Kuryłowicz 1966: 169; Bartmiński 1979, 1985), and covers musical as well as verbal and dance media, illuminating the symbolic connections of the topics and clarifying the structure under study by revealing superior 'texts'. For example, many songs were not as directly connected with the function of labour as was previously thought. Indeed, the purpose of such songs was often not to maintain the rhythm of work but rather to add splendour to rituals. This is the case with the ancient Slavonic harvest songs that, through their direct erotic symbolism, sanction the status of agricultural activities. Cross-textual examination, better than any other method, reveals the deep strata of the numerous gestures connected with a specific custom and helps to decode a barely comprehensible verbal text.

There is evidence to suggest that conventions of thought, together with the laws of structuralization, have survived longer in the consciousness of the performers of songs than they have in concrete artifacts. A psychosociological interview is therefore sometimes more useful than an analysis of cultural facts alone. Ethnopsychological studies show that social awareness has proved to be more durable than the systems and institutions that determined it (Czekanowska 1983: 28).

The results achieved by different kinds of comparative studies not only contribute to an understanding of the 'Old' Slavonic world (i.e., to an explanation of its geographical differentiation and historical stratification as traceable in the remnants of the past) but also help to reveal the structural properties of the culture, art and music as it is perceived and conceptualized by contemporary people. The main methodological problem centres on the dimension of the exploration to which it is subjected. The problem demands tools designed for an indirect penetration of the human mind. It demands methods adapted to concepts and ideas that have already been transformed and adapted to the mentality of people living simultaneously in the present and in the 'past'; namely, in the mundane reality of daily events as well as in the serious atmosphere of festivities, the latter being embedded in the culture of the 'olden' days and their paradigm (Żadrożyńska 1983).

2.1.3 Direct and indirect sources

The Slavonic foundations of Polish culture were seriously undermined the moment that Poland was converted to Christianity, and they now survive only as a trace, which can be perceived intuitively but cannot be characterized precisely. Extant sources, especially those relating to musical culture, contain comprehensive records dating from the fifteenth century onwards, and therefore offer evidence of music which features national Polish, rather than solely Slavonic traits. The culture of earlier periods, especially musical culture, is only fragmentarily documented. Thus, far less is known about it than about the culture of certain other western Slavs, for instance the Polabians, or even the southern and eastern Slavs. Archaeological records are of limited significance, since they merely confirm the existence of a handful of excavated instruments (see Figure 2). Among them is the *gęśle* – a primitive fiddle, excavated in Opole and dating from the eleventh century – as well as some kinds of pipes and drums originating from earlier times (Kamiński 1963: 555–8).

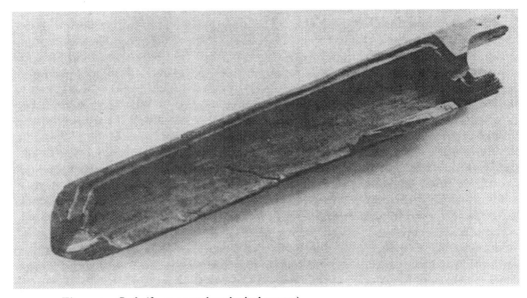

Figure 2   *Gęśle* (from an archaeological source)

Indirect sources in the form of musical material handed down by oral tradition are of especial interest to the ethnomusicologist.[15] Despite the fact that the folkloristic tradition underwent considerable transformation in the nineteenth and twentieth centuries, it still appears to be of assistance in the reconstruction of Slavonic culture. An investigation of folk culture and of the knowledge that its performers impart to the younger generation may yield a considerable body of data.

Nevertheless, material under investigation, and especially the texts of songs, does not offer direct evidence of the existence of the deities considered to be the Slavs' principal gods,

---

[15] Evidence of the first field research in Poland is provided by the questionnaire prepared for ethnographers by Hugo Kołłątaj in 1801.

namely the Sun god – *Swarog*, known also as *Swarożyc*, recognized by western Slavs – and the Thunder god – *Perun*, recognized by eastern Slavs. There is also no confirmation of the names of deities known in other sources, for instance in 'Vladimir's pantheon' which includes *Chors* and *Dadżbog* (Brückner 1918).[16] On the other hand, the song texts confirm the personal names of demons such as *Kupala*, a patron of festivals connected with the summer solstice, and above all *Lada* (see Example 73 below), the supposed patroness of fertility who appears frequently in song-refrains. There are also few clues as to the rôle of other names quoted in other sources, names such as *Yleli*, *Jassa* and *Tija* (Brückner 1895: 326), which may refer to Iranian deities (*Ileli*, etc.). Personal names of deities are at the same time recorded in indirect sources. They are especially significant in the case of the calls to *Lada*.

The folkloristic traditions include a variety of practices and magical customs and, more specifically, the calls, songs and refrains associated with them. This study, however, will focus on detailed analysis of the various media (including literature, music and dance) conveying the same or similar topics and concepts.

The basic material of our investigation consists of songs handed down by oral tradition, including both music and poetry, plus fragments of instrumental accompaniments, dance movements and gestures, and ritualistic behaviour. All these elements are best documented in surviving poetic song-texts and their refrains. The group of sources outlined above enables one to perceive the significance of a number of symbols typical of the ancient repertoire. This applies to both notions and abstract references, e.g., images of a circle as the movement of following the sun, and to concrete activities connected with such basic work as ploughing, sowing or scything rye, or with symbolic gestures such as drawing a snowman, i.e., expelling winter (Dlugossi 1964: 173). A study of the musical material and the principles of its formation also helps one to appreciate the general rhythm of the activities and behaviour. The rôle that music plays in the ritual repertoire is not so much one of direct illustration but rather of shaping the mood and rhythmical recurrence of the cycle, intensifying and relaxing tension, and shaping the final formula of a particular meaning. It should be stressed that effects intended for onomatopoeic transmission, such as emphasis on the crowing of a cock, the neighing of a horse or the arrival of a falcon, are not directly represented in music.

At the same time sequences of repetitions, their diversified character and the juxtaposition of repetition with principles of variation, complementation and contrast, contribute greatly to the re-creation of the natural rhythm of ritual behaviour that in recent times has been systematically reduced. In this case it is particularly fruitful to examine musical, gestural, and verbal transmission, which enables one to bring out the regularity of various 'deep' rhythms as well as concepts and their images (such as the wheel). It often illuminates bio-rhythms, including the annual cycle, vegetation or man's individual cycle, and the significance of particular processes, especially copulation and death.

The structures of song-refrains, in both poetic and musical terms, are especially important. Particular attention is paid to surrounding refrains and final formulae. In Polish song, final formulae and short musical refrains are usually connected with three- or five-syllable sequences. The degree of intelligibility of these syllabic sequences ranges from: realistic

---

[16] According to Łowmiański 1979: 113, in the treatises dating from AD 871 or 944 and later in AD 1068 some early information concerning east Slavonic beliefs can be found. The most important confirmation, however, is to be found only at the beginning of the fifteenth century in the so-called *Običnoe žitie*, see Sobolevskij 1888: 26.

descriptions, as in the refrain *Plon niesiemy plon* (Here we are with the crop); clear invocations to a magical herb, such as *Oj chmielu chmielu* (Oh! hop, hop); calls to a definite deity, *Oh! Lado, Lado*; and then to ambiguous calls such as *Lelija* or *Leluja* (see Figure 16), and sequences which are probably nonsensical such as *Oj to to*. The use of internal repetition as in the phrase *Oj chmielu, chmielu* (Oh! hop, hop) is very characteristic and enables one to imagine original folk concepts with their simplicity that stand in direct opposition to the invocations based on patterns of church sequences used in religious songs. One must, however, stress the existence of transitional phenomena representing the coexistence of both traditional and adopted ways of thinking, as for example the aforementioned *Lelija* that rhymes with *Maryja*.

From the features described above, one can define a repertoire of songs, which in the Polish material is usually limited to a group of seasonal songs or to strata connected with certain episodes in a wedding ceremony. There are winter and spring songs, as well as songs connected with the summer solstice, the harvest, and the gathering of hemp or linen (see Example 54). There are also family songs, especially wedding songs represented by a broadly developed cycle starting with the *zrękowiny* (engagement; see Example 4) and concluding

Example 4   *Niechaj będzie Chrystus*, Czekanowska 1956, no. 38

with the departure from the family home. Moreover, there is the interesting example of songs connected with childbirth dedicated to St Jeremy. The material described above appears to be relatively homogeneous. However, one may divide it into several levels, according to hypothetically different historical periods and to differing cultural backgrounds. Nevertheless, both the morphological and stylistic features of the songs under discussion include references to the repertoire preserved in other Slavonic cultures. These references enable one to detect features of the 'Old' Slavonic strata.

As is to be expected, the literary texts of the most ancient repertoire are intricately encoded and steeped in symbolism. This is particularly true of a small number of harvest and wedding songs from the eastern borderlands. Comparative studies between these ancient and later repertoires reveal that these songs underwent a process of reduction. The process is primarily concerned with restricting the rôle played by the performance mannerisms which in the past dominated this repertoire. Comparative studies show that these mannerisms highlighted the phonetic structure of the language and its instrumentational values, as is particularly evident in the case of shouts (Example 10; Czekanowska 1985). Moreover these shouts seem to have played a structure-generating rôle, which was later replaced by the function of melodic narration.

Example 5a *Pravo se pladne*, Stoïn 1931, no. 775

Example 5b *Żnece żnécyki*, Ewald 1979, no. 11

Comparative studies also allow one to discover the possible structure-generating influence of the *korovod* round dances, with their cycles and repeated but contrasting 'sections'. In general, however, such a study must remain fairly hypothetical since the *korovod* repertoire has become extinct in Poland and exists only as elements of games often connected with customs (Dąbrowska 1980). In the past, performances were usually collective, with techniques such as the opposition of contrasting voices and dance movements. The introduction of other voices may be considered as complementary to melismatic adornment (see Examples 5a and 5b). Both of these principles – the addition of voices and adornment – should be understood as having been subsequently replaced by a motivic shaping of the structural unit of melody.

Polish folk songs underwent considerable change in the fifteenth, sixteenth and seventeenth centuries. As early as the nineteenth century, when the first Polish folk songs were notated, they were presented as merely a single voice in monophonic structure. Yet, it is very probable that the songs were previously performed heterophonically, as is still practised in neighbouring Byelorussia. The changes in performance style apply especially to the small amount of collective participation and spontaneous reaction. Shouts therefore have nearly disappeared, though they can be heard in dance couplets in some regions. As may be expected from their transcendental character and orgiastic elements, shouts were suppressed by the church authorities (Dlugossi 1964: 178). They may have been replaced by embellished final formulae modelled on chorale melodies or on church sequences, thus acquiring the solemnity befitting a ritual (see Example 6).

In the regions of former Ruthenian Galicia and Volhynia, a number of particularly ancient

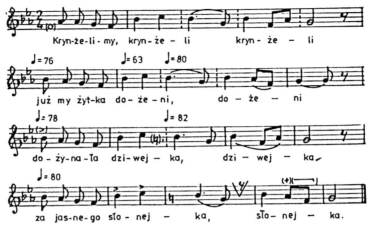

Example 6   *Krynżeli, my krynżeli*, Czekanowska 1961, no. 10

harvest songs connected with the ritual worship of the last unharvested ears of corn have survived. Fragments of summer solstice songs dedicated to *Kupala*[17] are also still preserved, as well as wedding songs which contain rich symbolism pointing to vestiges of solar and lunar cults and featuring particular animals, especially the cow (Ivanov and Toporov 1974: 255). One can point to groups of associations concerned with the concept of passage from one state to another, connected with the related images of danger and menace and featuring clear traces of transcendental communication. The songs of old customs are related to the culture preserved in certain residual regions which were isolated from cultural influences of Europe and the Orient.

2.1.4 Repertoire

Harvest songs

According to many scholars, harvest songs are unique in their close connection with ritual and in their survival in more or less traditional form until recent times. The extensive territory of their earlier distribution also demonstrates their importance to the Slavonic people. There are, indeed, certain kinds of Slavonic harvest songs in the Polish repertoire which can only be considered as remnants of 'Old' Slavonic culture.

They are of two types: the so-called 'narrow range' structure dedicated to the gathering of the last bundle of wheat, with its characteristic references to the east and south Slavonic repertoires represented by harvest songs in the Polish eastern border territories; and the structure of the Polish songs performed after the harvest which are found throughout Polish territory. Besides these two basic harvest song structures, there is a type transitional between the two.

The first, or 'eastern', type of harvest song may be regarded as representative of the Polish songs performed in the field and is probably connected with the customs associated with an

---

[17] *Kupala* is understood as a demon of summer with the typical symbol of the sun presented as a wheel, celebrated on 24 June.

invocation to the god of rye (*żyto*). The second type of song – which was and still is performed after the harvest – concentrates upon social events and entertainment rather than concern for the next crop. According to folk musicians interviewed in Poland and in neighbouring countries (Slovakia, Byelorussia), the distinction is also confirmed by the use of different terminology. The distinction between *żniwne* (relating to the harvest) in the first case and *dożynkowe* (relating to the post-harvest festival) in the second seems to be quite substantial and indicates two completely different traditions. The distinction is especially clear in 'border' territories where both structures exist side by side. The third, 'transitional', harvest song structure seems to be connected with the *żniwne* type (see Examples 7a and 7b and compare with Example 6) and probably represents later, transformed variants.

Example 7a   *Otwierajcie gospodarzu*, Sobieska and Sobierajski 1972, no. 89, p. 351

Example 7b   *Od zielonego gaju*, Kolberg 1865, no. 202, p. 167

The first melodic type connected with the structure of 'narrow range' is limited to tetra- or pentachordal skeletons and appears to present the most authentic version of the Slavonic harvest repertoire. This structure reveals its symbolism directly through its poetry (a direct invocation to the goat or to the sun) as well as through the cultural context, both manifested in accompanying gestures and activities which create a unique atmosphere based on circling movements and repetitions of short phrases and formulae. Nevertheless, only cross-regional studies can explain the ritual character and meaning of these customs. Analysis of these ritual situations begins with an exposition of their collective character. The mannerisms employed emphasize the clearly expressed concept of signal functions (see Examples 5a and 5b); while the character of intervals displayed in shouts and dialogue reveals the essential rôle of dissonance. The latter plays a crucial part in this structure, and confirms that the harvest songs were intended primarily as ritual songs (Czekanowska 1985).

The Polish versions of these 'eastern' structures described above, however, are hardly qualified to represent 'Old' Slavonic strata. They have been radically transformed and the origin of only some of the elements preserved today can be proved. A substantial alteration is in the performance style, which is to be found in contemporary recorded Polish versions of harvest songs. This reductional process is partly connected with the musicians' lack of professionalism; the songs are not performed by specially trained and skilled singers but simply by anyone who remembers the repertoire. Another alteration is the elimination of the highly trained shouting and the embellished drone with onomatopoeic effects, that are still preserved in Balkan and Polesyan harvest songs. Despite the substantial transformation of the Polish versions, remnants of the old structures can still be traced in the songs under study. Musical transmission based on the perpetual repetition of short phrases circulating within limited ranges of tetra- or pentachords, with a characteristic exposure of final and subfinal formulae (see Example 6), is practised in the style of traditional music. The second type of very popular post-harvest songs (Example 8a) typical of western and central Poland differ not

Example 8a   *Przynieśliśmy plon*, Sobieska and Sobierajski 1972, no. 71, p. 327

simply because of their pentatonicism but more importantly because of their reorganized form based on a dialogue between the dancing and singing groups, and because of their evident references to Polish Renaissance and Baroque music. This applies both to the poetry, exhibited in well-organized stanzas based on five verses (5+5, 8+8, 5) with characteristic refrain (8+8) and final invocation (5), and to the music which displays the rudiments of their form aa'ba', and a clear dance rhythm reminiscent of Polish Renaissance and Baroque dances (Stęszewska 1979). The character of these dance-songs corresponds perfectly with the merry atmosphere of the post-harvest entertainment held in the yard of the host, be he farmer or country squire.

The melodies of the third structure performed in the fields seem to be more closely connected with the 'Old' Slavonic heritage. This applies not only to the authentic 'eastern' version but also to some of the 'transitional' songs from Little Poland and Mazovia. The form of these latter songs was based upon the principle of parallelism (a,b), whereas their Slavonic roots with their typical fragmentation and concentration upon a repeated pattern (aa'ba') can still be recognized in certain tonal and melodic features. This aspect is also significant in certain harvest songs from Slovakia and Moravia (Demo and Hrabalova 1969). Similarities are revealed by cross-regional studies, but much more significant is the evidence of a common basis for the Slavonic harvest repertoire illuminating the features typical of this structure. In brief, it should be stressed that the double-verse stanza is based on a seven- or eight-syllable verse (7+7) or (8+8) with a characteristic rhythmic plan in duple metre, and includes principles of repetition which are typical of these Polish and Slovak-Moravian harvest songs (see Example 8b and compare with Examples 7a and 7b).

Example 8b   *Povej vetričku*, Demo and Hrabalova 1969, no. 22a

Solstice songs

Solstice songs are quite rare in modern Poland. The scarcity of folkloristic documentation, however, can be complemented by records preserved in written sources. The latter are well represented in this case.

The solstice repertoire is clearly divided into two typologically distinct strata. The first type is again connected with the eastern territories, whereas the second is connected with southern and central Poland. More particularly, the distribution of the second type of solstice song is connected with the River Vistula and can be traced from the mountains up to 'north Mazovia'. Relatively different variants of solstice songs are found in the regions of Kujavia and in Kurpie. The difference between these two basic types, eastern and western, is largely the result of a distinction between the symbolic persons to whom they are addressed. There is the demon *Kupala* in the first, or 'eastern' version, and a person named 'John' described as green, white or even as a saint, in the second version. The dedication to St John in the popular *sobótka* songs (Czekanowska 1972) indicates a correlation with the Christian calendar and recently with the feast-day of St John (24 June), although the solstice festivities, and even the actual night of solstice, were not limited to this date. The solstice was celebrated over a longer period corresponding to the last week of June. This also explains the popularity of the texts in the repertoire which were dedicated to St Peter (Example 9; Czekanowska 1972: 181) and

Example 9   *Już po świntym*, Czekanowska 1972, no. 14

which prevailed on the eastern bank of the River Vistula. According to sources, the songs performed at this time were connected with festivities held on hills or on the river bank and involving dancing around fires, shouting and calling to the pagan deities. Written sources are complemented by iconography dating mainly from the nineteenth century and by data preserved in the poetic and folkloristic tradition. All these sources describe the rôle played by magic herbs and by burdock and mugwort in particular. Iconography depicts girls in typical head decorations dancing around a fire (Kolberg 1865: 123; see Figure 3). The formulae and metaphors expressed by the poetry describe the significance of the choice of flowers and herbs for this ceremony. Cross-textual analysis also contributes to a better understanding of the function of these festivities. It reveals their deep sexual symbolism which, however, is presented differently from other Slavonic customs, and which in this case is not necessarily connected with the cult of fertility. The results of the analysis clearly differentiate this custom from the wedding ceremony and its symbols. The basic difference focuses upon the falcon and its symbolism (Kolberg 1865: 113).

The results of morphological and stylistic studies reveal the differentiation between eastern and central Polish versions, and in the geographical dimension display obvious references to the Slavonic repertoire. Speaking in more detailed terms, the eastern versions are limited to short and simple formulae with typical musical endings and are clearly related to the Byelorussian and west Russian materials (Możejko 1985: 198; K. Svitova 1966: 61; see Example 10 and compare with Example 5b). The central Polish versions are definitely Polish in style and they are complex in form and obviously articulated by their dance rhythms, which again have been clearly transformed by the Polish dances of the sixteenth and seventeenth centuries. The presence of the aa'ba' dance structure and even elements of

Figure 3   Solstice night, lithograph

Example 10   *Pora maty żyto*, Svitova 1966, no. 44

mazurka rhythm legitimizes this repertoire in historical terms and suggests again a connection with the music of the Renaissance and Baroque periods. Traces of the pentatonic scale, however, reveal roots that could extend back as far as the Middle Ages. Several points still remain obscure. For example, it is not clear how one should relate the data preserved in early records with recently gathered folkloristic material and their musical and poetic features. How can one correlate the atmosphere depicted and banned in homiletic texts with the hilarious social conditions of more recently described extant ceremonies? It is especially difficult to combine the libidinous 'orgiastic' dances accompanied by curving of the hands, shouting and clapping[18] with the mazurka rhythm and a rather formal way of dancing. There is a gap between the written sources dating from the Middle Ages and the documentation provided by folkloristic material from the nineteenth and twentieth centuries. Nor should it bee forgotten that our written information is a product of the 'official sources' of the time, supplied mainly by the church authorities, and that these formulations were dictated by a resolute struggle against pagan religion and its vestiges.

Solstice songs represent a tradition common to all Slavonic and non-Slavonic annual feasts. Two different strata – eastern and western versions – can be identified in the Polish material. Indeed, the substantial differences in the solstice material involve their dedication to variously nominated persons such as *Kupala* or John. According to Polish studies, the solstice custom, as opposed to other Slavonic rites, is basically concerned with the experience of sexual satisfaction not necessarily connected with the cult of fertility, which is the core of the wedding ceremony (Sobieska and Sobierajski 1972). The poetic texts of the songs clearly express this concept and stress an admiration for the promotion of sexual skills as well as disgust at sexual inefficiency. This is complemented by dance and acrobatic competitions involving the sizing-up of partners' potential. The surviving solstice material is not so concentrated on the concern with fertility and is free from invocations to definite demons. It differs from the songs and practices connected with other Slavonic rites. However, this seems to be a fairly recent phenomenon since *Lada* – the Slavonic goddess of fertility – was previously often invoked. This fact also indicates that the relation with the fertility cult in the repertoire may never be satisfactorily explained.

Spring songs

Spring songs make up a very limited group in the Polish repertoire. Their function is not socially demonstrated. In contemporary practice the surviving spring songs are limited to children's games. In contrast with the material previously described, their geographical distribution is not clearly differentiated and they are not divided into two historically distinct groups. In fact, an 'eastern' version of a spring song is not easy to find. The spring repertoire prevails today in the western and southern parts of Poland, where connections with Slovak and Moravian material can be traced. In these cases connections with the ritual calendar are also less direct. The structural connections with the ceremony dedicated to the end of winter symbolized by *Smrt* (Death) or *Marzanna* or with that dedicated to the coming of summer, symbolized by *Gaik* (Example 11), *Maik*,[19] and *Nowe Latko* (New Summer), have been transformed and recently have been connected with the celebration of Christian festivities such as the middle of Lent or the Easter period. Unlike the solstice songs, the spring repertoire was not so intensively depicted and banned in homiletic texts, despite obvious elements of idolatry which are sometimes negatively described in the texts of sermons (see Brückner 1918). This supports the thesis that the spring songs were part of the repertoire of the mediaeval *intermedia* which were organized primarily by church institutions (Seweryn

[18] It should be stressed that the solstice songs were also banned by the Orthodox Church in Russia. Several records of this fact exist. See Ivanov and Toporov 1974.
[19] *Gaik* is a diminutive of *Gaj*, meaning 'little forest'; *Maik* comes from May.

1928). The connection with the church probably contributed to the transformation and reduction of these songs to short recitations similar to the diatonic children's repertoire distributed throughout the European continent. However, comparative studies show many interesting symbols encoded in the verbal strata of the spring songs. They may also refer to the more distant east Slavonic (Russian and Byelorussian) repertoire connected with calling for spring (Popova 1962: 38; Możejko 1985: 182; Zemcovskij 1975). Nevertheless, the material under study presents a transformed or reduced form which demonstrates a process

Example 11   *Do tego tu domu*, Sobiescy 1973, no. 76, p. 290

of adaptation rather than preservation. This is probably the result of a severance with previous connotations and functions, and totally differentiates the Polish versions from the carnival and spring repertoires preserved in other Slavonic traditions.

   Unlike the harvest and solstice repertoires, spring songs do not contain sufficient common features to establish a basis for comparative studies.

Wedding songs

Within the richly developed and relatively well-preserved Polish wedding repertoire there are only a few musical structures which can be considered remnants of 'Old' Slavonic culture. Once again these are associated with the narrow-range structure distributed throughout the eastern border territory and with the structure of the most popular Polish wedding songs concerning crucial events in the 'capping' ceremony (see Map 3). Certain other songs can be regarded in comparative perspective only.

   The structural difference between the two basic types indicated above is even more spectacular in the wedding repertoire than in other Polish customs. These two structural types may also be referred to as the eastern and western Slavonic substrata of Polish wedding material, especially in the case of ethnohistorical interpretation. An instrumental interpretation of the wedding repertoire should, however, be directed towards different objectives, involving a more detailed analysis of the internal stratification of these substrata, with the problem of symbolic connotation receiving particular attention.

The narrow-range structure is represented in several varieties in the wedding material. This structure's internal division into subgroups is unclear. The material from the eastern territory constitutes a kind of amalgam where several strata of tradition are preserved. This may present a phenomenon of polydoxy. By contrast, the wedding repertoire from central and western Poland is well organized and designated in its functions (Czekanowska 1956).

A detailed cross-textual analysis of the songs under study reveals other interesting peculiarities, particularly regarding the 'deeply' symbolic poetry expressing the central rôle of the sun and the significance of animals connected with certain cults. Of the latter, the place of the cow appears to be quite crucial. The chicken and the rooster appear to have occupied a similar place in the past. No less important is the display of special gestures and behavioural patterns. The climax of the wedding cycle is marked by the famous ceremony of the *korovai*, the ritual cake.[20] The ceremony which is intended to safeguard the bride's fertility is divided into several phases connected with the preparation of the cake, its dedication, its symbolic decoration and finally its division among the participants of the wedding's drama. The bride's wedding costume also displays the symbols of the cow, shown by the fixing of her cap after marriage on the *hamełka* (symbol of fertility), the wheel made of the horns of cows (Figures 4a and 4b; Świeży 1952). Cow horns and a chicken made from dough are placed on the ritual cake, and sometimes a chicken is baked inside (Moszyński 1934, vol. I). The poetry and music accompanying the several episodes of the *korovai* ceremony transmit in deeply symbolic terms the description of ritual situations and supplement them with comments. The poetic text in turn stresses the significance of verbs such as 'rolling', 'flowing', 'crossing the bridge' and 'blossoming'. The atmosphere evoked by the poetry is articulated musically by the principle of repetition and is finally crowned by terminal formulae. Both the music and the poetry express that unmistakably serious, tense and gloomy feeling typical of the 'eastern' wedding and its mood of tears, crying and shouting, which is totally different from the merry, noisy atmosphere of Polish wedding festivities of other regions. Map 3 illustrates the different areas of western and eastern versions of the Polish wedding ceremony and its music.

Apart from songs with deeply symbolic texts, other variants may also be found. These differ in their manner of conceptualization and in their more direct addresses, as well as in their explicit associations and more transformed musical structures. The latter display features of parallelism and elements of causal thinking. The verbal transmission in these cases centres upon imperatives or conclusions addressed to the main protagonists of the wedding drama. The more general expressions articulate specific points in the ceremony and explain and evaluate motivations and judgements. Verbal analysis indicates the rôle of verbs and expressions such as 'go out', 'give some money', or 'do not forget'. This new manner of formulation illuminates the transformation of basic concepts and devices. The group of participants operates now in reality and the symbolic language and invocations to demons disappear.

The part of the Polish wedding repertoire that can be identified as a heritage of the West Slavonic tradition is quite homogeneous in character. It is clear in its symbolism, which is

---

[20] See above, footnote 12. See also Ivanov and Toporov 1974, in the chapter entitled 'K symbolike korovaja' (Towards the symbolism of *korovai*): 243–58.

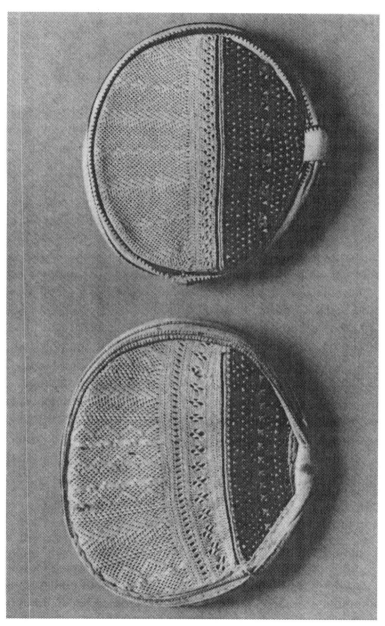

Figure 4a   *Hametka*, a wheel of cow's horn on which the cap should be fixed after marriage.

Figure 4b   Woman after marriage, District of Lublin

quite different from that of the eastern territories. The differences are still more obvious in the style, in the expressive qualities, and in the musical and poetic structures. As far as common points are concerned, these occur only in the symbolism of pine cones, and in the custom of placing the bride on a kneading-trough. This corresponds to the custom of placing the bride on a *korovai*, which is present in the eastern version of the wedding ceremony (Ivanov and Toporov 1974: 258). In both cases symbols and gestures are obviously connected with concern for the bride's fertility. Finally, some very general similarities are also visible in the preoccupation with common concepts and particular associations, e.g., magic herbs and birds representing the bride and groom. The differences in the western version involve a manner of thinking with more concrete visualization and description of the ideas which they transmit. Verbs such as 'unwinding', 'creeping in, up and down', 'tendrilling' or just 'sowing' and 'ploughing' dominate the poetry of the most important songs – especially of those accompanying the central 'capping' ceremony and the episodes of 'unplaiting' the braids, which are understood as a preparation for the main ritual of 'capping'. Very much the same can be said of the musical structures of songs accompanying the ceremony. They exhibit a clearly segmented musical form based on unequivocal structural principles, i.e., exact repetition, clear contrasts, and the elaborate relations of tonal endings. These phenomena may be interpreted as expressing the obvious dichotomy between 'yes' and 'no' or 'either' and 'or', which is so characteristic of the causal thinking of modern man.

The Polish wedding repertoire of western or central Poland, which was comprehensively described by the Polish ethnographers of the nineteenth century (Kolberg 1865–1907) and interpreted in the twentieth century as social drama (Baudouin de Courtenay-Ehrenkreut-zowa 1927), may be summarized as being concentrated on three main complexes of episodes. The 'capping' ceremony appears to represent the climax of the ritual. The time of performance (midnight), and the social status of the custom which co-exists with remnants of previous rites and magical connotations, elevates the central episode to the level of the extraordinary. All the events described by the songs and gestures centre upon the loss of virginity and the 'passage' to another sexual and social status that is connected with the basic concern for fertility.

By contrast, the other two complexes of Polish wedding songs are based on social rather than ritual situations. In the case of the pre-wedding ceremonies they are devoted to a farewell to the group of girls to which the bride belonged, and in the post-wedding events they concern the episode of departure from the family home. However, it is still quite difficult to isolate these socially dominated events from elements of symbolism and traces of transcendency. This is indicated by the preoccupation with magic herbs such as rue, periwinkle and rosemary, the evergreens chosen for the bride's wreath. It is also articulated by gestures and ceremonies such as the carrying out of the wreath (*wyprowadzenie wianka*), its rolling over the table (*kulanie wianka, toczenie wianka*; see Example 12 and compare with Example 22a), and

Example 12   *Siadaj Kasiu*, Czekanowska 1972, no. 16

the comparison of the bride to an apple tree. All these activities and associations display remnants of ancient magical thought and traditional gestures. It is, however, extremely difficult to distinguish between the 'capping' and the 'wreath', i.e., pre-wedding ceremonies, which both deal with the issue of virginity. The similarities and differences are articulated by the music that accompanies both groups of songs, but which in more recent performances can be exchanged.

To sum up, the central or western Polish wedding repertoire is accompanied by three different complexes of music and poetry. The most significant 'capping' ceremony is articulated by pentatonic melodies and prominent dances such as the *Polski* (Polish)[21] (see Example 13 and compare with Example 4) or the *Wielki* (The Great). From the musical point

Oj, ty dziw-czy-no,   oj, ty mo-To-da,   ne zaj-me te-be

by-stra-ja wo-da,   oj, zaj-me te-be   czu-mak mo-To-dy,

szczo-byś   wo - dy - Ta   wo-Ty do   wo - dy.

Example 13   *Oj ty diwczyno*, Kolberg 1968, no. 94, p. 135

of view it is obvious that both these facts – the preservation of traditional tonal strata and the adoption of a highly dignified dance – crown the central episode of the wedding sequence involving the 'capping' ceremony. The pre-wedding ceremonies are sometimes also accompanied by melodies which include pentatonic turns. These melodies, however, are limited to short models and neither their rhythm nor, to an even greater extent, their form displays elaborate musical or poetic structures. By contrast, the post-wedding ceremonies and some episodes before the departure to the church are accompanied by songs with well-organized stanzas and with the musical form of 'reprise' or repetitive aa'ba' sequence. At the same time the post-wedding ceremonies usually include quite substantially transformed melodies related to major tonality.

The identification of 'Old' Slavonic elements in west Slavonic music is a difficult task. The difficulties of identification are a consequence of the structural transformation that affected both Polish and non-Polish music between the fifteenth and eighteenth centuries, and this is the reason why the distinction between the west Slavonic and west or central European elements is so hard to identify.

However, comparative examination of the material can be helpful in detecting general properties of significance for this Slavonic repertoire. These general properties become evident when other kinds of non-Slavonic songs are considered, as for example European ballads. The expressive melodic qualities and the rhythms characteristic of the west Slavonic strata set it apart from the music and concepts of non-Slavonic groups. Despite intensive transformation, the Slavonic strata have preserved a style and manner of phrasing, conceptualization and structure very obviously opposed to the style and characteristics of other European currents, although the rudiments of west Slavonic structure have altered. The latter basically reflects the strong influence of the Roman Catholic church music that

[21] See Kolberg, vols. XXV, 1886, no. 739, and XXVI, 1887, no. 115.

dominated in the Middle Ages. But even more significant was the total restructuring of traditional music by Renaissance and Baroque secular music. Nevertheless, the emotional and expressive qualities of Slavonic songs have persisted, and have successfully resisted foreign, officially accepted ideas.

The Slavonic material examined above, and the set of wedding songs in particular, presents a vision of multi-dimensionally differentiated and variously stratified resources that are basically divided into two main groups identifiable as representative of the west and east Slavonic traditions respectively. This material is at the same time differentiated and modified by other cultural impacts and influences. This is why the ethnic identification of the Slavonic heritage involves at least two different methodological approaches. The first concerns the exploration of traditional elements and concentrates on the analysis of remnants and relics, whilst the second is directed more towards the exploration of contemporary peoples and their attitudes, perceptions, feelings and concepts. Both approaches employ different methods and tools, but are at the same time complementary.

2.1.5 Towards a synthesis of Slavonic structure

The heterogeneity of deeply rooted Slavonic and non-Slavonic elements is of crucial import- ance in the formation of psychological components of artistic creativity and in the perception of the differences between Slavonic culture and other European traditions. At least three or four basic differences in perception and creativity can be distinguished.

First, there is the mannerism of associations and the degree of directness with which the appellations and comments are formulated, as well as the way in which the reflections are exhibited. All of these patterns of conceptualization rooted in traditional structure may be regarded as showing transformational processes in which certain remnants of direct trans- mission, for example onomatopoeia, are preserved. These may be in process of continuous transformation into an advanced code based already on a language system operating on syllables and a musical system operating on intervals, whereas the role of directly perceived sound with its signal values disappears.

Second, there is an evident difference in time perception, tempo, kinetics and behavioural responses. In Slavonic music a fairly slow tempo and a tendency towards contemplation is balanced by a tendency towards spontaneous responses. These attitudes are often found side by side, and they are clearly opposed to the behavioural patterns of central and western Europe.

Third, there are obvious differences in participation and in the situational character of performance. This applies both to solo songs and to songs performed as interplay between groups or between individuals and groups, in which the process of engagement in the act of performance is clearly determined by the cultural context.

Finally, differences in repertoire and in song content should not be overlooked. The traditional and ritual chants and the lyrical and moralizing songs which predominate today present the basic topics and ideas. The former emphasize a climax which focuses the whole dramatic content of the plot on the subject of fertility, both in annual and family cycles. These two categories of repertoire seem to form the basic topics of interest to Slavonic people. Most attention, however, is paid to the loss of virginity; Slavs are really excited by this and regard it as the most crucial point in a woman's life. They reflect upon and even interpret this event in a more abstract dimension, while copulation, death and birth are interpreted as phenomena of the 'passage' to another state which needs transcendental protection.

Examining this in greater detail we must again stress the differences in attitudes. This involves a substantially different comprehension of an isolated sound and its directly measured length of time. This also requires concentration on the sound and its acoustic phenomena, such as effects of overblowing and overshouting, in particular. These obviously play an important rôle in mass heterophonic performances and contribute to the differences between the repertoire of Slavonic music and that of other European traditions. Very much the same applies to the perception of time, regulated in the repertoire by directly measured time and such fundamental relations as 1:2, 1:3 and 2:3 (see Example 5b). The latter may be found in the rhythms not evidently transformed by the European convention of the metric unit. This applies especially to the repertoire of 'old' ritual songs performed in slow tempo and in relatively 'free' rhythm, in which the prolongation of fermata plays a decisive rôle.

Many similar features apply to the dance structure that was originally rooted in mass performances. These were dominated by a paradigm of perpetual circulating movements, as well as by several stopping and balancing movements typical of the *korovod* dance ((Vladi-kina)–Bačinskaja 1969). Whatever the accompanying music, the latter gradually evolved towards a more transformed form of performance. This involved the elaboration of several kinds of dialogue and monologue form. The obvious difference between mass and chamber styles of performance is emphasized by the terminology used by performers in transitional areas (Rudneva 1957). This stresses a clear-cut opposition between the *korovod* (round dance) and the *tanec*, where the latter term applies to forms of a chamber character.

A structural analysis of Slavonic art reveals the basic structural properties directing all kinds of transmission: music, poetry and dance. The fundamental principles seem to be rooted in the concept of repetition with variations and in the case of basic formulae. The idea of interplay in two, three or even more dimensions, including verbal, musical and gestural media, should be thought of as a process of mutual complementarity, articulation and crystallization, whilst all manners of transmission should be taken into consideration. In discussing the principle of repetition in more detailed terms, we have to distinguish its various forms in the light of their changeability and their evaluation by the performers; in other words, how are they perceived, more or less consciously? This question concerns the basic difference between perpetual repetitions performed almost subconsciously and repetitions applied consciously, as a structural manipulation. Similarly, we can differentiate between the concept of formulae practised in a symbolic way, with their rich spectrum of connotations, and formulae perceived in purely constructional terms, as the mark of a system we should like to manipulate. It is clear that in both cases the type of involvement in the cultural context is quite different. We can distinguish systems that are more or less dependent from those that are more or less autonomous, whereas only in the case of the less autonomous can we speak of the preservation of an 'old' modal concept in its essential form.

A cross-cultural examination of Slavonic folk material exhibits tendencies of unification and differentiation. The former can obviously be demonstrated by comparison with material from the non-Slavonic heritage; the latter can be confirmed by cross-regional studies within Slavonic territory and reveals a diversity clearly rooted in geographical and ethnohistorical differentiation. In brief, we can summarize the basic Slavonic characteristics as tending towards lyricism and a predominance of emotional qualities (see Example 14). We should also

Example 14   *Oj lato, lato*, Sobieski 1955, vol. 2, no. 27

mention their loyalty to the concept of mode, as a subordination to a general context and its dominant rôle. This means that the concept of mode can be interpreted as being quite different from that of a pure, autonomous system rooted in the causal and linear manner which prevails in European thought. At the same time, it is quite clear that Slavonic systems and ideas were shaped in different ways in different periods and surroundings, and can be summarized as being based on two different paradigms. The 'eastern' form is subordinated unequivocally to the general context and includes a certain margin for subconsciously perceived impulses and responses, whereas the 'western' form can be interpreted as the interplay among, or even the manipulation of, the different systems, whether traditional or adapted. These systems might be differently articulated in rhythm, tonality or texture, but they are typically organized in dialogue and response forms. These dialogues refer as much to singers as to instrumentalists and dancers, and to their interplay in different mutual interactions (Lange 1978: 82). Finally, it must also be added that the substantial differences and contrasts in this kind of activity are related to the changeability of moods. The latter obviously stimulated the performers into a manipulation of the various conventions and stereotypes, that is to say of the elements representative of the various systems so diversely differentiated in the historical sense.

   Nothing reveals the character of Slavonic music and its stylistic features more clearly than does comparison with non-Slavonic music. This is most clearly observed in the contrast between Slavonic and western, especially German, music and in the difference between Slavonic music and that of the Carpathian newcomers, particularly the Polish mountain people of Walachian descent from the Podhale region who came approximately 500 years ago from the Balkan peninsula. In the case of German music, the difference is manifested by a totally different type of conceptualization based on rational thought and motivic evolution, and on the principle of preservation of the musical system. By contrast, in the music of the mountain people the principles of group performance seem to be of greatest significance; they organize the development of the whole performance on the basis of primary harmony, and on the principle of separating the dance and song sequences, ordering them into a whole cycle clearly divided into separate parts.

   Indeed, in the mountain area, where male performance dominates, the instrumental music of a typical ensemble (two or three violins plus double bass) has a really decisive rôle in shaping the basic skeleton in the tonal sense, as well as in projecting the whole structure and its division into several acts separated by instrumental interludes. The whole cycle is dominated by the idea of group performance, although it is true that in the case of the couple dance (*góralski*) the whole collective assumes the rôle of passive audience. But in this case even the concept of the couple dance is different, and it concentrates on the projection of sexual play and exhibition of acrobatic skills of the male partner, whereas the social group is involved as a passive but still important participant. The function in social 'civic' entertainment is clearly overshadowed by the context of ritual. The music and dance of these nomadic people directly reflect the behavioural patterns of their societies and may also be regarded as the best illustration of their ethnic identity, admiration of male performance and, last but not least, awareness as to how different they are from neighbouring groups. The internal differentiation of Slavonic music is clearly related to regional structure, geographically, socially and ethnohistorically shaped. These differences can be contemporarily interpreted as the areas of western style dominated by Polish and Czech elements and eastern style displaying the obvious impact of Russian elements.

Despite the evident regional and national differences, certain substantial features of a Slavonic structure can be formulated. This appears to be rooted in the concept of mode so characteristic of Slavonic culture and to be connected with the domination of the concept of cultural context over the concept of a system understood in a more autonomous sense. It is important to stress that the concept of mode dominated by cultural factors was formulated in Russian theory back in the nineteenth century by Peter Sokalskij. To be specific, it is a concept of an equivocally determined balance between musical and non-musical factors and their mutual interaction which shapes this music and its structure (Sokalskij 1888). According to this concept of mode, we can distinguish two basic kinds of structure in Slavonic music. One follows the dynamic projection of ritual and largely depends upon non-musical factors and their rhythmicity. The other, on the contrary, indicates greater autonomy, while its deepest strata seem to be determined by changeability of moods and responses, that is to say, it definitely possesses a situational character. It is clear that the interplay between different systems interrelating both traditional and transformed ways of thinking plays a decisive rôle in this Slavonic structure.

2.2   Polish tradition

2.2.1   The concept of 'Old' Polish culture: conjecture or fact

The rudiments of Polish culture and its national character are rooted in mediaeval culture and appear to have crystallized between the twelfth and fifteenth centuries AD against a background of two quite different traditions. The first may be described as a Slavonic folk culture centred upon the system of pagan Slavonic beliefs, and the second as a European culture principally imported by Church institutions after Poland accepted Christianity in 966. Certain other secular cultural elements, mainly connected with the western ballad and dance tradition, should also be taken into consideration. Indeed, the instrumental music of the time seems to be limited to the rôle of accompaniment, and was chiefly used for enriching court and military events. According to well-known sources the gap between these two basic strata of Polish tradition was immense, and only since the turn of the twelfth century do we observe any evidence of correspondence between them. The isolation of the adopted culture may best be confirmed by the well-documented total silence that accompanied the triumphal entrance of Emperor Otto III into Poland in 1000 AD. His route was strewn with carpets and lined by crowds of people, but the folk remained totally mute. According to sources, the people were not even able to greet the emperor with the *Kier les* (*Kyrie eleison*), which had been common practice in neighbouring Bohemia and Hungary during the visits of emperors in earlier times (Feicht 1975: 376). The beginning of communication between the strata indicated above is usually considered to have resulted from the activities of particular convents not earlier than the twelfth century. It was also connected with the establishment of a system of parochial schools in the thirteenth century. Both these activities strongly influenced the acknowledgement of words and formulae in Latin, of melodic models accompanied by texts translated from Latin into Polish, and, far more important, of models of western thought related to this kind of creativity. At this point a repertoire of western tropes, sequences and cycles infiltrated the local tradition of singing. The practice of following Latin models and adapting them to local society is naturally not exclusive to the religious tradition; the latter, however, played a dominant part in the early centuries of Poland's political existence. The phenomenon of bilateral exchange and the subsequent adaptation of local and imported cultures can be understood as a process similar to many others occurring in mediaeval Europe, whilst the mediating rôle of the repertoire of Church sequences is also found in other countries, in France and Germany in particular (Pikulik 1973: 13–35; see Example 15). The Polish counterparts to this kind of repertoire, however, were delayed by about two hundred years in comparison with the French and German versions.

The French and the more numerous German sequences, from Limoges, St Gall and Metz in particular, penetrated the Polish song repertoire and transformed it to a certain extent. This was above all the case with the elaboration of the final formulae visible in Polish folk songs to this day, and to a lesser extent it also applies to the structure of motifs. Movement patterns and general structural properties, however, remained unchanged. We can assume that the general development tendency influenced by other traditions also preserved its autonomy. This particularly concerns the general projection of form clearly shaped by patterns of reciting, singing and moving. A comparison between the different traditions – indigenous and adopted – highlights the two tendencies, towards adaptation and towards preservation, which often exist side by side. The former is obvious in the transformation of final formulae, the latter in the preservation of small, isolated phrases.

Nevertheless, there is no doubt that the sequences and tropes, and their structures, not only influenced but also shaped the rudiments of Polish modal tonality. In fact, sequences obviously contributed to the creation of Polish emotional qualities, and to a certain extent to the elaboration of the Polish national character. This phenomenon precisely distinguishes Polish modality from Russian, and other Slavonic modalities. At the same time, however, two points should be stressed: first, that a clear change in melody, re-orientated in the late Middle Ages towards rising movements, cannot be explained by the influence of western music and the so-called 'Church modes'; and secondly that the basic structural tendency towards perpetual circulation, repetition and elements of variability is still preserved in folkloristic material. Indeed, many facts suggest that the development of Polish tonality and folk tonality, despite their adaptational processes, retained a considerable autonomy as far as their

Example 15   *Christus surrexit*, Jan z Lublina 1964, 32 v., p. 220

deep structure is concerned. This applies above all to such residual traditional and isolated regions as Kurpie, where traditional folk music developed forms and patterns that were much more elaborate (see Example 48) than their counterparts from centrally located areas such as regions of Sandomierz. It is obvious that contacts with developed centres of European culture, and the inclusion of the Polish cultural legacy in the mainstream of cultural changes, not only transformed and enriched the folk tradition, but to a greater extent contributed to its gradual disappearance and halted its natural development. This will become clear when we compare the Polish folk tradition with its other Slavonic counterparts, and with the Balkan and Russian traditions in particular, which developed strong emotional qualities and evolved into extended and complex forms and performance media.

The scarcity of records leaves several 'dark areas' and unanswered questions. We are surprised, for example, by the mastery and high artistry of *Bogurodzica* – an anonymous work dating from as far back as the thirteenth century (Woronczak, Ostrowska and Feicht 1962). We are also surprised by the scale and popularity of particular social phenomena, such as the popularity of certain Polish songs, despite their sophistication and difficulty of performance. *Bogurodzica*, which was widely performed or chanted by the Polish knights in the fifteenth century, is one such example (see Example 16). Another surprise is the training provided in

Example 16 *Bogurodzica*, Feicht, Ostrowska and Woronczak 1962, p. 85

schools, and later at the university (after 1364), which attracted so many people from such a broad social spectrum. Finally, there is the unique phenomenon of the Polish dances which unexpectedly spread throughout the whole of Europe and were accepted by at least three social strata. The Polish dances (Figure 5), so comprehensively discussed in the literature under consideration and well documented since the first half of the sixteenth century,[22] indirectly reflect the essence and substance of gestures which later came to be identified as unequivocally Polish (see Examples 17, 18 and 19). As has already been documented, the roots of the Polish dances are to be found in mediaeval culture and in those indigenous elements that attracted Poland's neighbours as early as the beginning of the fifteenth century (1406) (Stęszewska 1977). From the viewpoint of the folk tradition, however, it is difficult to determine which kind of element, indigenous or adopted, played the most decisive rôle in the Middle Ages. They both contributed to the creation of Polish dances of a national character. But there is no doubt that the imported western dances of the Renaissance period, the pavane and saltarello in particular, were thoroughly transformed in Polish surroundings although certain structural properties of this stratum can still be recognized. Significant also was the influence of rhythmic patterns of poetry, such as trochee, dactyl and especially minor Ionicus – (∪∪– –) which is close to the Polish mazurka rhythm. The impact of western songs, and of the ballad in particular, is something of a mystery. This involves the relationship between the Celtic ballad and the west Slavonic tradition, whilst some German ballads appear to possess more advanced and transformed strata (Rogowska 1974). The scarcity of records is especially noticeable in the case of the folk and quasi-folk traditions. This affects the documentation of the activities of the 'Vagants' and 'Ribalts' who played a vital intermediary rôle in the late Middle Ages (Feicht 1962). It also applies to the activity of the early generations of university

---

[22] The first records of mazurka rhythm appear in the sixteenth century, and it dominates in the seventeenth century (after 1640).

Figure 5   Polonaise, after a lithograph by F. Grenier, drawn by A. Zaleski

Example 17   *Żołtarz Ładysława*, Lissa 1966, p. 358

students, the *Żaki*, who were apparently involved in the popularization of both the native and the imported traditions (see Wyczański 1976).

The spread of the upper-class secular tradition, and the court tradition in particular – such as the practice of multi-part singing and instrumental music – has also been of vital significance. Reference should be made to records of excavated instruments (Kamiński 1963, 1971; Feicht 1962) as well as to those mentioned in written sources. Both records confirm the existence of court and civic instrumental activities (Figure 6) which appear to be quite significant in the later development of folk instrumental music, and also in the tradition of

Example 18   *Taniec Polski*, Stęszewska 1966, no. 1

Example 18   (cont.)

chamber ensembles (Figure 7). Nevertheless in the case of multi-part singing it is hard to speak of the adaptation of court patterns. Polish folk music, apart from that of certain Carpathian territories, remains limited to monophony, which distinguishes Polish folk culture from other Slavonic traditions. It must be assumed that the substantial transformation of the indigenous Slavonic strata in the late Middle Ages was linked with a decrease in multi-part singing, which in 'Old' Slavonic days was probably based on heterophonic mass performances. There was probably a connection between the decline of heterophony or primary harmony, with its acoustic phenomena and harsh sound effects, and the powerful bans imposed by the Church authorities. It must also be assumed that these proscriptions probably shifted folk performance towards chamber and individual activities, in part following the patterns of city and court performance practices. Very much the same was true of the dance tradition which had developed since the Renaissance period, such as processional dances, in which dancers organized in couples followed the leader, whereas the old traditional mass performances and *rey* (round) dancing circles decreased.

Example 19   *Der Polnisch Tantz*, Stęszewska 1966, no. 40

Example 19   (cont.)

Figure 6   Shepherd playing bagpipe, fragment of a copperplate 'Boże Narodzenie'
(Christmas) by Samuel Kochanowski, 1598

The substantial transformation of Slavonic elements in the Renaissance period involves
various artistic media – music as much as dance and poetry. The latter were penetrated by
widely adopted poetic models, while the patterns of Latin versification (such as from
Horace), and the models of eight- and thirteen-syllable verses in particular, generally
accepted in the literature of the upper and middle classes, were also important. Indeed, where

Figure 7   Feast in an inn, after a woodcut by J. K. Haur, 1693

poetic structure is concerned, two facts must not be overlooked: first, the rôle of sequences and their models, second, the successful development of artistic Latin, which in Polish literature and scholarship reached its highest level in the Renaissance. All this contributed to the development and transformation of the genuine mediaeval tradition, while certain elements of the oldest Slavonic strata could still be traced. The latter may be found in particular performance patterns of folk singing and in the ways in which the repetition and refrain are employed. Nevertheless, the complexity and heterogeneity of background that can be distinguished in Polish Renaissance culture cannot submerge its most characteristic feature, which is its tendency towards unification. Unlike the culture of previous periods, Polish Renaissance culture is a product of clear cultural unification and presents a relatively well-elaborated and consciously appreciated national character.

An interesting methodological question is, however, how to relate the officially recognized and unified culture of that time to the phenomena of spontaneous ethnic identity felt and expressed by the local people. There is no doubt that it was the fashion of the day to sing and dance in a 'Polish', 'allemande' or *haiduck* style. It is not easy, however, to say to what extent those fashions or programmes, colouring the repertoire with local barbs, were representative of broad social acceptance. It is quite obvious, for example, that the popular *haiduck* dance recorded in the oldest Polish tabulature (*c.* 1536) (Jan z Lublina 1964; White 1963, 1964–6) (see Example 20 and compare with Example 88b) had no direct connection with the

Example 20   *Hajducky*, Szewykowski 1964, no. 44, cf. Chybiński 1948, no. 31

Carpathian nomadic dances labelled *haiduck* and performed to this day; its presence in the Polish source seems to be a result of inter-court or inter-city exchanges, but at the same time the folk dances called *haiduck* were popular throughout Poland, even until recently. The latter, however, seem to present quite different strata. Very much the same applies to Polish dances and their international careers. Indeed, it has to be stressed that this officially recognized and distributed culture was very open, a situation typical of the tolerance of Polish culture towards other social and religious traditions in the Renaissance period. This can be

confirmed, for instance, by the fact that David's Psalms (Perz 1981), translated into Polish by
Kochanowski and set to music by Gomółka, were intended for use by both Roman Catholic
and Protestant communities. It should also be stressed that the Jewish people and their
culture were highly esteemed by the Polish people of the day (Goldberg 1985). This
international and inter-social tolerance can be explained by the development of a national
consciousness, well rooted and crystallized in mediaeval times and well balanced by the
strong impact of western humanist ideas and by several patterns of classical thinking and
elaborated forms. The latter can be traced in the transparency of the clearly segmented
musical form and the obvious principle behind its construction, where clear contrast
contradicted exact repetition. It is also visible in the domination of the principle of a regular
syllabic form as well as in the obvious parallelism that organizes the poetic structure; it seems
to have left traces in folk art to this day, while its pure simplicity and balance of moods, which
can be recognized as the most characteristic features of Polish folk structure, seem to be
determined by the Renaissance paradigm. Clearly, the phenomenon of equilibrium which
balances the melancholic parts of the structure with the vivid and hilarious sequences, and the
obvious tonal contrast between modal and major phrases, or pentatonic and minor, can be
interpreted as a typical Renaissance feature (see Example 21 and compare with Example 63).

Example 21   *U mej mamy przed sienio*, Czekanowska 1956, no. 10

The concept of dialogue as well as a tendency towards 'reprise', i.e., towards the musical
expression of rounded sequences confirmed by the repetition of the first phrase at the end,
such as an aa'ba sequence, have also contributed to the crystallization of the 'new' structural
concept of the Renaissance and, even more, the Baroque period. In the latter period,
however, it became more autonomous, and was conceptualized in a purely musical sense. It
can be assumed that even at this time the principle of manipulating different musical systems
and the balancing of different and often contradictory moods was already being consciously
practised.

    The spontaneous development of merry entertainment music did not limit the significance
of the serious religious songs which flourished in Renaissance and Baroque times. This kind
of music, already performed partly in the Polish language, continued and developed several
new forms. The latter also played a vital rôle in the confirmation of the national elements in
artistic religious music. This involved the development of Church concertos and masses
based on the material of very popular Easter songs broadly adopted by several social strata

and rooted in the tradition of the mediaeval sequences discussed above. It was this repertoire that was chosen by the leading Polish composers of the Renaissance such as Franciszek Lilius (d. 1657), and more especially of the Baroque period such as G. G. Gorczycki (d. 1734), as a factor representative of Polish identity in artistic religious music. This even applied to masterpieces of the *concertato* style that were popular until the eighteenth century (Szweykowski 1966, 1977), and which played such a significant intermediary rôle in transmitting the Italian style as far afield as Byelorussian, Ukrainian and Russian music. The religious component of Polish musical culture still seems to be vital in both artistic and folk works, and this tradition in particular seems to confirm and re-evaluate the substance of the modal concept, which is still rudimentary in these forms. It should be stressed that, unlike the rhythmic and formal patterns which were thoroughly transformed in the sixteenth and seventeenth centuries, the tonality remains basically loyal to modal concepts. Nevertheless, it has to be understood in very broad terms and is not evidently connected with formulaic principles. It does not exclude, however, several 'new' ideas exhibited in this highly artistic music (chromatics).

Polish culture in the Renaissance and Baroque periods, despite regional differences, displays an unquestionable unity which can be identified in both the national and the temporal sense. It exhibits a definite style which is also evident in musical terms. The differences between Poland and other neighbouring countries, even other Slavonic nations, at that time are obvious and readily explicable in historical terms. This definitely also applies to Polish folk music. The latter reflects the richly differentiated, often contradictory, but still well-balanced reality of the period under study. From indirect sources it can be presumed that folk music, as well as folk poetry, reflected and depicted the cultural life of the sixteenth and seventeenth centuries in a very comprehensive way (see Figure 7). It is also quite evident that folk art reached its highest artistic and evolutionary stage during that period. Indeed, since the eighteenth century there has been a noticeable decline in folk art in general and in folk instruments in particular.

As has already been mentioned, the richly developed folk art can be perceived as a mirror or chronicle of its times. This shows the prominent rôle of the cities and institutions reflected in folk art and poetry. The texts of folk songs document the beauty of market squares, churches and their towers, the development of trade, commerce and skilled crafts. They also mention 'the King's men' (pages) or army dignitaries (marshals), whereas the names of specific individuals and historic events tend to pass unremarked. The general atmosphere of the life depicted in the songs is, however, dominated by family problems and moralizing sentences (Badecki 1936), while the central problem of virginity and its loss returns as a main topic (Kolberg, vol. XXV, 1886: 69; vol. XXI, 1888: 40). This and other phenomena indicate that, despite changes and transformations, the basic paradigm remains unaltered, revealing the under-development of social consciousness of these people, which is not documented in the folk art of that time. Indeed, basic social problems pass unnoticed by folk poetry, and even when problems emerge they are usually filtered through the channel of family affairs. Evidence of social conflicts appears in texts which can be identified as being of a later date, and this kind of comment usually emerges as a 'new' addition to old formulations and standards.

The music quite faithfully conveys the atmosphere created by the literary texts and complements the reflection of events and social interactions expressed in words. It documents, for example, the emergence of a new class – the minor gentry with its specific tastes, temperament and characteristic behavioural patterns. It is also possible that the very specific atmosphere surrounding this society contributed to the creation of certain Polish dances, in particular the *Polski* (Polish) or the *Wielki* (Great), which reflect psychological attitudes and especially the pride typical of this class. At the same time, however, several negative features of the minor gentry also appear in the music and musical culture, namely the limited interest of this class in music and its members' tendency to copy the style and dress of the upper classes, a tendency which is often lampooned in the folk song texts.

The atmosphere of social contact and interaction between different strata and social groups in the period under study is well documented by the folk repertoire and by the *przyśpiewki* (short dance-songs and ditties). This involves several situational moments characterized by an epigrammatic formulation often maintained in the form of a dialogue describing a given situation and based upon the principle of response. This kind of concept, containing elements of humour and satire, is perfectly illustrated and complemented by the music. The latter expresses a variability of moods, often exhibited and strengthened through effects such as interruption or suspension (see Example 62). This can also result in musical compression or, on the contrary, expansion and development, as well as concentration on certain basic 'topics' and their 'comments'. Consequently, this leads to an emphasis of contrasts by means of a perfect manipulation of the opposing tonal or rhythmic systems. Directness of reflection usually expresses changing moods, also articulated by the manipulation of different stereotypes of musical conventions rooted in a variety of formulae and their endings, or of basic motor patterns and their contradictions. The mastery of performance in this music, however, was judged according to the skill in spontaneous reaction, and according to a perfect feeling for the context and its conventions. Through this kind of folk music and through 'longer' narrative and moralizing songs, one can sketch a vision of traditional life in 'Old' Poland. The songs under discussion, through their poetry, moods and the behavioural patterns articulated by the music, convey the atmosphere of those crowded villages of Central Poland with their conflicts, problems and social events encompassing merry-making, the solemn and the sad occasion. The atmosphere of noisy markets is accurately reflected by folk art, which depicts heated quarrels and discussions, rumoured gossip and the pleasures of broad social gatherings at which music was heard and poetry was distributed in the form of leaflets, which today are an excellent documentation of this kind of social activity. Nevertheless, an analysis of the actual music leaves certain questions unanswered. These concern above all the problems of establishing an exact chronology. It can be assumed, however, that the indirect sources presented by sixteenth- and seventeenth-century tabulatures recording popular stylizations of the so-called peasant style, as well as the documentation transmitted through literary sources and the poetry of the bourgeoisie in particular, can be accepted in these cases as a proper indirect source for the folk style and behavioural patterns of the peasant class. The intensive development of the *przyśpiewka* (ditty) repertoire in the Renaissance, and particularly in the Baroque period, is a peculiarly Polish phenomenon and seems to have been shaped by the structure and dynamism of the society of that time. It cannot be compared with the development of the dialogue counterparts in other Slavonic countries and with the Russian *czastuszka* in particular. Indeed, the Russian repertoire of the sixteenth and seventeenth centuries tended towards other 'new' forms, apparently concentrated on historic and lyric topics, whereas the Russian *czastuszka*, a counterpart to Polish *przyśpiewka*, may be identified as a later historical phenomenon and never attained the same rank and function in folk music that it held in the Polish literary and musical repertoire.

The unification of Polish culture during the period of the Polish Commonwealth (1386–1772) did not negate the phenomenon of regional diversity. This still exists and is especially noticeable in folk culture and can be discussed at several levels. Disregarding for the moment the problem of the clearly distinct and isolated regions in the far south (the Carpathian area) and the far north (Kurpie), we should point out certain obvious differences between the two spheres of cultural influence which can be interpreted as the zones of 'Old' and 'New' Poland. In other words, this is a question of the cultural differences between the territories placed on the background of Polish and west Slavonic heritage ('Old' Polish), and those areas with east Slavonic heritage Polonized since the late Middle Ages ('New' Polish). These differences are still visible in the stratification of the folk repertoire and in the rather literary style of the Polish language which is spoken in these eastern highly Polonized territories while the western 'Old' territories preserved old dialect verbs and forms. So far as the problem of repertoire and its stratification is concerned, the obvious difference must be stressed between the traditional repertoire concentrated on rites and customs on the one hand, and entertainment and narrative songs on the other. The former is still marked by clear elements of 'Old' Slavonic culture, whereas the latter obviously belongs to the general Polish repertoire of the Renaissance and Baroque periods. Nevertheless, the unifying power of Polish culture in the fifteenth to eighteenth centuries is still the most striking phenomenon. This is confirmed especially by its transformational power that penetrated and infused new qualities into the old patterns of Slavonic tradition. The specific features of Polish music are once more confirmed by the results of comparative studies highlighting the basic differences in the cultures of Poland's Slavonic neighbours Russia, Ukraine and Byelorussia to the east, and Bohemia and Moravia to the west. In the case of Byelorussia the differences are especially significant and demonstrate a tendency towards the preservation of traditional strata in this area. In the case of Bohemia and Moravia, on the other hand, comparison will demonstrate a more advanced transformation of these west Slavonic cultures. The comparison with Russian music reveals a significant difference in the projection of form which in the Polish repertoire is clearly crystallized and transparently segmented into small units, while in the Russian it is much more expanded through the variations and repetitions. The comparison with the Bohemian repertoire, by contrast, elucidates the vital changes in this more highly developed music and in its instrumental tradition in particular. This concerns above all the principles of city ensembles and this kind of tradition.

It should be mentioned that Polish culture, despite its mediatory function between east and west European culture, developed many specific features and trends which can be identified as typical of its own societies and representative of their traditions alone.

2.2.2 Basic Polish sources and research tradition

The earlier records of Polish folk music are of an indirect character and occur primarily as the brief comments of chroniclers and travellers and in a sparse iconography which includes excavated musical instruments (see above, p. 20). A significant amount of information can be traced in the music and poetry of the Polish bourgeoisie clearly involved in the popular song and dance tradition of the Renaissance and Baroque ages (Badecki 1936). This is confirmed by several references, together with the presence of dance melodies in Polish and non-Polish tabulatures (Stęszewska 1962, 1977, 1979) and by the poetic texts of popular and folk songs distributed in the form of leaflets. All of these indirect sources document the existence of a social folk stratum and confirm that its culture was identified as distinct and specific. The sources, however, are too meagre for one to be able to create a vision of this folk culture and its music. Consequently, its reconstruction must be based upon the assumption that the folk legacy which was preserved until the beginning of the nineteenth century, and which is already well documented, can be considered representative of the folk tradition.

Indeed, the progress from the eighteenth into the nineteenth century has already been well documented by scholarly works which included the recording of folk culture and its resources. This was a result of the obvious growth of a national identity or, speaking more generally, of the development of a social consciousness. It is a sorry fact that only during the final years of the independent Polish state – and to an even greater extent after its decline – has the growth of national consciousness been confirmed by a proliferation of scholarly and artistic achievements. This applies to the phenomenon of the first Polish opera and to the founding of a national theatre.[23] It also applies to several academic institutions and initiatives, and especially to the beginning of the systematic documentation of folk culture and its resources. As is well recorded, folk culture and its musical features had by then already been interpreted as the background to a national identity and as a mark of national stylization. This progressed to conscious stylization and displays of typical Polish rhythms and melodies of Polish folk or popular songs, and to national topics purposely stylized and recognized for their 'new' and revitalized expressive values. These new artistic trends supported by scholarly interests and endeavours contributed to a proper evaluation of national resources and set the scene for a comprehensive and well-documented recording of Polish folk culture and its music, culminating in the excellent studies undertaken by Oskar Kolberg and edited in the latter half of the nineteenth century.

The beginning of folklore studies

The history of the documentation of Polish folk culture is usually interpreted as being divided into three or four periods. The first covers the years 1801–57, and the second the period 1857–90; the later periods are variously interpreted. Thus, the period regarded as the beginning of Polish documentation is marked by the first questionnaires prepared by Hugo Kołłątaj in 1801 (Strumiłło 1954: 164); the second sees Kolberg's monographs subsequently confirmed by his first scholarly presentations of Polish ballads, followed by his regional studies; the last two periods represent the development of Polish folklore research in later years. The division of these last two periods, which encompass nearly a century, may be variously interpreted. The most reasonable approach, however, would be to divide this time interval into two parts – 1891–1950 and after 1950 – by emphasizing the social and cultural transformation which followed the substantial historical and social changes that occurred in Polish society in the middle of the twentieth century. At that time an attempt was made to record and to preserve folk traditions before violent social changes connected with acceptance of a new social system could distort their image.

---

[23] Especially important was the famous theatre of Wojciech Bogusławski (Warsaw 1799–1814).

The first period of documentation (1801–57) is marked by the isolated initiatives of individual composers (Karol Kurpiński), scholars (Wacław Zaleski) or travellers (Zorian Dołęga Chodakowski) who were fascinated by the nature of folk phenomena and their expressive power. The general idea of Pan-Slavonic culture also stimulated the interests of these early folklorists. Polish interests and activities were closely related to the various European trends concerned with orally transmitted culture and literature. The discovery of a new world of folk culture is one of the great achievements of this epoch.

These early Polish records and investigations failed to notice the most characteristic regions, and were frequently orientated towards the culture of the non-Polish inhabitants of the previous Polish Commonwealth like the Ruthenians or the White Croatians (Zaleski 1833; Wójcicki 1836). The rather poor musical quality of these early notations, their manner of presentation (usually complemented by a harmonic accompaniment) and their scant documentation limits the historical value of this legacy; its documentary significance, however, remains undoubted. The variety of these earlier documents reveals the emotional involvement as well as the intellectual power of their authors. This applies especially to Karol Kurpiński – a well-known composer of numerous operas and other works – who propounded a survey of Polish folk music in a paper of 1820 (Strumiłło 1956: 106). More fascinating, however, than the information conveyed by these early collections is their visionary power, which contributes to a better understanding of the Polish intellectual and artistic climate of the first half of the nineteenth century, the epoch of Chopin's and Kolberg's youth. It is clear today that this rather amateurish research undertaken in part by young people on excursions to the Warsaw suburbs (Strumiłło 1954) produced the diversity of approaches seen in the comments of these amateurs and travellers. Oskar Kolberg drew extensively upon the materials of his predecessors and exploited these in his monographs, treating this legacy as comprehensively as possible. The atmosphere of this first period can also be traced in Chopin's stylizations, and particularly in his first mazurkas composed in these early years (op. 6, op. 7), in which both popular and folk inspiration exist side by side.

Oskar Kolberg and his work

Oskar Kolberg's monumental work was without equal in the scholarship of his day and distinguished itself *inter alia* in its emphasis upon musical material being approached and discussed within the comprehensive context of the folk culture (see Figure 8). His basic studies published between 1865 and 1907 are presented as a set of descriptive monographs on folk culture regionally orientated and organized according to the functions of different folk genres, and according to the content of the poetic texts and musical features (Kolberg 1865). Kolberg's monographs were prepared over many years, and his approach is well documented in his correspondence and particularly in his letter of 1865 to the *Biblioteka Warszawska* (Kolberg 1965b: 102–5). The correspondence gives detailed clarification of Kolberg's objectives as well as his attitudes to Polish folk culture.

The first edition of Oskar Kolberg's scholarly collection, i.e., the volumes published in 1857 and later between 1865 and 1907, comprises 38 issues containing the transcriptions of 10,000 folk melodies and 12,500 song texts. For the first time these songs were complemented by a relatively precise documentation of the places from which the material originated, together with copious comments, references and quotations displaying the author's scholar-

Figure 8   Oskar Kolberg, after a woodcut by W. Rzewuski

ship. The references to material in the press and periodicals of the day shed light upon Oskar Kolberg's perspective of interpretation and reflect his increasing understanding of his subject, documenting both the evolution of his approach and his perfect understanding of selection. The materials collected betray Kolberg's musical, historical and sociological passions and clearly confirm his interdisciplinary perspective. Unfortunately, Kolberg had not personally visited all the provinces described in his monographs. This fact is apparent from the quality of the documentation and the criteria of selection, as well as from the parameters of his interpretation. Indeed, the realization of this immense work was made possible only by the co-operation of other researchers who delivered material by correspondence, although their information was inevitably often limited and incomplete. This applies especially to the last volumes (1891, 1907, edited after Kolberg's death), which document material from rather remote areas populated by mixed or non-Polish ethnic groups which Kolberg had not studied personally. The titles of some of the late volumes betray Kolberg's conscientious and modest attitude to his subject: 'Images', 'Schemes' or simply 'Materials'. Kolberg was undoubtedly the foremost expert on the Polish folk culture of those central areas which he knew personally and whose music resounded in his ears in a number of local variants. Nevertheless, his documentation of the more remote regions, and especially of non-

Polish materials, is of great historical value and frequently is the only source for particular regions and cultural phenomena.[24]

The historical value of Kolberg's publication was celebrated on the centenary of his first volume (1857) by new editions of his works and publication of previously unpublished manuscripts. This took the form of a reprint of 38 virtually unobtainable volumes and, most importantly, the first edition of Kolberg's letters and writings deposited after his death in the *Akademia Umiejętności* in Cracow. This legacy, including prolific correspondence, descriptive articles and discussions, compositions, commentaries and several indexes only began to be published in 1961. The whole edition is destined to encompass 80 volumes containing 17,000 folk melodies, and has reached, to date, 67 volumes. Thanks to this source Polish and non-Polish folk culture of the second half of the nineteenth century has been documented in a thoroughly scholarly manner.

The years directly following the period of Kolberg's research, although well recorded thanks to several ethnographic and folkloristic institutions and university initiatives, were not productive or successful in the field of music. This was a result of the generally low level of musical education, which is best reflected by the quality of the musical notation. The same applies to the quality of the selection and documentation of musical material published in periodicals of the time. The selection of material tended to concentrate upon those highly popular non-folk songs which were the easiest to notate. This rather disappointing 20-year period (1890–1910) was at the same time successful in the area of local initiatives, with the publication of material from such barely studied western provinces as Silesia and Pomerania. It also saw the establishment of regional journals and periodicals transmitting data and information into the social conscience. The information supplied at that time documents many cultural artifacts which were rapidly disappearing from the scene, for instance unique Polish folk instruments (Karłowicz 1888) and non-Polish instruments from the territory of the historic Polish Commonwealth. Information supplied at that time also describes the authentic form of the folk dances and music of the mountain people (Kleczyński 1888).

The birth of Polish ethnomusicology

The academic study of Polish folk music started to develop a decade before World War I and was accompanied by other manifestations of the intellectual and artistic enlivenment of Polish society. Poland witnessed the development of various cultural institutions supporting and organizing cultural life in modern terms. Polish musicology was established as a university discipline (1912 and 1913) at the leading universities of Cracow and Lvov. Polish scholarship had been solidified by the foundation of the *Akademia Umiejętności* as early as 1873 in Cracow. However, the Academy's research like that of Warsaw and Poznań was still concentrated territorially on the areas controlled by the three foreign powers administering Poland and could not draw up a nationally unified programme. Nevertheless, this period has to be characterized as the beginning of the scholarly study of folk music. The first phonograph recording was undertaken as early as 1913, accompanied by attempts at the classification of folk melodies (Chybiński 1907).

---

[24] It must be added that Kolberg's study stimulated documentation in other Slavonic countries, particularly in Bohemia (Ludvik Kuba) and Croatia (Franjo Kuhač).

Nevertheless, an appreciation of modern methodology and its rigorous discipline some-times succeeded in underestimating previous collections, and went so far as to criticize Kolberg's work. Kolberg's materials, although not always perfectly notated, preserve their value to this day, whilst professionally trained musicologists have never managed to produce a well-organized modern collection. They clearly lag behind their Finnish (Ilmari Krohn), Hungarian (Bartók and Kodály) and Ukrainian (Filaret Kołessa) colleagues involved in collection on an extensive scale. On the other hand, the interest in folk music and the well-trained taste of Polish musicologists and musicians, who at that time were connected by close contacts and personal friendships – Z. Jachimecki, A. Chybiński (1959), K. Szymanowski (1982: 88, 174) – contributed to a re-examination of the approach to folk music and formed the background to the concept of a national style.

The first academic studies were not, however, the products of traditional university professors. They were undertaken by a highly educated, excellently trained lady who never obtained a university post. Helena Windakiewiczowa started to publish as early as 1897, with a study concerning the rhythm of Polish folk music. Her interest in prosody, versification and rhythm shaped the basic trends of the research which she continued throughout her life, and which led to her being awarded membership of the Polish *Akademia Umiejętności* (1948). Helena Windakiewiczowa's interests and investigations are documented in one of the best contributions concerning the deep strata of Chopin's stylizations, i.e., her discovery of Chopin's deep roots in Polish folk music (1926). She was the first to consider Chopin's structure as being determined by behavioural patterns of dialogue and responsorial corre-spondence (see Examples 22 and 23), altering the dimensions of analysis and breaking the

Example 22 *Zakukały kukaweczki*, Kolberg 1857, no. 20, p. 314

conventions of morphologically orientated analysis in favour of general concepts of structure, their functions and situational context. This was successful thanks to her perfect knowledge of folk material and its cultural determinants.

Cultural life developed in restored and independent Poland after 1918 with renewed vigour and in totally new conditions. The latter were primarily concerned with efforts towards territorial and administrative integration, but this was also visible in cultural policy. Greater energy was directed towards educational programmes which rapidly overcame the alarming illiteracy of Polish people in certain areas of the country. Educational programmes were addressed towards primary and secondary schools as well as the rapidly expanding univer-sities, and finally the musical conservatories. The dispersed and, initially, often amateur initiatives gradually gave way to better organized, institutionally supported systems. This also applied to musical life and to the interest in folk art and culture. On the other hand, the situation in the traditional Polish village, despite its economic difficulties, started to change much faster than previously, not without consequences for the transformation of folk culture.

Example 23   F. Chopin, op. 30, no. 4, Paderewski's Edition, Cracow 1961, no. 21, bars 17–25

This was a result of the cultural integration, which distorted the former provincial or regional borders, but it was also caused by the intensive educational processes stimulating greater mobility of people and their openness to the new mass media. The growth of social awareness announced by sociologists led to the transformation of the basic hierarchy of values. It also influenced scholarly investigation and resulted in the modification of methodological approaches. The latter evolved towards concepts stressing the significance of social structure and towards the re-examination of folk culture and the analysis of its durable values. It should be added that even at that time traditional art was approached not merely as a national treasure or resource but as a well-spring of creative inspiration. However, these ambitious programmes resulted in the artistic achievements of poets, painters, dancers and musicians and in the area of decorative art in particular, but their influence upon scholarly endeavours was rather limited. Actually, for a long period, folk culture and folk music fascinated ethnologists and anthropologists more than musicologists; indeed, the first syntheses of Slavonic and Polish folk music and dance were accomplished by ethnologists and not musicologists. It was also the ethnologists who explored the culture of non-Polish ethnic elements in the multi-national Poland of those days.

The situation changed when two universities began intensive work in the field of ethno-musicology. These were the new University of Poznań (1921) and the lecturer's post inaugurated much later (1936) at the University of Warsaw. These two university departments led by musicologists Lucjan Kamieński and Julian Pulikowski initiated systematic sound-recording in Poznań (1930) and Warsaw (1935) and designed research programmes

linking them with teaching programmes. The ethnomusicological centre in Poznań led by
Lucjan Kamieński is recognized as the first Polish school of musical ethnography, concentrating primarily on the exploration of the practically unknown music of northern and
western Poland, and of Great Poland and Pomerania in particular. A survey of the studies
undertaken there elucidates the interests and methodological concepts of this school, and
traces of Kolberg's tradition are clearly visible. This applies especially to the topics of its
dissertations (Czekanowska, 1958: 147) which typically stress an interest in ballads and the
wedding repertoire. The discovery of the almost unknown folk music of Pomerania must be
regarded as the greatest achievement of the Poznań centre.

Other achievements of the Poznań school are its establishment of standards for the
recording, documentation and transcription of folk music, together with its initiative in
organological research successfully accomplished by Jadwiga Sobieska's dissertation on the
bagpipe in Great Poland (J. Pietruszyńska (Sobieska) 1936). Thanks to the studies organized
and undertaken by Kamieński in conjunction with his students, the ancient strata of this old
Polish north-western tradition have been discovered. This also includes the documentation of
the old, authentic versions of west Slavonic 'capping' melodies from Great Poland notated by
Lucjan Kamieński, and his discovery of the Pomeranian trumpets (*bazoune*) and other folk
instruments.

Unfortunately, many of the results and achievements of this brief period were destroyed in
the ravages of World War II. The war annihilated the song collections of both universities
mentioned above, as well as the collections gathered by ethnologists from the University of
Vilnius, which are no longer accessible. Nevertheless, the basic standards of university
training in ethnomusicology had already been attained and were to result in the establishment
of a university programme after World War II.

So far as the gathering and recording of music is concerned, it should be stated that the
most fascinating and artistically compelling material was discovered not by university staff
but by musicians fascinated by the music of the Polish mountain people (Stanisław Mierczyński, first edition 1930) and by amateurs and local personalities exploring the unknown
music of Kurpie (X. W. Skierkowski, edited in two volumes divided into fascicules, 1929,
1934). It was the expressive quality of this music which contributed to the creative stylization
of folk music in the modern sense and, as mentioned above, contributed significantly to the
creation of the idiom of Polish folkloristic stylization (see Example 24).

The restoration of national resources and the academic tradition after the losses and
tragedy of World War II dominated the activities of Polish scholars in the immediate post-war
period (1945–55). At the same time, however, the consequences of the alarming social
changes and migrations which took place during the post-war years made the need for
documentation more vital than ever before. It was generally acknowledged that the changes
in the social structure would transform, if not utterly distort, the balance of traditional
culture. The new centralized institutions of the socialist state with its policy of cultural
intervention, created new situations for massive undertakings on a global scale. The idea to
compile a general inventory of folk art emerged as early as 1948, and was organized primarily
as a series of summer work-camps focusing on the documentation of folk art. This idea
subsequently expanded into the establishment of an institute and periodicals specializing in
folk art and the foundation of folk music and dance ensembles modelled upon Soviet patterns
and ideas. The background to these 'new' ideas was clearly rooted in the 'inter-war' concepts

Example 24   K. Szymanowski, op. 50, no. 1, Kraków 1982, no. 1, bars 1–28

Example 24   (cont.)

of decorative art described above, and thanks to this tradition the results of this initiative have been crowned with many successes. Nevertheless, it should be stressed that folk music in Poland, unlike in many other Slavonic countries, never attained great significance. The documentation of Polish folk music has been basically an academic enterprise, and unlike dance and decorative art the musical resources of Polish folk music which have been collected have had a limited influence on contemporary art. In brief, the objectives of scholars, composers and popularizers (including folk ensembles) have been clearly divergent. This is especially true in the case of the music of recent decades; contemporary composers have not devised new proposals for the proper stylization of folk material and apart from a few attempts have remained aloof from this music and its inspirational power. At the same time popularizing movements have found authentic Polish folk melodies difficult to perform and stylize. All in all, recording and documentation have been limited to basic academic goals.

The recordings intensively made during the period 1949–53 laid the foundations for the second Polish national collection. The latter must be compared to that of Oskar Kolberg. It entailed the recording of 60,000 folk melodies undertaken at the very last moment before general social changes and upheavals overturned the traditional structure of Polish culture. Indeed, the plan to produce a modern national documentation of folk music which had been attempted several times since 1920 only succeeded in the middle of the twentieth century. This was made possible thanks to central organization and massive state support, additionally strengthened by the protection of local authorities. The documentation of dance, although included at the beginning of the programme, was finally directed independently. The dance programme was linked to teaching and training programmes to an even greater extent. The differences in the programmes and documentation objectives of music and dance have, with the passage of time, become more and more obvious.

Among initiatives of that time the work undertaken by the ethnologists who compiled the *Polski Atlas Etnograficzny* (Polish Ethnographic Atlas) should also be mentioned. In contrast to the activities mentioned above, the latter was furnished with more elaborate programmes and clearly dominated by the comparative approaches and historically orientated consider-ations which had flourished for many years in the tradition of Polish ethnology. Indeed, the investigation of the distribution of cultural artifacts and their cartographic documentation held out great promise and attracted many Polish scholars, among them ethnomusicologists. The basic interest was concentrated upon the distinctive cultural areas of Polish territory, including their relations to other Slavonic and Baltic cultures. Nevertheless, the ethnological approach, though crowned by spectacular results in the area of material culture, gave limited access to musicologists, who were attracted by different methodological trends.

Centrally supported documentation, including the initiative to re-edit Kolberg's work, may be generally interpreted as one of the hallmarks of the period and its enthusiastic belief in the power and importance of centralized initiative and state support. A comparison of the inter-war period (1918–39) and the two decades following World War II (1945–64) reveals obvious differences both in ideology and concept of organization. It also reveals the advan-tages and disadvantages of both programmes, although elements of a common tradition can be traced in both concepts.

The gathering of documentary evidence, however, was not always successful in its long-term consequences. This applied to the generalized models of standard questionnaires current at that period, which tended to level out and suppress the character of the information obtained. It also resulted from a scarcity of documentation sufficiently adapted to the different conditions of research. The inadequacy of the information supplied by these traditionally descriptive methods has now become evident since new methodological approaches concentrating on the analysis of performance practice and behavioural patterns came into prominence. Nevertheless, thanks to the massive documentation of the mid-twentieth century, Polish folk culture of that time can be seen in its realistic dimensions. The existence of many 'grey zones' and 'bridge territories' have also been documented, together with the restriction of the authentic folk tradition to confined enclaves. In the twentieth century the image of Polish folk culture created by Oskar Kolberg was re-examined in its geographical, historical and sociological dimensions.

Methodological aspects of contemporary research

Neither the ethnohistorical discussion, with its hypothetical conclusions, nor the standards of documentation provided by traditional scholarship satisfy contemporary scholars. The explosive changes in modern Poland have stimulated new interests which are clearly visible in research trends since the 1960s. These have resulted in temporary co-operation with sociolo-gists; and the questions of cultural change led the field in the 1970s, overtaking the previous diachronically orientated perspective, which had regarded the material under study mainly in its regional diversity. At the same time these sociological methods have revealed certain limitations, especially in so far as the interpretation of the creative element in art is concerned.

By contrast, the application of mathematical methods in ethnomusicology has gone beyond mere ordering and systematization procedures, as practised in many east European countries, Slovakia and Hungary in particular (Elschekova 1966; Bartók 1951). Polish scholars utilizing mathematics and concentrating on structural integration through the discovery of statistically demonstrated clusters (Czekanowska 1972) and the exploration of its nature have contributed to a better understanding of the material under study. Although these methods, like many others, have contributed to a fundamental re-examination of the tools and approaches previously used, they have not yet revealed the basic principles of the creative process in music. This applies to the employment of mathematics in the modelling process (Żerańska-Kominek 1986), to the exploration of the correspondence between syntactical units and their distributional aspects, and finally to the confrontation of the results yielded by analytical procedures with the information contributed by psycho-sociological interviews. The latter have centred upon a reconstruction of the conceptual system that exists in the informant's mind (P. Dahlig 1983). The development of theoretical thinking has contributed in particular to an understanding of the aesthetic criteria and processes of assessment. On the other hand, the application of mathematics has advanced the discovery of proper structural ties (Czekanowska 1986), and consequently has helped to explain not only syntactical properties but also their relation to the phenomena of perception and to the processes of social acceptance. The final result is a further integration of the isolated research programmes concentrated on the one hand on syntactical analysis, and on the other on the cultural interpretation of both the creative perceptual processes and the processes of social acceptance.

To conclude, it should be stated that Polish ethnomusicology – originating concurrently from musicological and ethnological traditions – has been associated both with the general development of theoretical thinking within the humanities and with the traditional workshop of the empirical disciplines (measurements, tests). Polish ethnomusicology has also been engaged socially and has developed strong links with more pragmatically orientated research projects. The influence of west European methods in Polish ethnomusicology has generally been stronger than those of eastern Europe. The latter, however, have been and remain significant and contribute to the distinctiveness of Polish scholarship.

One of the toughest dilemmas facing contemporary ethnomusicology in Poland is the re-evaluation of the material which has been collected so far. Thanks to this basic material the modern synthesis of Polish folk music has been made possible, but the introduction of the analytical approach towards transformational processes of the repertoire still remains a responsible task. It must also be stressed that these basic studies have to be complemented by contributions concerning the musical culture of those non-Polish ethnic groups which still exist within the framework of Polish society.

The basic resources of Polish folk music are represented today by three different kinds of collections. The first is that of Kolberg, the second was made during the mid-twentieth century, whereas the third refers to recent materials collected and presented since 1970 by various university staffs, the Research Institute of the Polish Academy of Sciences and certain regional institutions and includes altogether about 100,000 melodies. The materials indicated above already present a relatively high standard of documentation, although they are evidently individual and follow diverse orientations depending on the possibilities of research in the field and the needs and objectives of particular institutions. For example, the Catholic University of Lublin has concentrated on selected areas such as the documentation and investigation of Polish religious songs in the folk tradition. Other universities have more varied programmes which attempt to combine an exploration of both Polish and non-Polish cultures, leading to a better understanding of the complex cultural structure of contemporary times. The work of Silesian scholars such as Kopoczek, Dygacz and Marcinkowa, concentrating on regional culture, holds quite an important position amongst the various research and training programmes.

The results of contemporary research clearly indicate that Polish culture has now become homogeneous nationally and socially, though rooted in both a Slavonic and non-Slavonic cultural heritage. As is well known, the transformation of contemporary folk culture is still under way and evidently depends upon changeable trends overbalancing the temporarily achieved equilibrium. The social rôle of the folk tradition and of folk music in particular is also changeable and contributes variously to the general transformational processes. As has been indicated, the complicated nature of the subject matter demands differentiated and appropriately selected methods. This applies especially to the sociological tools and instruments which up until now have not been successfully exploited. The latter are full of promise particularly where studies on contemporary youth movements engaged in the popularization of folk music are concerned. This also applies to research into the rôle of music in recently repopulated areas, and those of western and northern Poland in particular, as well as to the music of different groups of émigrés. The results of these investigations, however, cannot be expected before a longer period of systematically conducted research has elapsed.

2.2.3 Regional aspects of Polish folk music

The regional diversity of Polish folk culture that so fascinated the chroniclers and scholars of the eighteenth and nineteenth centuries is in evidence to this day. Recent changes, however, especially the enforced migrations of sections of the population, and the processes of industrialization and urbanization, have broken down the traditional regional structures which had hitherto been preserved for hundreds of years. These changes are basically the result of a decisive shift from a class-stratified to an open society, and from a state comprising many national groups to a structure dominated by one nation.

Remnants of regional culture are mainly to be found in some isolated enclaves, which usually contain not more than 20 to 25 villages or even fewer, and are dominated by a specific, vital tradition. Although this tradition is limited, it has survived the deluge of modern Polish culture and civilization. It has to be added, however, that not only the folk culture itself, but also our view of it, has changed, and this has also contributed to the fact that we need to make a different evaluation of regional reality today. Kolberg's study was motivated by his documentary and descriptive approach to what he understood as his patriotic duty, and it has succeeded in creating a vision of the pre-partition Polish Commonwealth which is reflected in its folk and peasant culture, and was described against this background. By contrast, contemporary studies are usually restricted to Polish ethnic territory and are presented in a series of monographs dealing with the folk culture of closed areas, justified by the fact that they possess a homogeneous legacy or that there is an obvious sense of identity among the inhabitants. These studies are concerned with parts of historical Polish provinces such as Great Poland, Silesia, Kujavia and Mazovia, which have preserved their cultural homogeneity to a certain extent. They also deal with some border regions which are clearly ethnocentric or just distinctive by reason of their traditional legacies. The conservative culture of the Polish eastern border territories presents a different case. The archaic features of these lands have fascinated many generations of scholars, but it remains difficult to interpret them in regional terms. Indeed, well before it became a homogeneous entity, this rather conservative folk culture revealed a dispersed conglomeration in which remnants of different cultural strata existed side by side. To a certain extent it is even easier to detect some elements of the 'Old' Slavonic culture of prehistoric times in these border territories than it is to identify the local centres that are integrating cultural activity in the regional sense. Polish culture, evidently younger in the eastern border territories, obviously had greater effects on representatives of the upper and middle classes, while representatives of the folk culture remained true to the 'Old' Slavonic tradition for many hundreds of years. It may be surprising, but the results of anthropological studies indicate that cultural radiation from the historical Polish centres flourishing in these eastern areas since the Middle Ages has not altered the folk culture there. Although they have definitely been Polonized linguistically, they have remained loyal to traditional behavioural patterns and the people have preserved their different ways of thinking. The results of various studies also indicate that the rôles of small local centres can be more easily comprehended by means of their material culture than through their music or dance.

A different, even more complex, problem is posed by the regional identity of the inhabitants of the western Polish territories. Disregarding recent changes and migrations, it must be stated that the remnants of Polish culture in this area should be regarded as an 'Old' Slavonic stratum that has survived the pressures of rigorous Germanization. This is especially the case with the culture of some parts of Silesia (Opole Silesia – Opolskie) and of northern Mazovia (Mazuria). It was recorded immediately after World War II that the latter regions still retained at that time the features of a homogeneous culture with an obvious regional character. Ethnocentric and national feelings supported the preservation of vernacular culture in these areas until the middle of the twentieth century, and only the most recent changes and migrations destroyed its unity.

The regional identity of central parts of Poland presents yet another situation, which has resulted rather from the homogeneous nature of the traditional culture than from the ethnocentric feelings of the inhabitants. By contrast in these central provinces the sense of regional identity usually has a different function; and it is motivated not by feelings of ethnocentricity but rather by local pride and by the conviction that this culture is superior to others. These feelings in the central Polish region are not, however, further intensified by a sense of strangeness, and they evolve towards feelings of self-satisfaction. Indeed, feelings of self-identity and self-satisfaction, usually more intuitive than conscious, favour and support the preservation of traditional culture, even in those territories where ethnocentric feelings have already lost or never developed their significance. In many cases considerable responsibility attaches to the task of interpreting such regions. The classical approach of explaining regional integration as the product of historical events, that is as a legacy of previously existing and often privileged regional units (Crown territories, properties under episcopal management), cannot be regarded as sufficient or satisfactory in many instances. The prosperous past and the conditions then pertaining, even if they really were favourable, cannot sufficiently explain the artistic sensitivity of the people and protect the structure of cultural transmission which can still be identified as an active force. As has already been mentioned, the phenomena of social consciousness and homogeneity of culture do not often coincide, nor does the distribution of material artifacts overlap that of spiritual phenomena. The distribution of musical and dance phenomena usually covers a much more extensive area than does that of architecture or of folk costumes and, to a certain extent, it only covers the distribution of dialects and their phonetic features.

The distribution of folk musical instruments presents a further problem, especially as regards the context in which these instruments are produced, in which musical ensembles are created and some stylistic peculiarities still preserved or, conversely, altered. In fact traditional instrumental practice is today restricted to limited enclaves that still exist in a few regions. In these areas both the traces of the production of musical instruments at home and the tradition of creating musical ensembles within the family circle are still to be found. This is also the case with the principles of musical education, the social status of musicians, the ways in which economic support for musicians is organized, and the way in which spare parts for musical instruments are purchased; patterns of musical transmission and, of course, performance practices have also been preserved. However, alongside these enclaves where the best musical traditions have been retained, many more extended 'bridge' zones can be identified. The latter, usually located close to the most traditional areas, are at the same time relatively open to innovation and transmit their legacy in more altered versions. This means that they adapt the current fashions, modern instruments and peculiarities of performance which a neighbouring area might articulate. This kind of distribution is especially typical of centrally located areas dominated by the Mazovian violin ensemble, accompanied by a drum and harmonium and specializing in dance music of the *oberek* type. A similar phenomenon can be found in southern Poland, the Sub-Carpathian area in particular, where ensembles of modern string and wind instruments, specializing in *polka*-type dances, have gained a certain popularity. The dissemination of these quasi-folk ensembles and of that quasi-traditional repertoire is obviously contributing to several transformational processes occurring today, as well as to the levelling out of definite regional differences. This is especially evident in those territories where ethnocentric feelings do not support regional identity. At the same time, however, the activity of these quasi-traditional ensembles, more than many other factors, continues to keep the Polish folk instrumental tradition alive. Thus, the disappearance and the territorial limitation of purely regional instrumental music, such as for example that of the bagpipe and violin from Great Poland or of the violin ensemble from Podhale, is an indisputable fact. It must nevertheless be stated that the roots of regional identity are preserved today in a great variety of ways. They may create more homogeneous units, that are consciously perceived or that have recently been dispersed and are only intuitively felt. They may also be created by political factors and adapted to local realities in varying proportions. This is precisely the reason why Polish folk culture today presents such a regionally diversified picture.

Great Poland (Wielkopolska)

Great Poland, not without reason sometimes called 'Old Poland', is the region of Poland which has been best documented historically. Its musical culture has been traced back as far as the end of the tenth century in written sources, and much earlier through archaeological excavations. By contrast, the folk culture of this historical province is not obviously archaic, although both vocal and instrumental traditions have been well preserved, and some remnants of ancient dances and customs and certain features of the local dialect can still be found (Sobieska and Sobierajski 1972). Although the culture of Great Poland is not archaic, it has been deliberately preserved and is regionally distinctive. The way in which the people move, dance, communicate or formulate their ideas particularly emphasizes those regional characteristics that obviously set them apart from the people of other Polish provinces. This is also evident in their provincial pride, differences in temperament and sense of humour. It must be said, however, that the roots of this regional distinctiveness lie very deep. According to historical linguists, in fact, the culture of Great Poland was already recognizably different in early mediaeval times, and it would be a mistake to explain its specific features as having been formed by recent historical events and migrations. The musical culture of this highly civilized part of Poland, and the way in which it is organized, are also different. This is particularly so with the practice of instrumental playing which is one of the best preserved in Poland. It is of a semi-professional nature, although it still tends to be considered a family business. Indeed, the conventions relating to how the journeys of the instrumentalists are organized are reminiscent of the activities of a guild rather than of the habits of east European society. A traditional culture that has preserved some continuity and possesses a definite regional character indicates an obvious ability to adapt and to accept the standards and patterns of modern civilization; more than any other Polish province Great Poland has adapted its culture in these ways, thereby consciously preserving it. The earlier pattern, rooted in old beliefs and symbols, no longer exists in the present day, although several remnants of the old strata can still be traced.

The traditional instrumental ensemble of bagpipe and violin dominates the music of Great Poland. This is demonstrated by the social status of the musicians, the presence of the ensemble at socially significant events, the variety of these instruments, the way in which they are made and decorated, and finally by the degree to which the musical structure is influenced by the tuning and scale of the various types of bagpipes, and the techniques employed in playing them. The sound of this instrument can even be detected in the timbre of human voices simulating its sound.

Among these traditional instruments the noble bagpipes known as *koziol* deserve particular mention (see Example 25 and Figure 9). Its importance is confirmed by its size, lower tuning and shape, good aesthetic design, and by its inclusion in the school curriculum. In fact, the art of playing the bagpipes was promoted by local schools of music in the 1950s. The limited success of this initiative, however, only indicates the heavy responsibility attaching to external intervention in cultural policy and how difficult it is to predict the trends according to which a tradition will develop.

The most characteristic regional features of the instrumental music are those relating to performance style, since other east European versions of the bagpipes from Great Poland, despite their different tunings, sizes, scales (Pietruszyńska-(Sobieska) 1936) and technical details, do not display organologically many specific local characteristics. Indeed, the performance style of Great Poland is to a certain extent unique and cannot even be compared with other Polish traditions of playing the bagpipes. Its stylistic features seem to be rooted in a fast tempo and in the timbre of an instrument clearly dominated by the effect of a rather high tessitura and in the constant 'rotating' repetition of a short melodic pattern and emphasis on these repetitions by the addition of certain final formulae. The basic melody, played by the

Example 25   Melody of *kozioł*, Sobiescy 1973, no. 7, p. 253

bagpipes and supported by its drone, is simultaneously accompanied by violin, playing in the same register and as far as possible following the same melody. There are vocal parts and dances that correspond to the instrumental music, but this last is also performed as a purely instrumental solo. The vocal part consists of various short repetitions inserted in the framework of the constantly repeating melody. The singer can also demonstrate his invention by manipulating the time units in a particular way within regularly pulsating bars and with a special way of gasping for a breath. The pattern of rotation, repetition and pulsation is also expressed in the accompanying dances: in the rapid circulation of the couples balanced by the wide-spread skirts of the dancing women. The expressive character of the music and dance is

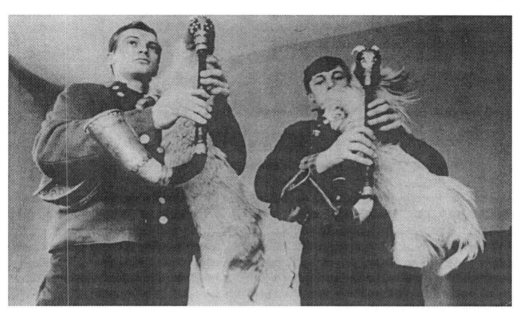

Figure 9   *Koziol* of Ziemia Lubuska played by boys

emphasized by the atmosphere conveyed by the texts of the songs. These are equally gay and robust, and maintain a mood of equilibrium, underlining the common sense, sobriety and steady nature of the inhabitants, so obviously different from the changeable, lyrical atmosphere of east and central Polish songs. Balance, control and good humour clearly dominate the performance style; generous accepted norms are never exceeded in tempo, dynamics or tessitura, though these can be high and strained.

Dance music performed by instrumental ensembles and accompanied by short dance songs, or *vivats* (see Example 26), definitely dominates the folk repertoire of today. It does

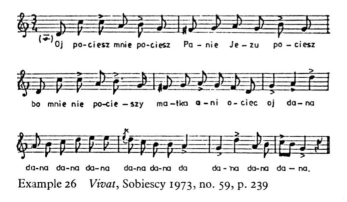

Example 26   *Vivat*, Sobiescy 1973, no. 59, p. 239

not, however, exclude other strata; both customs, accompanied by chants, and so-called 'common' songs exist. The first of these clearly depict the 'old-world' Polish character and focus on wedding (see Example 27), harvest and spring ceremonies, whereas the 'common'

Example 27   *Oj chmielu, chmielu*, Bielawski 1970, no. 102

songs concentrate on moralizing subjects, ballads, and professional songs and dances charac-teristic of this area. The touching mood of east Polish lyrics is of limited appeal to this reasonable society, and although the text might contain a mournful element this is dispelled by the spirit of the accompanying music. Moments of deep emotion are very rare, and are usually restricted to certain genres and situations. These occur during the 'capping' cer-emony which is the climax of the traditional wedding, or they can also be found in the mood of professional songs dedicated to seasonal workers who lose their jobs in the autumn. Never-theless, the gay atmosphere of dance gatherings does not preclude the more serious moods as preserved in the remnants of ancient customs. This especially applies to wedding episodes accompanied by the outstanding *Polski* (Polish Dance) and by the melodies devoted to the 'capping' ceremony, authentic versions of which were preserved in Great Poland until the middle of the twentieth century. By contrast, the most recent strata reveal a different type of repertoire, obviously influenced by west or central European traditions. On the other hand, seasonal customs and their songs, and those connected with hay-making or harvest in particular, are definitely west Slavonic in character (see Example 28).

Example 28   *Kośniczki stojum*, Sobieska and Sobierajski 1972, no. 58, p. 276

The different character of the culture of Great Poland is further emphasized by the open relationship between the cultures of the city and the village. Unlike the eastern and central regions of Poland, the border between town and country does not really exist in Great Poland, and the best of the musicians that accompany weddings and other social gatherings usually do not live in villages but in small towns.

It should be stressed that an awareness of the strength and continuity of local culture dominates the mentality of the people and helps preserve the cultural resources of the province, although the old pattern of earlier traditions no longer exists.

The differences within Great Poland point to the differences between the south-western, eastern and northern areas. For example the music of the northern regions does not exhibit such vitality, although it is still rich in tradition and preserves some typical customs and dances (see Example 29). This is also the case in eastern regions of Great Poland and in neighbouring Kujavia, which are culturally less dynamic today, although historically they developed activities that have been confirmed as being the oldest in Polish territory. Today, however, this area reveals how folk culture, including musical activities and even the bagpipes, has progressively disappeared. The bagpipes have been replaced to a certain extent by the Kujavian style of ensemble, and by changes in the musical and dance repertoire. Thus the culture of the south-western provinces, located between Great Poland and Silesia and concentrated around several local centres such as Kościan, Leszno, Międzyrzecz, Zbąszyń, Krobia and Gostyń which played a significant cultural rôle in the past and have preserved their traditions to this day, remains the most vivid and authentic in cultural activity of this province.

The coexistence of archaic remnants typical of Great Poland, evident in language, dance, customs and performance style on the one hand, and in the ability to adapt on the other, is an unusual phenomenon in Polish contemporary folk culture. This fact reflects the deep historical roots of a tradition that has flourished in this province for many hundreds of years. It is also a record of the vital contacts between privileged centres and their surrounding villages, and of the reasonable character of the inhabitants who have consciously preserved their own traditional treasure.

Silesia (Śląsk)

Silesia is one of the most civilized Polish provinces where Polish, Czech and German cultural influences have competed and coexisted for many hundreds of years. Historically speaking, the national differences in this area were connected with the question of social and religious identity. The organic unity between the towns and the countryside, typical of Silesia in the Middle Ages and the Renaissance, was progressively replaced by marked social differences. This was especially the case in the larger towns, and on the big estates which, in time, came to be dominated by the German population, whereas the villages and smaller towns remained loyal to Slavonic and Polish culture. The links with the Polish state were broken as early as the fourteenth century (Davies 1981), although some areas were ruled by Slavonic princes right up to 1675. It is surprising that the rulers of Poland did not strive for the cultural incorporation of Silesia into the area of Polish domination, although it was famous for its printing enterprises (Brzeg 1880) and contributed in the seventeenth and eighteenth centuries to the dissemination of Polish language and culture. At the same time we find that the records, particularly in relation to this, reveal that prominent Polish citizens were totally ambivalent towards, if not downright ignorant of, Silesian problems. There is, for example, the well-known story of some Polish citizen (Franciszek Karpiński) who was surprised (c. 1770) by the fact that the people of Silesia still spoke the Polish language (Kolberg, vol. XLIII, 1965a: v). By contrast, the Austrian and German rulers devised programmes of intensive acculturation, which were especially strong in the so-called Prussian partition occupied by the Germans since the middle of the eighteenth century, while in the southern part, governed by Austria, the policy was more liberal and supported cultural autonomy to a certain extent.

Historical events clearly contributed to the regional differences of the province. The most culturally active regions can be divided into three parts: the area around Opole in the so-called

Example 29   *Kujawiak*, Krzyżaniak, Pawlak and Lisakowski 1975, no. 491, p. 224

'lower' part, the mining area of Katowice and Rybnik in the 'upper' part, and the mountain region close to Cieszyn. The basic historical division makes a distinction between the areas of the lower and upper tributaries of the River Oder, which were the result of provincial dispersal by Bolesław Krzywousty (the Wry-Mouthed) who divided this province among his sons as early as the twelfth century (see above, p. 5). It seems that there are traces of this historical event in the cultural structure to this day. Nevertheless the regional diversity of Silesia is balanced by many features that apparently unify this western province. The background, above all, is that of an obviously west Slavonic culture possessing well-preserved wedding and seasonal traditions, additionally documented by strong cultural links with Moravian and Czech culture (see Examples 30a, b, c). There is the music and dance

Example 30a   *Ruža som ja ruža*, Sušil 1860, no. 2,318

Example 30b   *Wyleciała dusza*, Bobrowska 1981, no. 132, p. 219

Example 30c   *Oj płakałam ja wczoraj*, Bystroń 1934, p. 701, no. 636

performed for entertainment which convey a gay, robust atmosphere, as well as a rich repertoire of ballads and narrative songs – better preserved here than in any other Polish province (Bystroń 1927; Ligęza and Stoiński 1938) – and many professional songs. Finally, the balance between diversity and unity can be seen in traditional spring customs and their obvious references to the repertoire of Little Poland (see Example 31). These seem, however,

Example 31 *Smrtna nedela*, Sobieska and Sobierajski, 1972, p. 172

to be closer in character to church mysteries than to traditional pagan rites. Indeed, the influence of Roman Catholicism has been strong in this province since the Middle Ages; many religious orders founded monasteries and convents in this area (Pikulik 1973), and their influence has remained especially strong among the peasants who did not accept the Protestant reforms. The strong link with the Roman Catholic church was also characteristic of several professional groups, the miners in particular. In fact, the miners' loyalty to their religion (see Example 32) and their professional pride even dominated regional feelings. In

Example 32 *Robota stanyła*, Dygacz 1956, no. 4, p. 12

brief, the vernacular culture and its oldest strata are preserved today in the area of Opole (see Example 33) and in the territories surrounding Rybnik.

Example 33 *Młoda pani cepca ni mo*, Dygacz and Ligęza 1954, no. 94

None of the Silesian regions, however, has such a clearly individual character as the area around Cieszyn, and its mountain districts in particular. This applies both to the local culture that has developed in this economically privileged area, and to the culture of the mountain people of the western Carpathians which is that of highly acculturated nomads, some of whom came from very far away, since the Cieszyn district is the last point to have been reached by the Walachian[25] migration. The coexistence of different cultural trends, and even religions, together with the obvious influence of the Protestant tradition in the Cieszyn area, resulted in the preservation of a rich traditional culture which combined pastoral, agricultural and even urban elements and united them into one relatively homogeneous entity. The most characteristic features of this culture are to be found in the music of the mountain villages and in their instrumental tradition. The latter can be seen in the variety of wind instruments the shepherds played, although the convention of playing in an ensemble or of creating a repertoire has not been preserved so consistently in Silesia as it has in the Podhale region. The instrumental tradition here is also cultivated in family circles, but the rôles of the performers are not categorically circumscribed and women are now accepted in instrumental ensembles within the transformed pattern of a nomadic society. The rich sound of flutes, trumpets, pipes and whistles (Kopoczek 1984), the elaborate Silesian bagpipes, and the variety of communication and love dialogues (the so-called *hellokowanie*) underline the pastoral nature of this culture. Those songs that retain remnants of topics dealing with robbery (*Ondraszek*) and the dances also reinforce this style. In this area these have obviously been transformed and have developed into several specific forms uniting Carpathian (Walachian and Ruthenian), Polish and central European elements. This has especially been so with sung and danced forms, which combine slower and faster sections that also contain contrasting metres. These features can be found in the coexistence of slower parts, displaying a Polish national character, and in fast ending sequences that are clearly dominated by Carpathian melodies and rhythms. They can also be traced in several games and dances which contain opposing double and triple metres, as in the so-called *zwie fachen* forms (see Hoerburger 1956).

The historically significant province of Silesia is still an entity despite its obvious divisions and differences. The transitional character of Silesia is revealed, on the one hand, by the rôle of this territory in transmission of Polish dances to the west, and on the other, by particularly spectacular absorption of western ballads and dances.

The province of Silesia must be interpreted as being the most typical south-western Polish border region, deeply rooted in a west Slavonic and Polish background of mediaeval culture but structurally different; its traditional patterns, like those of Great Poland, have been adapted to modern civilization and to its ways of cultural transmission. The particularly hard living conditions and the problems of preserving local vernacular culture in Silesia have resulted, however, in the partial disintegration, if not liquidation, of traditional strata. At the same time these difficult conditions have contributed in various instances to the development of more intensive feelings of ethnic and national identity than in many other areas.

Pomerania (Pomorze)

The folk culture of Pomerania has been preserved predominantly in the region of Cassubia (Kaszuby), particularly in the southern part of this area. This culture previously had much in common with that of the neighbouring Slovinians (Słowińcy) who have practically ceased to

---

[25] The most important migration of the Walachian shepherds began in the fourteenth century. Later some Walachians moved throughout the country, becoming professional shepherds engaged in sheep-breeding on the many big farms of the nobility.

exist now. The Cassubians could be considered to be the group most representative of north-west Slavonic culture; they have preserved their language and the culture of west Pomerania well, despite an extremely powerful flood of Germanization. This was linked not only with processes of acculturation but also with a number of events that devalued Polish and all of Slavonic culture. There was, for example, the widely known statement that 'Pomerania non cantat', which was spread around by German priests, and by Parson Lorek from Cecenów in particular, condemning the people of a parish for their ignorance of German religious songs (Bielawski 1973a: 2). At the same time, however, the regional movement was actively maintained in Pomerania, and this resulted in several conscious initiatives to support the preservation of the vernacular culture. This movement intensified, especially at the end of the nineteenth century, by means of several publications and the creation of a regional journal (*Gryf Pomorski* 1907–39). Nevertheless, only in the last 50 years have contributions been made to systematic research and collections, and to sound recordings of the music from the area being studied. It is clear today that the music of this region is basically governed by the prosodic and versification patterns of the spoken language (Bielawski 1985b; see Examples 34 and 35), and to a lesser extent modified by the structure of Polish national dances, that is, by

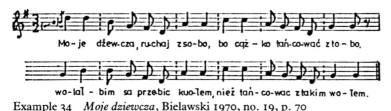

Example 34   *Moje dziewcza*, Bielawski 1970, no. 19, p. 70

Example 35   *Bibi dzecz*, Bielawski 1970, no. 27d

the rhythms of the mazurka or *Polski*. The influence of these dances was probably never very strong and was later diminished by that of modern dances such as the *polka, shot* (écossaise; see Example 78) or waltz (see Example 36). As a consequence, obviously Polish dance

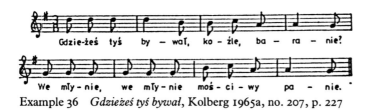

Example 36   *Gdzieżeś tyś bywał*, Kolberg 1965a, no. 207, p. 227

rhythms have survived principally in the more traditional sung versions of ballads and wedding songs, but not in the dances.

The regional character of Cassubian music clearly differs from the vivid atmosphere conveyed by the music of central Poland, which is dominated by fast tempi and short dance songs based on dialogue and situational responses. This Cassubian music contains quite moderate 'walking' rhythms with classical initial accents and strong downbeats, far removed from the German upbeat model; at the same time this rhythm is not transformed to any great extent by the central Polish type of syncopation associated with the paraxytonic accent, which was typical of the Renaissance and Baroque periods (Z. and J. Stęszewscy 1963). The local Cassubian repertoire and the principles according to which it was formed are also characteristic of the region. The repertoire today focuses on traditional religious songs and particular chants devoted to funeral rites and to the tradition of the so-called *puste noce* (empty nights) in which the community gathered in the house of a dead person to keep watch and sing religious songs. Many of the songs sung on other occasions also have a narrative character, obviously influenced by general Polish or European ballads; some also have moralizing or satirical subjects, or deal with certain activities, particularly fishing. Local characteristics can also be traced in some unique musical instruments still in existence. A wooden trumpet called the *bazoune*, and documented in sources since the eighteenth century, has been preserved; according to Łucjan Kamieński it played a significant rôle in the establishment of the local tonality based on a triad. There is also the so-called *burczy bas* (screaming bass; see Figure 31), the name of which obviously refers to the north European tradition of *rommelpot* (Bielawski 1985a) which played a vital rôle in winter customs, and in carnival games and songs.

Finally, the culture of Pomerania, and of the Cassubian people in particular, can be described as being a homogeneous entity which has retained several elements of the old Polish and Slavonic strata, and which is defined by the patterns of the spoken language of the region, and by walking dances not unrelated to the *Polski* or *Okrągły* of Great Poland or Kujavia. This traditional culture, with its well-preserved wedding and seasonal customs, was later enriched by ballads and religious songs. The latter often evolved into relatively modern versions and became superficially Germanized, principally through the use of the Gothic script (the so-called *Shwabakha*) in which the Polish religious books of this region were usually printed. Nevertheless the language and repertoire remained Polish and traditional. Very much the same happened with the style of performance, especially that of the men and their traditional manner of recitation (Bielawski 1970); this applied not only to the pattern of accentuation, but also to the ancient style of prolongation and use of fermata typical of northern Poland. The coexistence of different cultural influences with a well-preserved and consciously articulated sense of identity, resulted in the creation of a highly individual regional culture of a very different type. Thanks to these specific features it is possible today to re-create an earlier picture of the north-west Slavonic and northern Polish folk culture and music. The preservation of local character also played a decisive rôle in the foundation of a regional and national image, and is still very helpful in creating local or regional programmes today.

Little Poland (Małopolska)

The folk culture of Little Poland, also called 'New' Poland, which is younger than its older sister (Great Poland) by a few years according to the records, possesses quite an archaic legacy. The highlands of southern Poland have been inhabited for many thousands of years, and their folk culture today reflects life in past centuries. The areas most representative of this region lie closer to its border, however, than to its historical centre, Cracow. In fact no more than three areas in this historical province have maintained their traditional culture to this day. The first of these is an extended zone covering the north and north-east of the region, with such historical centres as Sandomierz, Kielce and Opoczno; secondly, there are some totally different areas with an obviously ethnic culture situated in the Carpathian Mountains. Finally, there are some eastern parts of Little Poland in the western parts of the Lublin region which have preserved many features of the culture of Little Poland.

Surprising though it may seem, the concept of regional culture in the area of Cracow, so richly described in post-romantic Polish literature and such an important element in many patriotic programmes in Poland and in émigré communities abroad, does not fully exist today. Even local festivals of the Cracow area are now supported by folk performers specially imported from distant areas, mainly from the conservative district of Opoczno.

In contrast to Great Poland, Little Poland cannot be regarded as a homogeneous entity. This is partly because of the heterogeneity of its background, especially where the eastern border and Carpathian areas are concerned, and partly because of the limited regional function of Cracow, the character of which has been more national than local.

The area of the Świętokrzyskie Mountains is regarded as being the historical northern frontier of Little Poland. This territory did not just separate the province from its neighbours, it also provided a link with them and absorbed many cultural influences from the north (Mazovia), south, east and west. As a result one of the most vital folk traditions has been created in this area, and its popular instrumental ensemble still exists to this day. The traditional short dance song, called *przyśpiewka* (ditty), has also been preserved and plays a crucial rôle in social communication. In contrast with the music of Great Poland, that of Little Poland reflects the realities of daily life. It is not the product of conscious programmes, nor the result of a deliberately preserved and filtered legacy. The culture of northern Little Poland is still authentic, although it is steadily being diluted and is disappearing. It is, or at least it was until the middle of the twentieth century, not restricted to festivals and ceremonies, nor was it artificially revived just for certain events.

The musical instruments, like the national costumes and architecture, were constructed from raw materials in Little Poland, partly from home-produced elements. They were totally different from the fine artifacts hand-made or manufactured by outworkers in Great Poland or Silesia. The way in which they were made affected not only the specific details of their construction but also their expressive qualities. Although this culture was not consciously shaped and filtered, it was the only current culture. It preserved its character and maintained its speed of evolution for many hundreds of years. But unfortunately this folk culture will probably not be strong enough to survive in the future, since it is not being promoted. It nevertheless played a part in all serious social situations and was accepted by all generations until at least the middle of the twentieth century; this applied to its music and dance in particular. It owed its vitality to its variety of form and loyalty to traditional patterns, and to the fact that it centred on family events or the rhythm of the seasons. Very much the same applies to the music and its performance conditions, in a variety of genres, which were used to accompany such ordinary events as gatherings in a house or inn (see Figures 10 and 11). Musicians, more precisely violinists who are still quite numerous, command some social

Figure 10   *Krakowiak* in an inn near Cracow, after a drawing by W. K. Stattler, first half
of nineteenth century

respect in this area, but have never received the sort of recognition in Little Poland that they
have in western parts of Poland. In central Poland the musician was treated as a regular
member of society and tended not to be sufficiently appreciated. He would be engaged from
one event to the next, provided with food and vodka, given transport by a neighbour; he was
appreciated if he could fulfil the expectations of the audience and peremptorily dismissed if he
failed. Musical education was also spasmodic. In these areas, playing an instrument, singing
and dancing created an indivisible whole based on the communication patterns of constant
dialogue and responses. The music here is not, and was not, elaborate in form but concentrates on concise formulae that display the essential rhythmic and tonal framework. The
actual performance depends upon the manipulation of changing moods and on their correspondence to appropriate musical and poetic models. When they both perform, the
musicians and dancers compete in demonstrating their skills, and also together create a
common situation. There is no actual division into actors and audience in this region; the
villagers, even including those who have remained out-of-doors and who are looking in
through the windows, and who are joining in the event with their responses, are all active
participants in the social entertainment.

Traditional pieces, played or sung, usually consist of small units of just eight bars,
corresponding to a short two-line stanza, and are clearly based on a vocal pattern. This
pattern is constructed parallel to a background of two small units, of four bars each, bound
into one whole (see Example 37). The elements of contrast are expressed by musical
oppositions between falling and rising melodies, or between tonic and dominant harmonies.
These may also be accompanied by oppositions within the poetic text, juxtaposing metaphoric concepts with descriptions of concrete situations. The music oscillates between

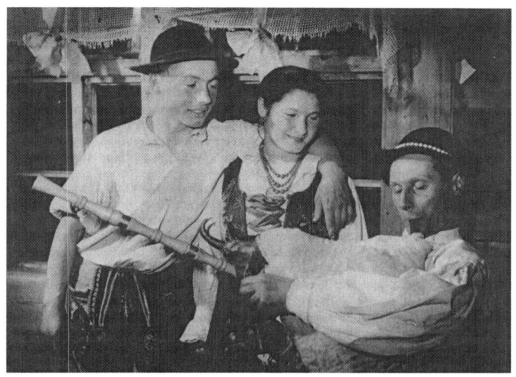

Figure 11   The bagpipe player of Podhale

Nie   ru-szą   ko-ni-ki,   nie ru-szą, nie   ru - szą,

a   da   jak   im   za-gra-ją,   to mu-szą, to   mu - szą.

Example 37   *Nie ruszą koniki*, Czekanowska 1956, no. 26

progressive sequences of tensions and resolutions in a particularly flexible manner. Such sequences of performed pieces and their improvised passages can form quite long chains, fluctuating between the different kinds of dances and moods, and the various melodic, rhythmic and tonal patterns that the performers have at their disposal.

The skill in performing activities is to be found in the virtuoso manipulation of time units and in shifting the accents, modifying patterns of phrasing (Szachowski 1974). This use of *tempo rubato* results, in Central Poland, in obvious variations in bar placement and in a characteristic oscillation between duple and triple metre. This style of performance is achieved intuitively, and corresponds to the general tendency of fluctuating tempi expressed in the music, a feature that is clearly demonstrated by the vocal sections. These are freer in nature and can even cope with variations in the basic rhythms; they oscillate between the different rhythms of the major national dances, like the *oberek* (see Example 45) and the *krakowiak* (see Example 63), and this usually gives rise to one fluent sequence with erratically shifting accents. This style of performance is best demonstrated by the traditional way in which the singers move during their presentation, that is, the accompanying gestures that sway the body from the shoulders to the lower parts. Although the danced sections keep to the basic metres to a greater extent, they remain open to innovation, and are also influenced by the variety of figures and gestures created by the singer and instrumentalists. The stamping and shouting are also of structural importance, and are socially appreciated. As spontaneous actions, physiologically motivated, these gestures have unfortunately been disappearing in recent times.

Contemporary changes are clearly destroying the authentic manner and rendering the traditional style of performance progressively less common. They particularly affect the manipulation of time units and rhythmic patterns as limited by regular sequences of tempi. This also applies to the spontaneous reactions, responses and natural feelings of social communication, to which people are no longer so sensitive. Consequently, the organic unity of music and dance is beginning to be distorted and has been replaced nowadays by an acceptance of reduced standard patterns which are constantly repeated to an increasing tempo. Contemporary changes are even more visible in the purely instrumental repertoire. They affect the introduction of new dances and new ways by which the structure can be transformed. The new instrumental pieces are different in that they possess widely developed forms extended by several repetitions and interludes, and therefore modify the previous proportions of the vocal model in the direction of a multi-sectional musical form.

The variety of music in this area has been created by the obvious coexistence of different strata and varied traditions. This is especially evident in the Świętokrzyskie Mountains, where the tradition of the *krakowiak* has been, and still is, systematically reduced by the more recent impact of the *oberek*. A similar process can be traced in the tonal character of this music, in which the previous modal and pentatonic skeletons are being replaced by major scale patterns and cadences. This, however, applies more to the vocal music, which is conservative by nature, while the instrumental music is clearly aiming towards the major-minor system (see Example 38), both in melody and in formal structure. It concerns also the style in which instruments are played, how members of an ensemble co-operate, and finally which kinds of instruments are generally accepted today.

It is not only the music of entertainment that creates an image of regional culture; traditional customs and their music also demand particular attention. This repertoire was well developed in the past, is still preserved to this day, and is clearly connected with specific episodes of certain customs. The largest family event, the wedding, was a complex affair and lasted for many days. More recently the wedding ceremony, which has today been reduced to two days or even to one day, would be accompanied by traditional melodies and texts performed in many local variations. The main episodes, such as those in which the young couple bid farewell to their parents and to their contemporaries, or the 'capping' ceremony, and the departure for the new house, were connected to a set of basic melodies known to everybody and regarded as conventional patterns (see Example 39). These melodies were usually performed by female groups singing in unison or with a set of responses. This vocal music was primary to the whole ceremony, and was accompanied by a violin and interrupted

Example 38   *Ober*, E. Dahlig 1982, no. 20

by more improvised instrumental interludes. Analysis of this repertoire has revealed many archaic elements, still preserved in the melodies and definitely connected with certain episodes in the customs (Czekanowska 1956). By contrast, analysis of the repertoire not connected with the customs confirms that this legacy is a rather recent development. This repertoire reflects the everyday image of the Polish village and the atmosphere of its social events, conflicts and situations better than other repertoires.

Those customs connected with seasonal feasts are also well represented in the northern part

Oj, Ta – dny wia ʳ– nek mam,   oj, Ta – dniem

go   wi – Ta,   oj, da wie – le   ja

za tym wia – ne-ckiem   tru-dno-ści   u — .zy – Ta.

Example 39   *Oj ładny wianek mam*, Kolberg 1865, no. 7, p. 25

of Little Poland, and reveal obvious regional differences. In the eastern regions of Little Poland they tend to be very archaic – as in the harvest songs from the Sandomierz district (see Example 7b) – or they are much more transformed as in the west; they might be connected with well-preserved customs – such as the solstice songs that are especially popular in the villages along the Vistula – or more transformed, like the spring songs from the western and northern regions of this province.

None of the Polish territories presents such a close ethnic entity as the mountain region of Podhale. The complex of less than a dozen villages identified in detail in several monographs obviously differs from the surrounding area, although the districts of Orawa, Spisz and the more distant Gorce, Pieniny and even the western Beskidy, have retained many features in common. These similarities and differences can be confirmed by the music and dance. The music of the mountain people tends towards multi-part singing, and their dances towards complex patterns that demonstrate the acrobatic skill of the dancers.

In the Podhale region the folk culture still retains a fresh power and creativity which defends it successfully against any standardizing trends. This is a consequence of the function of the music in the life of this ethnic group and of the strong sense of ethnocentricity among the inhabitants. The distinctive character of Podhale can be explained by the isolation of the people living in the highest mountain areas, and by their loyalty to the traditional work of the shepherd. Finally, the ethnic background of these nomads, who came partly from the south, must not be forgotten. These 'strangers', however, also absorbed considerable influences from the Polish settlements in Little Poland. In fact it was basically the environment in which they had been living for years, and their profession, as well as the privileges granted to them by Polish kings (Potkański 1922), that contributed substantially to the creation of this unique mentality of Polish citizens and their culture. The artistic and musical abilities of the Polish mountain people are well documented in several ways. Questionnaires have revealed that every third inhabitant of these villages has a musical instrument (Przerembski 1979), and almost everybody sings. This is also the case with people living as émigrés in large Polish towns or even abroad. The people from Podhale retain their own tradition and practise music even when in different surroundings. The structure of the musical culture is clearly different in Podhale, as are the repertoire and principles on which it is formed. The musical education, the social position of the instrumentalist and, above all, the unwritten rules according to which music is performed, also deserve recognition. To the mountain people music is an echo of their basic responses. They identify themselves with their musical activity, they relax by dancing and singing, they meet each other at musical events, and they simply enjoy themselves.

In Podhale, as in many other Polish regions, music is intended basically for collective performance (see Example 40). But in Podhale alone this collective, though relatively open,

Example 40   *Snieg hale okurzył*, Kotoński 1956, no. 6, p. 23

approach presents a coherence which is visible in the way the group is organized and in the concepts behind certain rôles and functions. This applies above all to the various parts of the instrumental ensemble, which is divided into first and second violins and double bass, as well as to the idea of correspondence between the instrumental and vocal parts, and between the music and the dance sequences.

It should be stressed that the repertoire of the mountain people concentrates on everyday events and social gatherings. The seasonal or family cycle that so dominates the repertoire in other parts of Poland is not so important in Podhale, and even the wedding ceremony, which is very popular today, does not have any associated sequence of a specific character. Similarly, the 'wandering' motifs of many ballads or narrative songs, which have spread all over Europe at various times, have not noticeably penetrated this area. The verbal texts of Podhale songs usually describe concrete social events in this group: the activities of the shepherds, depictions of nature and subjects dealing with robbers. The musical structure of the vocal parts is established by the principles and conditions (performed walking in the open air or during indoor gatherings) of common performance, and by the place of a given piece in the whole cycle. The complex cycle of sequences played and danced obviously varies and can be identified by its detailed terminology. The basic principle relies on the concept of co-existence within the social group. This is realized by multi-part playing (see Figure 12) and a common tendency towards harmonies set out in vertically projected chords. The rôle of a particular instrumentalist is predicted by his functions, by the fact that he maintains a drone (previously of bagpipes) or ostinato (double bass), or that he leads the basic melody (first violin) or supports the chords (second violin). The leading (melodic) and supporting (harmonic) functions can also be observed in vocal performances, although they are more loosely structured. There is a fixed stock of melodies that is commonly known and easily identifiable. They can more readily be understood as being a source of inspiration than a collection of definite pieces. Individual creativity is welcomed, as long as the basic patterns are those that have been traditionally laid down, and the music of the repertoire has a definitely social and collective character.

In this area, unlike other Polish provinces, a number of pieces are identified according to the names of individuals (see Example 41), although these are often more legendary than real.

Figure 12   Highlanders playing

This close, well-defended repertoire and the style of music do not preclude certain transformational processes which occur even in this region. An example of this is a variable sense of tonality as expressed in the characteristic flattening of the raised fourths (Chybiński 1926) and the clear domination of thirds which replace earlier fourths. The traditional sense of harmony is also pervaded by the standard conventions of school harmony. Recent changes can also be observed in the case of instruments whose authentic forms are disappearing. Unusually, however, the basic principles remain unchanged, and play a decisive rôle in the creation and social appreciation of the musical repertoire. They have been preserved like a spoken dialect kept alive by the people.

The morphological features of this regional music indicate several distinctive characteristics: the vocal forms are short, and the music is restricted to an even metre (duple) which clearly disregards the rhythmic patterns of many Polish national dances, while the dances are designed and organized in a totally different way from other Polish dances. The poetry of the songs is restricted in this area to the principle of parallelism and there is also the style of multipart singing, discussed above.

The cultural distinctiveness of the group is indicated chiefly by its style of performance. This is based on the harsh, raw timbre of male and female voices performing in the same register; it also involves uncontrolled dynamics and dancers moving at wild speeds and with considerable skill. The wide range of tempi and the volume of sound are exhibited in a

Example 41 *Sabałowa*, Chybiński 1951, no. 1

spectacular way by cycles, played and danced, that preserve the traditional sequences and respect the distinctions between rôles referred to above. The cycle usually begins with the moderate tempo of *Ozwodna* melodies (see Example 42), performed relatively freely and richly embellished by the first violinist; the final sections of these pieces are augmented in a typical fashion, thereby transforming a four-bar phrase into one of five bars. The following sections of the cycle are individually identified (*Krzesane, Zielone*) and present different tempi and other performance attitudes. In all parts of the cycle, however, the basic idea remains the same. The accompaniment by the second violin – often performed by two violinists – and the double bass maintains the basic pulse, while the rhythmically mobile upper voice fluctuates between the more lively and the more sedate movements of the cycle. The general idea depends to a certain extent on the invention of the first violinist and on his concept of the traditional pattern; he is able to accept and to re-examine, demonstrating his own power and sense of identity, which help him to resist a standard, routine performance. Nevertheless, the basic rôle is to produce harmonic effects by means of vertically projected chords which function as pillars or blocks of sound, but which at the same time are shaped by the development of the melody. Indeed, the general concept of harmonic sequence combined with that of direction (rising or falling) of melodies, defined as *nuta* in local terminology, plays a decisive rôle in the identity of the style (Kotoński 1953). This concept of *nuta* is more conventional and easily memorized, and of even greater significance in creating a repertoire than is the melodic pattern.

The musical sequence of different sections of the cycle is clearly divided and identified by special names as indicated above, and it is dependent upon the traditional, collective pattern. The danced sections, on the other hand, provide wider scope for a more individual approach. The traditional *góralski* (mountain) dance, performed by a couple, displays a considerable range of characters, and the rôle of the male partner in particular has attracted the attention of chroniclers and tourists for many years, and has been compared to the love-play of birds (Kleczyński 1888).

Example 42   *Ozwodna*, Mierczyński 1973, no. 35

Example 42   (cont.)

Dances performed by male groups deal with different subject matter, relating to the traditions surrounding robbers and outlaws, stories of which have been well documented in this mountain region since the Middle Ages. Comparative studies indicate that such features as the melodies to the *Zbójnicki* (robber dance; see Example 43 and Figure 13), marches, and

Example 43   *Zbójnicki*, Kotoński 1954, Mierczyński 1949, no. 100, p. 85

Figure 13   The dance *Zbójnicki*, fragment of a woodcut 'w Tatrach' by E. Gorazdowski

dance patterns clearly point to a background that is common for many Carpathian dances; these studies also reveal diverse, specifically local features and the figure of so-called *krzesanie* in particular (Kotoński 1956). The spectacular nature of these acrobatic dances is a factor in their popularity today. Unfortunately, these productions are usually exploited commercially (for tourists) and neither contribute to the preservation of traditional patterns nor stimulate their creation. Nevertheless the full complexities of the cycle of dances revolving around robbers have still to be reconstructed; the cycle forms a long chain of sequences, and is a multi-layered structure that combines and unites several elements such as the type of step, dance patterns, the position of the body, and the direction and type of movement into one whole (Kotoński 1956).

Artistic creativity in the Podhale region is not limited to collective performances. It also exists in individual and chamber forms, and in vocal and instrumental music-making. Especially popular in the past were the individual performances of instrumentalists playing shepherds' pipes and trumpets, often to create various kinds of signals and melodies in their music. One still quite unique vocal form is the love signal or love dialogue (*wyskanie*; see Example 44).

Example 44   *Wyskanie*, Bielawski 1973b, no. 10, p. 62

The culture of Podhale has developed against a heterogeneous background and with a variety of influences; those of Little Poland and neighbouring southern countries, including the Walachian strata, have, for instance, had a decisive influence. Any links with other Carpathian cultures, whether western or eastern, cannot be ignored, including the impact of the gypsy ensemble on instrumental music in particular (Kovalcsik 1985, 1987). In spite of its varied background, the culture is exceptionally homogeneous and creates a strong sense of ethnic identity which cannot be compared with any other region in Poland.

It should also be reiterated that the artistic quality and inspirational power of this harsh-sounding music has not been properly appreciated until the last 50 years. It is well known also that the stylized music of Podhale contributed significantly to the creation of a concept of Polish folkloristic style by Karol Szymanowski but it must be remembered that this was not achieved successfully until quite recently.

Mazovia (Mazowsze)

It is difficult to compare the cultural variety to be found in the region of Mazovia with that of other historical provinces. This is one reason why Oskar Kolberg divided his monograph on Mazovia into so many parts; it is very likely that this is also why he changed the title of his monograph and, in the case of this province, called it only an ethnographic 'image' and not a comprehensive monograph. Evidently, it is not easy to deal with the folk culture of Mazovia as a regional entity. Its old centres, for instance Czersk, have never achieved very great importance; Warsaw is a comparatively recent phenomenon, capital since 1611, and like some other industrial cities has contributed to the transformation, even possibly the destruction, of the traditional culture, rather than to its creation. This is particularly noticeable in the immediate neighbourhood of the city. At the same time, however, Mazovian folk culture remains conservative and can still be found no more than some dozen or so miles from the capital. It is an obviously varied culture and demonstrates the classical divisions proposed by Kolberg: it is clearly divided into *Polne* (field), *Leśne* (forest), *Stare* (old) and *Pruskie* (Prussian) parts (Kolberg 1885/6, 1887, 1888, 1890). The realities of contemporary life have also clarified many 'grey' areas and 'bridge' territories, and the traditional culture is nowadays restricted to some small regional enclaves. The transformation of the traditional structure has to a certain extent been caused by substantial changes in the geographical environment. The large forests and marshes of the north-eastern parts of this province have been totally cleared today. This is one reason why some isolated enclaves have preserved only the ancient traditional strata, while Mazovian culture in general represents the current legacy of the Polish village tradition. There is a connection between the later tradition and the popularity of recent popular songs and dances, and certain quasi-folk instrumental ensembles and their repertoires. The songs of Mazovia are still dominated by the entertainment repertoire and are performed at various social gatherings, in particular at weddings. The lyrical influence is much stronger in this region and flourishes in different ways. The songs about love, the loneliness of the life of the soldier or orphan, are quite clearly lyrical in atmosphere, and obviously reflect east Slavonic fashions and moods. Despite the fact that the whole area possesses some common features, there are regional differences in the Mazovian repertoire.

The area known as 'field' Mazovia is more clearly defined by its material culture, its costumes, architecture and some kinds of decorative art, but is not exactly confirmed by musical evidence. The *oberek* music, however, demonstrates some local varieties which may be identified as regional idioms. There is a distinction between the western area where the *kujawiak*, with its longer phrases and richer embellishments, among them the typical triplets, prevails (Wójcik-Keuprulian 1930), and the central Mazovian zone of the *oberek* (see Figure 14 and Example 45). Finally, there is the distinctive, most traditional sphere of the south-eastern 'border' areas where traces of the *krakowiak* are still to be found. A description of the Mazovian instrumental tradition, and that of 'field' Mazovia in particular, could also include

Figure 14   *Oberek*

Example 45   *Oberek*, Kolberg 1857, no. 364

elements of Jewish instrumental music. This is known today from sources only, but there is clear documentation that Chopin knew this music personally. Contemporary records unfortunately do not document this tradition any more, and our accounts are limited to a few descriptions and letters.[26]

Musically, indeed, 'field' Mazovia is clearly connected with the name of Chopin and is recognized as being the country of his musical inspiration (see Example 46). Chopin spent

---

[26] See Chopin's letter to his parents (1824) from Szafarnia known as 'Kurier Szafarski' explaining the convention to call Mazurka opus 17 (A Minor) *'Zydek'*. Sydow 1955, vol. 1: 45.

his childhood there, coming back later for holidays, and he remained loyal to this part of the Vistula region until his death (Sydow 1955, vol. 1: 45); many of his letters record his homesickness as well as his dedication to the folk music of the region which he still remembered. The folk music that Chopin so comprehensively stylized has been preserved until this day, and some of the motifs, melodies and structural principles that he intuitively discovered and re-worked so effectively in his mazurkas can still be found in the current repertoire (see Sobieska 1976). The folk tradition has changed as has the reality of contemporary village life, but some traces of the basic ideas, moods and styles still remain.

The musical ensembles of this part of Mazovia (see Figure 15) are also usually considered to be typical of the accompaniment of Polish national dances and of the *oberek* in particular. This dance usually occurs in instrumental versions today, performed by violins, drum and harmonium, and accompanying circulating couples. Such a dance, with the partner in a characteristic slumped posture, is enhanced by several stamping and kneeling figures which are articulated in the musical accompaniment. The music oscillates freely in *tempo rubato*, erratically shifting the accents of the beat.

The culture of 'forest' Mazovia, located at the eastern part of this province, possesses quite different features. Unlike other parts of this area, this poor region is dominated by a vocal repertoire, and by 'longer' songs of narrative and lyrical mood in particular. These convey a totally different atmosphere, in obvious contrast to the atmosphere of social gatherings in central Poland, which are full of humour and dialogues between the performers. The east Mazovian style is abstract and lyrical, especially in wedding episodes which are sometimes accompanied by women weeping and bemoaning human fate from a certain distance, actions that are not without some symbolic connotations. The timbres of the female voices play a fundamental rôle in the transmission of specific moods (see Example 47). The female voices are well rounded, soft and precise in intonation, which is why they are ideally suited to this kind of lyrical repertoire. It must be stressed that this tradition, although still in existence, is limited today to members of the older generation and will probably disappear as a consequence of recent changes. It is unfortunate that after a singer has spent just a few years in the city, or when he has sung in church or in some other type of choir, the timbre of his voice undergoes a definite change.

The rich tradition of 'forest' Mazovia is famous for a variety of harvest songs, which include several variants – west as well as east Slavonic – and which also include some unique songs dealing with the cultivation of hemp and other customs connected with agriculture. The substratum of an ancient legacy is still to be found in the traditions of these areas which were previously forested. It is evident in tempi, in a moderate volume of sound and in the different timbres of voices. It can also be detected in the different ways of conceptualization, in the richness of symbols and in the variety of diminutives. The poetic content of the texts and the principles behind the musical structure are concentrated in small units of intense expressive qualities easily perceived by the listener. These form an obviously different type of song tradition.

By contrast, the legacy of the villages belonging to the minor gentry, which are very numerous in this area, presents a totally different musical situation; it is relatively poor in songs and in instrumental music, and the drum is noticeably absent in local ensembles. The gentry have also not preserved many customs with their seasonal and family cycles, but their

Example 46   F. Chopin, op. 59, no. 3, Paderewski's Edition, Kraków 1961, no. 38, p. 140, bars 135–46

repertoire is rich in narrative songs which often recall historical events. It is possible to trace student songs from the 'old days', dedicated for example to St Gregory, in the tradition of the oldest people in these gentry villages. This group, which held many privileges in the 'old days', also possesses national dances such as the *Polski* and the *krakowiak*. By contrast, there are no settings of texts depicting social conflict, especially those between the gentry and the peasants. These songs, usually transmitted by short dance melodies, circulate exclusively among peasant groups.

It was not without reason that Kolberg called Kurpie, the region located in the north, the 'older' part of Mazovia. The folk tradition still preserved in this area is one of the most archaic in Poland (see Example 48). Mazovian settlement, however, reached this region relatively late, in the fourteenth century; this forest area was inhabited much later than were other parts of the province. It should also be said that Oskar Kolberg did not know this culture well, and its music had not been discovered in his day. Studies began no more than fifty years ago, and a more scientific approach was first made as late as the 1950s. In addition this culture has recently been disappearing very rapidly, despite the high recognition given to

Figure 15   Instrumental ensemble from the Łowickie area

Example 47   *Za las słońce*, Stęszewski 1955b, no. 1

it, and today it is restricted to a few places and only to an aging generation. The disappearance of the culture is being accompanied by the destruction of the landscape, because no part of Mazovia has undergone as much geographical transformation as Kurpie. Neither *biała* (white) nor *zielona* (green) virgin forest exists any more, nor do the marshes or even the rivers so picturesquely described by Oskar Kolberg. The social status of this territory,

Example 48 *Jaś koniki poił*, Kolberg 1857, no. 5, p. 57

previously protected by the privilege of kings who defended its autonomy for many hundreds of years, is also being destroyed by recent changes and migrations to the city or abroad. Remnants of the traditional legacy (see Example 49 and Figure 16), as well as the local pride and dignity of the inhabitants, can still be observed, however, and fortunately there was more activity fifty years ago when ethnographers and musicians visited this region for the first time.

The Kurpian repertoire possesses at least two strata: the first is clearly Mazovian in character and contains a basic stock of wedding songs and dance music; the second is focused on lyrical and narrative songs and some wedding songs. A basic factor in the systematic study of the repertoire in question is performance style, and its diversity and richness. Current folk terminology as used by performers confirms the different elements of the repertoire and distinguishes between so-called *leśne* (forest) and *skoczne* (jumping) chants (see Examples 50 and 51), dividing the songs according to the conditions and circumstances in which they are performed.

The stylistic and morphological features of the 'forest' songs, which are greatly valued by the inhabitants of this region, are obviously different from those of other Polish chants. This part of the repertoire is similar to some genres of Lithuanian or Byelorussian traditions, although the Kurpian songs present many quite unique traits thanks to their rich instrumental sonority. This is expressed by many peculiarities of performance and by special timbre of female voices and by different resonance effects. Pitch and time are often not precisely articulated and present a rather fluctuating sequence. The sound is enriched by certain effects, such as the swallowing of syllables, whispering or slurring. The time units could also be manipulated by various kinds of fermatas. The concluding time units are especially augmented and often enriched by certain sound effects so they may be perceived as separate musical sections. It is to be found even in those cases when the 'sections' are limited to isolated sounds. The initial sounds are often supported by whispering effects, whereas rich embellishments occur throughout the whole melody. Thus, this particular type of performance style is a rather peculiar combination of basic qualities of musical structure and an authentic rich content, resulting in elaborate, rich melismata and a variety of metro-rhythmic patterns which combine regular and prolonged time units in well-organized and regularly pulsating models: 2 + 3, 3 + 2 and above all 3 + 2 + 3 (see Example 51; Czekanowska 1971: 126).

The best-developed musical structures are the lyrical and the older strata of Kurpian wedding songs, owing above all to their melody and form, creatively woven and rich in sound. The highly artistic musical style of these songs is a unique phenomenon in recent Polish folk culture.

Figure 16   Papercut of Kurpie *Leluja*

Example 49   *Jadźwa Jasiulu*, Sikorska (Jankowska) 1986, no. 7

The first Kurpian songs to be published immediately captured the imagination of artists and scholars alike, and this led to Karol Szymanowski's highly artistic stylization of songs from Kurpie (see Example 24). Expert assessment came later, and the structural properties of the music remained undiscovered until the first sound recordings were made in this area. Access to sound material as well as to the authentic 'field' context stimulated studies of this

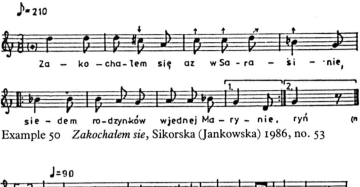

Example 50   *Zakochałem się*, Sikorska (Jankowska) 1986, no. 53

Example 51   *Bicem konia*, Bielawski 1970, no. 56

repertoire, studies leading to analysis of performance style. Musicological analysis discovered several of the properties of these interesting structures, and pointed out the existence both of ancient tonal strata (pentatonics and church modes; see Examples 48 and 52) and the sound qualities of some modes of performance such as glissandi, whispering, swallowing and gliding (see Example 53). These rich sound qualities are really quite unique to Kurpian vocal music and in this respect the area cannot be compared with other Polish regions. It should be stated, however, that the accompanying gestures, and in particular the dances of this isolated region, have still not been sufficiently explored (Dąbrowska 1980), although the authentic strata of the traditional culture are disappearing almost before our eyes. The instrumental tradition, which is rather restricted and undefined, is in a similar condition. The relics of traditional dances, such as *żabka* (frog) and *konik* (horse) (Chętnik 1983), or some collective gestures accompanying songs (the so-called *przytrampywanie*) and the already forgotten idiophones, called *diabelskie skrzypce* (the devil's violin; see Figure 23), can only be regarded as museum pieces and not as phenomena that are still in use.

By contrast, the Mazovian culture of the 'Prussian' region, and that of Warmia as well as of some areas lying on the north-eastern border of Mazovia (the district of Suwałki and Augustów), have been influenced by the cultures of neighbouring areas. There is also evidence of some remnants of the oldest Baltic strata, which can be more readily traced in the general atmosphere than in morphological features.

As has already been mentioned, the 'Prussian', or Mazurian, culture survived almost untouched until the middle of the twentieth century. This unique culture possessed the 'Old Polish' character and its repertoire differed from that of Kurpie and from the songs of the Suwałki region. It was rather western in style, as demonstrated by its repertoire, particularly by the richness of the ballads which dealt with almost all the topics common to each of the Polish territories (Czekanowska 1954). The west Slavonic nature of the repertoire was also

Example 52   *Nie spodoba sie*, Skierkowski 1934, no. 707

Example 53   *Wkoło mego ogródecka*, Jankowska 1986, no. 17

revealed by narrative and satirical songs that were also typical of Pomerania, and by the stronger influences of music for such dances as the *oberek*, and the presence of classical Polish 'capping' melodies and post-harvest songs, as well as songs connected with the cultivation of linen (see Example 54). Some stylistic phenomena were, however, closer to those of the old

Example 54   *Ach lanku, lanku*, Sobieski and Sobolewska 1955, no. 12

Kurpian tradition, contrasting this regional culture to its western counterparts in Pomerania. The culture of Mazuria developed in isolation for more than a hundred years; links with vernacular Mazovia and Poland were cut (see Example 55), and the region was subjected to intense Germanization, rendering it closed to other foreign influences. This led to the creation of specifically local features, which were clearly audible in the music and in the spoken dialect. This was especially so in the districts where there was a mixed Polish and German population (in the district of Mrągowo, for instance). These places produced special genres, such as some of the church songs, in use among the local Protestants, and songs and

Example 55   *Po rogolach chodze*, Sobieski and Sobolewska 1955, no. 73

calls of fishermen. Nevertheless, the basic structural properties remained Polish or Mazovian in character, as is best demonstrated by German studies of both sources and folkloric evidence (Müller-Blattau and Jeziorowski 1934; Borowski and Lukač 1931). Unfortunately, it needs to be stressed that this well-preserved culture must be regarded today as being a document of the recent past (see Example 56). The considerable migrations since 1956 have resulted in its disappearance.

Example 56   *Maja hu hu*, A. Pawlak field notation

Quite obviously, the north-eastern lake region (the Suwałki district) has not preserved its cultural entity. Unlike that of the other Mazovian regions, this culture was relatively open and welcomed the various ethnic, social and religious influences that often co-existed side-by-side there. The Poles obviously dominated in this area, but there are still several groups of Lithuanians, Byelorussians, Russian 'Old Believers' (see Example 57), and Muslims also to be found in this 'border' territory. The population includes members of the east Mazovian minor gentry. The social and ethnic heterogeneity typical of east Mazovia is as evident here as are elements of a national heterogeneity that was previously much richer and included Jews and Karaites, for example. Many of these people, especially the Jewish musicians, were

Example 57   *Och, ty młodost'*, Frasunkiewicz 1985, no. 4

famous for their skills in instrumental music. The tradition of dulcimer-playing is particularly well documented, and has been recorded in the national Polish literature of the Lithuanian area.

The folk culture of the Polish population in this lake region possesses east Mazovian characteristics. They are expressed in the rich lyrics, often called 'autumn', 'forest' or 'field' songs here, and deal with the beauty and melancholy of nature. Certain features of the local poetry, especially its diminutives and sound effects, also stress the character of this folk culture. The specific features of the tradition are balanced, however, by the rich impact of the general Polish repertoire, its narrative songs and the dances with their *krakowiak* elements. Indeed, links with the historical capital of Cracow and its surrounding area can still be traced in the dance rhythms and in some of the song texts of this remote territory. On the one hand, co-existence with other national and religious groups facilitates acculturation which, for example, affects the distribution of some songs and motifs. The foreign groups, on the other hand, preserve their identity very carefully and tend to absorb new trends from their distant mother countries rather than assimilate a Polish repertoire. This state of affairs can give rise to quite new phenomena, such as Lithuanian multi-part singing which was unknown in this territory before 1950; and there is also the case of the dissemination of recent Russian soldiers' songs among orthodox Old Believers (Frasunkiewicz 1985; see Figure 17).

A general survey of Mazovian folk culture reveals its considerable variety. Despite the differences discussed above, its overall character demonstrates the influence of Polish culture on this remote, conservative territory, which is deeply rooted in the 'Old' Slavonic or Balto-Slavonic tradition. This in turn has left some traces in the local repertoire, and in a performance style that reflects the different mentality of the people, different patterns of behaviour, and a different degree of artistic sensitivity. These features especially affect the older concept of distance and time still preserved by the people, and the way in which they formulate their basic artistic ideas. All this is to be found in the rich variety and variability of repetitions, and in the type of diminutives, comparisons and associations used. Indeed, analysis of the musical and poetic structures of these conservative regions highlights the conceptual foundations of the culture and contributes to a better understanding of the traditional art that is still preserved there.

The south-east border country

The south-eastern territory (mentioned at the beginning of this chapter, and described as an area with a varied background) is not culturally homogeneous. As in the eastern Mazovian regions the south-eastern area reveals the coexistence of at least two different cultural strands, east and west Slavonic, later engulfed by the stronger influence of recent Polish

Figure 17   The 'Old Believers', District of Białystok

culture. It is also clear that these different cultural elements often coexist within a single repertoire and might be performed at the same social event. There is also a connection between social consciousness and religious identity in this territory. In those areas where a different rite is observed (Greek Catholic or Greek Orthodox) the sense of identity is firmly east Slavonic (Ruthenian or Byelorussian) with an east Slavonic dialect, as well as some other cultural phenomena. This is especially so in the northern part of the Lublin region (the district of Chełm) where different ethnic and religious groups exist side by side.

The vast territory under discussion can be divided into three zones: northern, southern and Sub-Carpathian. The first of these areas is also represented by the so-called *dyftonizujące* (diphthong-dialects) of the Polish language, and the second by the so-called *ikające* (i-dialects) (Kuraszkiewicz 1932). Studies carried out by both Polish and Ukrainian scholars (Kolessa 1916; Czekanowska 1961) have detected obvious differences in this traditional culture at the deepest level. As has been stated, the culture of the northern territories can be related to that of Volhynia and the culture of the southern to the Galician legacy. It is also clear that the Sub-Carpathian area was fundamentally transformed by the culture of Little Poland, and its deepest strata preserved only a few remnants from the previous proto-Polish culture. This was quite a heterogeneous culture, and was dominated at different periods by various components of the shepherds' legacy, in which Ruthenian and Walachian elements prevailed (Kolessa 1923, 1929).

Remnants of the 'Old' Slavonic background can still be found in the 'eastern' versions of the wedding, harvest and solstice repertoire, often co-existing with their western counterparts here. By contrast, the music of entertainment is definitely Polish and demonstrates either the Mazovian tradition of the *oberek* with its modernized waltz derivatives, or the new wave of *polka* music. Some Ruthenian dances such as the *kołomyjka* and *kozak* (Cowell 1950) and also some Czech dances (*polka*) have also entered the repertoire of the Sub-Carpathian and Lublin regions (Czekanowska 1961).

Studies made of the culture in this interesting border country reveal several often contradictory results, especially contrasts between analyses of ancient strata and the views of the contemporary inhabitants. The most traditional strata show clear references to the music of other Slavonic groups, those of the east and south in particular. On the other hand the present-day inhabitants of these regions consider themselves Polish, with the music of the *polka* (see Example 58) as a mark of their national identity.[27] It should be added that the

Example 58 *Polka*, Sobiescy 1973, no. 120, p. 310

[27] This phenomenon is particularly noticeable among Polish émigrés from the Sub-Carpathian area to other countries, especially those now living in the United States.

inhabitants of the poor Sub-Carpathian area produce the highest number of Polish economic émigrés who are often identified by non-Polish groups, Ruthenians above all, as 'Mazurian', which has falsely come to be considered a synonym for Polish nationality. Thus, the terminology as has been applied may lead to a total misunderstanding, while the inhabitants of this Sub-Carpathian province have very little in common with those of the provinces of Mazovia or Mazuria; Mazuria is not a synonym for Polish nationality nor is the *polka* a Polish dance.

The results of comparative studies are making it easier to identify the preserved legacies and especially the differences between the northern and southern strata of the 'Old' Slavonic culture, in a very different, more concrete way. They deal above all with the tonality of traditional songs, and refer to south-eastern versions of the widely-distributed 'Old' Slavonic strata which even reached the Balkans; they refer also to the north-eastern versions of the Byelorussian and Balto-Slavonic legacies. Comparative studies have also contributed to a better interpretation of Slavonic modality, connected with obvious musical influences of different religious groups – Roman Catholics in the western areas and Greek Catholic or Greek Orthodox in the east – and with the specific melodic formulae that have been preserved in the traditions of these churches. It should not be overlooked also that several features that are totally unknown in other Polish provinces have been found in this south-eastern area. They include the remnants of funeral laments, and some unusual instruments discovered by Polish ethnographers about sixty years ago, in particular the so-called xylophones and the musical bow (Figures 18a and 18b) described by Kazimierz Moszyński (1939: 599, 627). These have not since been confirmed by other studies and must therefore be regarded with some scepticism.

Figure 18   (a) Musical bow

Figure 18   (b) Musical bow, detail

Surveys of this heterogeneous south-eastern culture reveal both changeability and a traditionalism that still exists. A balance between these two tendencies can be achieved by different means, depending upon political programmes and cultural policies, which play significant rôles in this area. Nevertheless, the creation of a regional identity in the modern sense also depends upon the power and attraction of local culture for contemporary society.

There is unfortunately no doubt that folk culture and music today are being transformed, if not degraded. This applies to the reality of the contemporary Polish situation more obviously than to that of some other Slavonic countries, such as Russia, Byelorussia or Bulgaria, which have concentrated on their traditional legacies to a much greater extent. The transformational processes which will be analysed in the next chapter have not, however, destroyed national or regional identity, both of which remain vital and functional, albeit with varying degrees of effectiveness, in contemporary society. It is even possible that the traditional paradigm will be accepted once more within the framework of a modern and already balanced society. This would be especially clear with a culture that possessed a varied ethnic or social background, as well as with those people who have totally changed their surroundings, professions and concepts of life. This last point applies above all to people from previously poor and conservative regions who have obviously changed their way of behaviour superficially but who remain rooted in the old beliefs and conventions, which, though partially forgotten, still exist to a certain extent in their consciousness. The results of sociological studies confirm the existence of these deeply rooted habits, which still preserve their power of integration despite the changes that have occurred. It can be expected that tradition will still have a rôle to play and that it will integrate people with common or similar cultural backgrounds. Finally, it seems highly possible that the simplicity of folk culture and the directness of expression exhibited in its way of transmission will continue to be significant for future generations.

2.2.4 The concept of national style in Polish music: a reassessment

The problem of national style in Polish music has been widely discussed and recorded, though not definitely resolved, in literature on the subject. This applies to research on both the art and the folk music of Poland. Two factors seem to present the main difficulty: the historical changeability of evaluations and feelings in the field, and the strong connection between Polish musical culture and changes in the music and musical culture of Europe and the world. As a result, Polish music has never developed a set of very individual or specific features as in the case of isolated cultures.

It is for this reason that an obvious difference between Polish and Russian music occurs as far as the relation between artistic and folk music is concerned. In Poland attitudes towards folklore are limited merely to periodic trends in interest. In addition, folklore has never been used as material for music theory, something that did in fact occur in both Russian and south Slavonic scholarship (Czekanowska 1981b). Current aesthetic, philosophic and even religious and magical concepts in Poland have never directly enriched understanding of the essence and rôle of sound in the sense of its basic power, its function, and the possibility that it might directly influence people.

Of all the factors mentioned, it is easier to speak about and elaborate on some stylistic phenomena than to define criteria of national style in a more abstract and theoretical way. So far all attempts at defining national identity in music have been limited to indicating: those musical features that are determined by the specific character of the Polish language, and by its accentuation in particular (Stęszewscy 1963: 624; Perz, 2nd edition 1981: 215); those that are determined by morphological patterns, that is the melodic and rhythmic motifs in the music (Windakiewiczowa 1926; Wójcik-Keuprulian 1930; Lissa 1958; Kamieński 1918/19; Sobiescy 1963), and dance and tonal patterns in particular; those determined by some expressive qualities, that is specific moods, as well as some behavioural phenomena transmitted by agogic and rhythmic means basically connected with performance habits (accents, *tempo rubato*; see Example 91; Windakiewiczowa 1926; Lange 1978).

Despite the achievements of traditional research, contemporary studies of national style require new approaches and several methodological changes. Modern interests centre on transmission, on the formulation of concepts and the discovery of the principles behind musical creativity; on the contextual determination of these processes and on social responses to them. This new approach stresses the necessity for more detailed studies on the processes of perception and reception of musical phenomena. It requires new tools and procedures, both psychological and sociological. The psychological element prevails in studies concentrating on general human abilities and sense of identity, while the sociological approach focuses on ethnically, nationally or socially orientated processes of identification, especially their contextual analysis. Nevertheless, the history of research into national style indicates that the most lasting basis for success comprises those expressive values that are perceived by the recipients as being personally addressed to them (Czekanowska 1982). The basis for perception is always to be found in the possibility and achievement of identification with the perceived musical work. This process, moreover, is more easily comprehended intuitively than through comparative studies or tests. Thus, in the Polish case the most fortunate solutions of national stylization seem to be connected with the use of two factors: specific expressions, and the emotional impact often conveyed by formulae with clear associations; and by specific types of kinetics and kinetically conditioned rhythms. These two factors, expressive and kinetic, are directly linked with basic human reactions, whether in the emotional sense through identification, or in a typical sequence that exploits the pulsating beat and phrasing which corresponds with the natural flow of human reactions. By contrast, in artistic music ethnic or national character is to be found in the more conscious stylization, whereby concrete references to national or folk music are found in the material chosen for stylization. Additional factors, complementary to the above, are those of innovation and inspiration, strikingly different ethnically, nationally and socially, and of perception, where there are exciting new possibilities.

The sociological method prevails in studies on the popularity and adaptability of the music and on its evaluation from the point of view of different possible opinions, especially when it is a question of different groups of recipients, inside Poland and beyond. Those general problems connected with research into national style require additional study – general or specific – as regards the general tendencies of a given period and the changeability of norms, which from the historical point of view lose their sense or at any rate their clarity.

In brief, the problem of national style should be discussed and investigated today: in psychological terms, focusing on the basic features of human reactions studied experimentally; in sociological terms, concentrating on its ethnic, national and social functions, as they still occur in contemporary society; and in historical terms, through re-examination of this concept and studying its connections with the general trend of the epoch. It is to be expected that this type of research will explain several phenomena as yet unsatisfactorily interpreted, such as the success of Polish dance music and types of phrasing, as well as the comparatively lesser popularity of Polish illustrational music, these phenomena, so dance-like in character as well as in type of phrasing, being at the same time characteristic of both art and folk music.

In attempting to clarify the position of a Polish national style in the history of world music, we have to answer the basic questions: to what extent do Polish musicians create and contribute to world music; to what extent do they only receive and adapt; and how much of an international response is there to Polish music? In order to clarify the problem it is worth looking at the success of Polish art music in the world and at the significance of the folk influence in those successes. From the historical point of view there are three periods during which Polish music achieved great success and popularity. The first period is connected with the spread of Polish dances throughout Europe from the sixteenth to the nineteenth centuries. The second period comes in the third and fourth decades of the nineteenth century and is directly connected with the work of Frédéric Chopin. The third period falls in the twentieth century, in the second half in particular.

The relation to folk music presents in each of these three periods quite different problems. In the case of Polish historic dances documented by about 1,500 source items (Stęszewska 1979: 16) the identification of folk strata is difficult to trace in a modern sense. There is not much direct confirmation documenting the social provenance as being current amidst contemporary people. The identity marks are only occasionally confirmed by terminology recorded in the sources (*Paur Tantz*, 'Peasant Dance'; Chybiński 1948). At the same time, however, it is quite obvious that the dances, confirmed by sources and mostly identified only as Polish, were widely distributed and accepted by several social strata both in Poland and in other countries. These dances should be recognized as representative of Polish national culture which, though in different proportions, was distributed across varied strata of society.

In the case of the work of Chopin the success of the synthesis of national elements is deeply rooted in the stylization of folk music. Although several earlier attempts in eighteenth- and early nineteenth-century music tried to highlight national features through stylization of folk elements, the great success in this field is truly Chopin's achievement. The ideological programme of Chopin's concept is also well documented in his biographies and correspondence. As is confirmed by analytical studies, Chopin's stylization is achieved by consistent attention to structural detail such as integrating and interrelating phrases. The emotional features of the Polish character so splendidly demonstrated and perfected by Chopin and so ideally suited to this romantic music – fluctuating moods, short conclusions and intensely expressive formulae – are undoubtedly rooted in Polish folk music. They are also shown by the clarity of texture and by the shape of some motifs psychologically motivated by patterns of human and social communication (Ottich 1958), which Chopin intuitively discovered and transformed.

In more detailed studies on Polish modern music, the changeability of concepts and ideas is dominant. This applies also to the relations between folk music and its use in modern compositions. The concept of creating 'a new musical language' based on folklore was precisely formulated by Karol Szymanowski in 1936 (see Szymanowski 1984: 44), not without reference to other concepts of that time (in Hungary or Russia). But these trends are in fact almost totally forgotten in Poland today. The reluctant relation to folklore of contemporary composers seems to have roots in modern trends of composition and their techniques. It concerns especially the techniques of serial compositions, as well as a general trend toward big forms, often connected with monumental topics. Nevertheless, interesting attempts to find inspiration in folk music are undertaken from time to time and present ways of using folk material in compositions created according to contemporary conventions, and using modern techniques.

From a historical perspective the relation between folk and composed music is clearly changeable, though links between these two strata obviously exist. Depending on the epoch and its trends, folk music was either a well-spring of inspiration, or provided a permanent resource of ideas for composed music which could be revived or stylized in new ways.

It is difficult to interpret all periods of Polish music against the background of one set of methodological procedures, however up-to-date and universal they might be. It is very difficult to find common references and establish some principles, even as regards the periods in which Polish music, and art music in particular, was most 'successful'. The reason for this is the large number of determinants and varying contexts including modifying approaches towards music, art and culture.

In focusing on a Polish national style one should mention the masterly use of opposition between different systems, tonal and rhythmic, as well as the characteristic inflections, suspensions and oscillations closely related to the basic behavioural rhythms. Expressive examples of the uses of interchangeable principles are mainly those of the emotional oscillation of formulae in both structures, which is often related to a fairly constant agogic-rhythmic discipline modified only by the manipulation of time units. The features of Polish national style as indicated seem to refer both to folk patterns and to the basic principles and habits of human perception.

There remains, however, the open question of the problem of the recipient's identification of these expressive values, that is of his deciding in favour of the ethnic-national qualities important for Poles, or in favour of general human qualities inherent in our perception and thus readily understood by everyone. The aim of research still not satisfactorily resolved is the establishment of the rôle played in the identification and adaptation processes by directly effective functional factors (tempi, pulsations, timbres) and by formulae which constitute the basic units of national language despite transformation. Moreover, it is necessary to establish which of these factors should be considered as variable characteristics functioning as exponents of adaptation, and which should be regarded as exponents of a fairly stable tradition.

The concept of national style should be regarded as an historical process; thus its changeability and variety of conditions need to be understood. The achievements of Polish music are closely connected with the general process by which composers improved and developed their skills and techniques, and the general development of musical culture in Poland. These conditions ensure the permanence and limit the sporadic occurrence of these achievements. In these processes and under such conditions, some innovative and inspirational values that are rooted in folklore and tradition seem to play a significant rôle. Individual genius has a direct influence on achievement and success. However, the fate of a nation and its traditional background are not without significance. The experience of having lived through periods of stress is linked with the dramatic content, intensity and expressiveness of the music produced subsequently. The genius of artists lies in their skill in transforming, reshaping and restructuring their own and national experiences into music of the highest artistic quality.

Turning to folk music and to its inspirational power, it should be pointed out that the most characteristic features of Polish folk music seem to be rooted in the patterns of accentuation and phrasing of the spoken Polish language, and in the basic patterns of movement and communication. Recently this pattern has clearly been articulated by paroxytonic stress, accompanied by the musical phenomenon of syncopation. The musical pattern indicated is additionally reshaped by a tendency to shift the accents within a phrase by *tempo rubato* (J. and M. Sobiescy 1963; Kamieński 1918–19), that is, in a manner that depends on the emotional impact of the musical message being transmitted. A general inclination towards the downbeat as well as towards a falling rhythm (Bielawski 1970) is consequently preserved, however.

The characteristic features of Polish folk music are evidently shaped by the rhythmic patterns of Polish national dances, that is, those developed during the Renaissance and Baroque periods. This applies both to concrete dance figures (stamping, kneeling), positions of the body and combinations of steps, and to general responses and patterns of interaction (dialogues, following a leader, solos). These last features articulate the general concepts of integration and composition, dominated by the basic idea of interaction as conveyed by the participants (couples, wheels, processions). All of these three systems, of language, dance and music working together, create typical patterns which can be identified as Polish.

If we accept the basic principle that style is to be understood as 'a quality and meaningful expression through which the personality of the artist and the broad outlook of a group are visible' (Shapiro 1956: 287) and as 'a vehicle of expression within the group, communicatory and fixing certain values . . . through the emotional suggestiveness of forms', or the 'manifestation of a culture as a whole, the visible sign of its unity' (*ibid.*), and finally, according to another author, 'the idiom in which a number of works speak recognizably the same language' (Shaper 1969: 248), it will lead us to the conclusion that it is precisely in this manifestation of unifying power that the rôle of national style is to be found; and that it is no surprise why in fact in the most significant periods of national history, prosperous or more often tragic, the treasure offered by different social strata can be recognized and integrated into one unity. Thus it is perhaps not so important to identify the various types of 'input' offered by different strata of society and even foreign nations, since it is precisely their mutual references and interplay, deeply rooted in basic human and social modes of interaction, that create the phenomenon of national style.

2.3   Transformation of Polish folk culture and music

2.3.1 Change of social consciousness: approaches and dimensions

The phenomenon of cultural change is one of the leading topics of contemporary social science, and is of great concern to Polish scholarship and ethnomusicology. Studies show that the evaluation of cultural change depends directly on which aspects of culture are studied and which methods are applied. In our experience, two phenomena of Polish contemporary folk culture seem to be significant, but both of them are complex and sometimes inconsistent. These are: the evaluation of tradition and of its importance for contemporary society; and the rôle of cultural identity, including the concept of regionalism. Finally, the ways in which both tradition and identity are perceived and understood by different groups in Polish society must be considered.

With the first problem it must be stressed that the results achieved gradually at different times and with various methodologies elucidate different aspects. Our first experiences are usually based on superficial observations and on intuitive feelings and those usually detect the obvious facts of reduction and of a global drop in repertoire. This concerns both the limitation of the traditional resources and the dilution of its morphological and stylistic features. By contrast, functional and structural analyses usually show continuing needs and social demands for folk material, despite the transformations it has undergone. These demands are usually psychologically motivated and prove the attractiveness of folkloristic material which is still to be found among many groups in Polish society. At the same time, however, there is no doubt that Polish folk culture in the last century has changed more than ever before and only in its deep psychological qualities can one find certain values remaining stable and significant for contemporary society. Indeed these psychological qualities of folklore, and their stabilizing effects in particular, seem to be the most decisive factors in certain choices and preferences of Poland's modern society. The nature of these decisions and processes of selection is obviously more of an intuitive than of an intellectual character. The evaluation of tradition is closely connected with the concept of time and its generally accepted dimensions. As has already been mentioned, psychological investigations have suggested that the Polish people, and people with a peasant background in particular, accept two quite different time dimensions. This is especially obvious in traditional cultural areas, in which traditional festivities are in clear contrast to the tempo and style of everyday life. To a certain extent this also concerns people who have now moved to totally different environments and living conditions, such as workers in large factories, and often includes highly skilled and successful individuals. Nevertheless, despite all the transformations people undergo, the traditional way of life is still preserved as a means of relaxation and of psychological stabilization. They coexist in some people's consciousness as a second level of reality.

The coexistence of different cultural traditions, including different perceptions of time, can be additionally tested by speaking to members of different generations and observing their concern for the stability provided by tradition. This is evident in traditional regions and among representatives of the older generation. It is especially evident amongst people returning to old customs and repertoires which they have not used for many years, and these habits and modes of entertainment are found not only as a means of relaxation, but also as marks of their age and of their socially accepted dignity.

The coexistence of national and ethnic strata in the processes of identification presents a second dilemma for sociological investigations which attempt to penetrate the consciousness of contemporary folk societies. For example, rural immigrants to urban communities, as well as émigrés to other countries or continents, use regional identities as an inspiration in the formation of new groups. At the same time, however, the new reality creates more general programmes for cultural unification in which national aspects dominate over ethnic sympathies and feelings. The simultaneous coexistence of two contrasting interests is especially visible in border territories, which in a long historical process were polonized or, on the contrary, depolonized or deslavonicized in more recent historical periods. As has been indicated, the nationally homogeneous Poland has a quite differentiated ethnic background.

In brief, we would stress that contemporary Polish people now living in quite different and transformed conditions still preserve some traditional patterns of behaviour. The contemporary folk culture preserves only traces of the old tradition, but the persistent demand for this kind of cultural activity demonstrates that the roots of traditional cultural patterns still exist and that they may be revived, especially in psychologically difficult or critical situations. This last phenomenon is evidently vital among social groups or individuals living away from their original homes. In all these situations, traditionalism and ethnicity play vital social rôles, and they highlight the significance both of folklore and of folk music in particular. Indeed, aesthetic qualities of artistic transmission seem to influence and move people much more directly than other ways of communication. Traditional thinking, with its withdrawal from time and tendency to solve contradictions in a very specific way which is so typical of folkloristic concepts and of mythical thinking in particular, seems still to be observed. This is the ability to communicate by media of highest abstraction. At the same time, however, these media based on associations express the concepts with striking directness and simplicity. As might be expected, these primary qualities, that play a significant rôle in communication processes, will preserve their functions in the frame of modern society.

The increasing use of ethnopsychological methods also shifted interest towards analysis of performance aspects, i.e., towards those qualities of folkloristic message which were undocumented in early musical transcription and for a long time were not considered in any comparative procedures. The research done thus far indicates clearly that peculiarities of performance contribute more than other features to the creation of national or ethnic styles. Indeed, owing to those qualities, even songs of non-folk origin can sound 'authentic'. The exploration of performance media also revealed that the identification of morphological features and of style are two completely different subjects for investigation. The morphological data usually mark the preservation of a long tradition easily discovered by scholars and recognized to be the cultural treasure of a certain group or nation, whereas the analyses of performance phenomena require the discovery of elements that are perceived directly and associated immediately, and which play a decisive rôle in the communication process. Nevertheless, the cultural significance of morphological features is often intuitively felt by professional folk performers and particularly by instrumentalists organizing their repertoire according to certain motifs and phrases. It should also be remembered that traditional comparative studies often reveal the vitality of certain morphological features such as rhythmic or melodic motifs which are very significant for ethnic identification. Basically this concerns data discovered by systematic comparative procedures not perceived directly by the recipient.

The preservation of tradition depends on two additional factors; on the character of the legacy which has been transplanted, including its degree of transparent traditionalism, and on the character of the new culture, and of the new conditions to which people had to adapt in their new homeland. This is why folk culture transplanted many years ago can be more lasting and influential; and why people living amongst other traditional groups, for instance Polish émigrés in Yugoslavia, preserve much better and more consciously their traditional though already transformed legacy.

Manipulation with different political programmes often stimulates the revival of some regionally or traditionally orientated trends. Depending on actual motivation, these programmes may be projected on a different scale and based on different ideologies in which either local or general national and social interests prevail. In all of these programmes, however, manipulation with psycho- and physiological factors plays a significant rôle.

2.3.2 Polish folk culture and music today, its conditioning and functions: preliminary conclusions and hypotheses

Folk song, folk music and musical folk culture in contemporary Poland (see Map 3) have been under study from several points of view and have been observed progressively at different times since 1970. This has produced a body of evidence which permits us to put forward some conclusions and to formulate preliminary hypotheses (Czekanowska 1975a).

The first results achieved in 1972–5 revealed four basic facts. At first, it became clear that the distance between the material currently in circulation and that preserved and represented in folklore has been gradually diminished, particularly since 1970. Secondly, it has been noticed that the spatial structure of culture and of folk music has undoubtedly been modified through a process of interregional levelling. Thirdly, it has been found that the functions of folklore in contemporary society have obviously changed: from communication in specific social situations towards the inspirational and functions of social identity (Czekanowska 1975a).

Finally, the transformation of morphological and stylistic features has revealed changes in musical repertoire as well as changes in the principles of instrumental accompaniment. The latter are evidently associated with the selection and composition of musical ensembles.

The conclusions of those studies have been derived from a comparison of historical and more recent collections, such as those of Oskar Kolberg (1857–1907), of the Polish State Collection (Institute of Art of the Polish Academy of Science – 1949–53) and current field investigations (since 1970) and they indicate the strong dynamism of recent transformations. Moreover, the material representative of the last period reveals the complex character of the changes in question. In an attempt at generalization it can only be stated that the first half of the twentieth century was a time of substantial change in the range of influence of big urban and industrial centres, and of a decline of the main institutional determinants in the traditional sense. In contrast the second half of this century is marked by changes in social consciousness, whereas the changes of the last few years are going simultaneously in different directions, thanks to the restitution of many traditional ways of life in present-day Poland. Clearly, social consciousness appears to be more resistant to change than are the social institutions and forms which are more easily transformable. The historical collections reveal a characteristic correlation between genre and spatial differentiation, as well as between morphological qualities, which could be located in time, and spatial structure. These correlations are confirmed by all comparative studies done so far. In recent years, however, substantial changes have occurred in these correlations and, indirectly, in the spatial structure and distribution of folk music. This is most clearly demonstrated by the example of the dance song which has now gained an interregional character owing to the flourishing of the amateur movement and the consequent popularization of some dances. Thus the dance song, which was once virtually confined to a region, has now crossed its former boundaries and, in many cases, has spread all over Poland. This is a very substantial shift, considering the fact that the genre in question is functionally the most important, especially in central Poland, on account of a deepening decline of the ritual song and of many common 'longer' songs (e.g., ballads). The phenomena particularly worth studying include changes in the range of influence of various categories of folk music which tend towards either differentiation or unification. Any conclusions in this respect will be premature, however, since they have to be preceded by detailed and cross-contextual analysis of representative material.

The social functions of folklore and of folk music are quite different in contemporary society. The main functions include recreation and relaxation often connected with reflection and mental stabilization. The other functions are of mobilizing type although the demand for that emerges only under certain conditions and in certain situations. This functional dualism of stabilizing and mobilizing, however, is not so much conflicting as complementary. Their integrative features become visible when the functions are considered in terms of a relationship between ordinary and unusual events. The first type, i.e., the recreational, is marked by its regular occurrence during periods of stability, while the second type gains significance occasionally, as a reflection of abnormal and eventful periods.

Quite different and even less conflicting relations can be observed in the case of the inspiring and identifying functions of folklore. The contrast between these functions is not exactly a matter of differently organized perception but rather of the degree of participation in the group (individual, collective, active, passive) with the resultant division into outside recipients (the inspiring function) and inside recipients (the identifying function). These outside recipients act as passive observers, perceiving folklore but with no inclination to participate fully and to identify themselves with it. In these cases folklore opens new horizons and acts as a catalyst for people to get to know other cultures and continents and to enrich their inner lives and artistic experiences. But folklore used in this way is never fully assimilated. Inquiries show that there is an ever-increasing demand for this as managers and administrators of mass media well know. As a rule, consumers of folklore perceived in this way do not come from authentic folk communities.

The function of folklore in social identity is gaining more and more significance today, but its analysis is complex. Generally speaking, the growing significance of this type of function is directly related to the growing prestige of different social groups, peasant and labour communities, who formerly played a minor rôle in the process of creation and perception, within the framework of an officially supported culture.

In conclusion, the functions of folklore in Poland and in much of central Europe have undergone substantial changes as a result of the prevailing demand for individual, and largely passive, perception as well as for recreation and relaxation. Moreover, folklore serves primarily as a means of getting to know other cultures and regions, and also as a source of inspiration. It is frequently stylized, with varying degrees of authenticity, but the versions that seem to be valued most are those which resemble the genuine patterns as closely as possible, with their expressive qualities being stressed and their scale adjusted, depending on the form of presentation.

Turning to the results of comparative studies based on morphological and stylistic features, it should be stressed once more that they reveal more than other kinds of studies how the repertoire has declined and been diluted. Particularly significant is the decline of narrative songs, and lyrical and moralizing ballads. The latter are associated with the vanishing generation of women-singers specializing in so-called 'longer' songs that contained specific types of reflection and were usually performed at social gatherings, such as peasant weddings or social gatherings.

Morphological and stylistic studies also show how the form has been extended, on the one hand, but at the same time how its internal structure has been atomized into smaller units. The phrases have been broken up into minor motifs or, at times, even into single, often repeated, sounds (see Examples 59a and 59b). It is worth studying to what extent

Na Po-do - lu   bia - Ty kamień, bia -Ty kamień,

Po-do- lan-ka   sie-dzi na nim, Po-do-lan-ka sie-dzi na nim.

Example 59a *Na Podolu biały kamień*, Sankiewicz–Frąckowska 1978, p. 74

Idzie żoł - nierz   bo-rem, la-sem, bo-rem, la-sem, przy-mie- ra - jąc

z gło-du cza-sem, z gło-du cza-sem, suknia na nim   o-bla-tu-je,

o -bla- tu-je, wiatr dziura- mi   prze-la -tu - je, prze- la-tu - je.

Example 59b *Idzie żołnierz*, Sankiewicz–Frąckowska 1978, p. 74

these formal transformations depend on the development of musical factors like the transformation of tonal or formal systems (see Example 60b), and to what extent they are directly caused by changes in the composition of musical ensembles and by principles of performance, and finally, to what extent they are influenced or perhaps merely accelerated by external factors.

The most recent research (1980–5), complemented by more detailed interviews and centring around some ethnopsychologically orientated questions, has brought a modification of our previous observations (Czekanowska 1983). This applies primarily to the continuity of tradition which, to a large extent, still exists in the minds of most performers and many receivers, and the rôle of ethnopsychological and ethnosocial factors in shaping the regional consciousness of Polish society. At the same time, the regional differentiation of Poland as perceived both by the contributors to folk culture and by their receivers does not correspond with the differentiation arrived at through a historical interpretation of morphological analyses. Moreover, the regional consciousness of the inhabitants is to a large extent independent of the degree of conservatism and traditionalism of culture, and of the consequences of urbanization and industrialization in modern Polish society.

It was previously argued that regional differences had been reduced as a result of the amateur-group movement and its repertoire disseminated by mass media, but this view must also be partially modified. According to the latest results, we now differentiate phenomena of interregional levelling as they occur among traditional groups from those among stylized groups popularizing folklore. Consequently, it is much more difficult to make any general statement about those parts of the population which are not involved in the amateur movement and which are acquainted with folklore only through mass media. In traditional regions, investigating the process of reinforcing regional distinctiveness requires more controlled measures. Field research conducted in traditional regions shows that regional consciousness comprises at least two strata which play a significant rôle in the process of identifying the vernacular culture. The first is that of genuine heritage. The second is that of the indirectly inherited elements which have either been modified from the original patterns or, by reinforcing the old tradition, clearly redefine the status of folklore: this is to a larger extent subject to external factors, such as fashion, regional pride, ethnopolitical motivation or even commercial factors. Through these latter processes, vernacular culture is adapted, being, as it were, a mere reflection of the wave of heritage and the attitude taken towards it today is less intuitive and more conscious.

Turning to more detailed analyses, the problem of principles of performance in instrumental ensembles and of instrumental accompaniment are of significance. In the traditional regions of central and eastern Poland, dominated by vocal music and individual violin performance both solo and as an accompaniment to singing, there still functions a particular model of musical thinking and style. This is a monophonic model clearly rooted in vocal music and its forms, enriched by ornamentation, with repetitions and elaboration of phrases, and with only occasional use of doubling and addition of sounds. The accompaniment in this model, realized by double bass or drum, is primarily rhythmic. More frequent, on the other hand, is what Kolberg described as a suspension on the fifth degree of the scale from which incipient functional thinking can be inferred. This model, which Kolberg described so well (Kolberg 1867: 7–10) and which was used by Chopin in his mazurkas (Windakiewiczowa 1926), is considered to be a basis of Polish national style and still functions, to a certain extent, in many regions. This model has not been affected even by the introduction into bands of factory-made instruments, such as the accordion, which seem to be predisposed to harmonized music. This manner of performing music has influenced the fairly common practice of reconstructing accordions, to reduce their registers or to make use of only a limited section of the scale, as is the case with village violinists who usually do not use the technique of changing positions (E. Dahlig 1982). The findings at hand favour the contention that the old model of shaping is still current and still functions among 'composers' and performers in traditional regions.

Finally, in those regions in which culture is in the process of transformation, but whose inhabitants are at the same time still aware of the values and distinctiveness of their vernacular culture (Cassubian, Silesian), questions of performance in instrumental ensembles and of principles of accompaniment are subordinated to principles of the common practice of harmony. The latter have entered the consciousness of the musicians so completely that they are also found to operate in vocal music.

The results of more recent research show both confirmations and refutations of earlier statements (P. Dahlig 1983). The most interesting are the results of exploration of folk terminology. They confirm that the basic rudiments of traditional thinking are preserved still in some parts of Poland. At the same time, however, they indicate also that the findings of morphologically orientated investigations are often in opposition to the results of research into regional consciousness. The traditional regions with the highest coefficient of archaism are not always characterized by a maximal interest in folklore. Recent research also shows clearly that the state of balance between stabilizing and modifying factors may be varied; the decisive rôle in this case is played by psychological factors which are not always appreciated or explained sufficiently. The detection of a proper balance between individual and social factors in their mutual conditioning should be the best way of understanding Polish culture in recent times.

2.3.3 Change or stability: analytical remarks

Contemporary researchers are particularly interested in studying cultural change synchronically. Cultural phenomena are now studied basically from the viewpoint of their structural and specifying properties and as sets of factors that are subject to transformations, particularly the relations between a subsystem (musical) and a system (cultural) that determines it.

Especially interesting is the changeability of folk songs due to levelling and the transformational processes that stem from essential changes in their functions. These may emerge in connection with adjustment to a newly accepted model, while processes of change consist both of mutual exchangeability of elements and of mixing of these elements and their gradual transformations. Processes of reduction and evolution often exist side by side.

To illustrate this, we shall use the results of studies of two closed sets of folk songs subject to transformations resulting from their connection with various historical functions: military songs of folk origin (Sankiewicz-Frąckowska 1978) and songs that function in the repertoire of song and dance ensembles (Grajewska-Harasiuk 1974).

Results obtained from these studies also display contradictions. Thus, in the military song studies, it appears that a review of sources points to a considerable outdating of ethnic, regional or local designates. Secondly, it seems that the selected repertoire consisted mainly of folk songs bearing features of recently developed folklore with definite stylistic tags, e.g., the domination of the major mode, stabilized periods of AB structure, marching rhythms, or equally distributed rhythmic values; and versification reflecting the influence of seventeenth- or eighteenth-century literary patterns (8+5, 6+5, 8+6). Consequently this repertoire is to a large extent characteristic of the eighteenth and nineteenth centuries, as included in collections assembled by Kolberg in his sections devoted to 'war', 'army', 'varia' and finally '*dumas*' and lyrical songs, and to a minimal degree in his section of short dance songs. The oldest and most authentic folk material accounts for a tiny percentage in the material under investigation, and seems to be basically from the eastern borderland of ethnic Poland.

Further conclusions stem from studies of the transformations of the formal structure analysed in detail. In the latter case the process of change was studied in two approximations. First, basic transformations were detected especially in rhythmical and melodic features, which changed from that of the mazurka into that of a march in about 50 per cent of all melodies (see Examples 60a and 60b), and to rhythms connected with an equal progression of values. Among fundamental transformations one should also include changes of interval structure, which was transformed from that of an oscillating character typically featuring

Example 60a   *A z góry, jadą mazury*, Sankiewicz–Frąckowska 1978, p. 80

Example 60b   *Hej z góry, góry*, Sankiewicz–Frąckowska 1978, p. 80

interchange of seconds and thirds with clearly archaic expressions, into chord melodies based on triads and other chords.

These changes are of vital significance since they reveal an almost complete exchange of one type of morphological property for another. It means that we observe neither the phenomenon of gradual change characteristic of a folk tradition, which is usually proof of a diachronic transformation of material, nor the phenomenon of the mixing of properties which is so typical for border regions between different zones of a country.

Alongside these fundamental changes, less vital changes were also studied by investigating another set of parameters. They primarily concerned transformations of form, especially in its external manifestations. From these studies it seems that the formal features present a relatively rich spectrum of diversification. We do not observe here such obvious formal changes as in the case of the influence of marching rhythms or of the use of chordal melodies that are easy to march to, to sing along with and to harmonize. There is rather an emphasis on repeated single sounds which are so typical of melodies recited or sung collectively. The diversification of forms shows that there exist a number of processes that stem from the mutual influences of the background of tradition, of the consequences of mass appeal, of form of performance, and finally of gradual adaptation and adjustment. Results of detailed studies may collectively be presented in the following way.

First, the maximal development of musical form is in its size: a short verse often in the form of a short couplet is extended by numerous repetitions, usually in the form of two and four 'bars', so that formats of 24 bars or larger become a rule. Secondly, a characteristic feature is a departure from the circular arrangements characteristic of songs in the folk repertoire (aa'ba' with a repetitive ending or refrain), in favour of two-part periodic forms, typically AB. Divisions into two parts prevail over divisions into three parts, and the symmetry of division and the use of two- or four-bar phrases instead of three-bar phrases as a basis may almost be considered a rule. Thirdly, extension through repetition is not achieved in the sense of gradual development. There is also a lack of variability, while simple repetitions of phrases and of phrase fragments predominate (see Example 60b). Fourthly, in the process of the extension of form, the exclamations or interjections do not play a rôle. The songs start with a downbeat, and have no breaks in the phrase, while frequent pauses play the rôle of inserts and complement the metrical regularity.

The body of information obtained in this way enables one to draw an outline of changes and of the factors that have brought these about. The distinction between basic and secondary transformations, and some quantitative information (e.g., the growth of the basic number of bars in a period), enables one to define crucial points and to draw conclusions on basic formats and features of particularly popular or characteristic songs. Analysis of the first set of material reveals that there is still an insufficiently diachronic overview for a full study of the process of change. Comparative studies taking into account the influence of the cultural context should provide material for the interpretation of these issues. Among the most significant is the departure from compact musical formulae of a folk song towards a new type of form regulated by diversified relations of cadences revealing basic structure regulated by sequence of harmonic functions. The latter break up the form of song that are largely devoid of individual traits and present a complex and differentiated structure, which corresponds slightly to the concept of construction characteristic of the traditional repertoire. In these cases the song is identified as a whole connected with a definite topic, rather than as reminiscent of old intuitively felt formulae, although fragments of previous motifs or phrases can still be detected.

The second set of conclusions obtained from studies of the authentic folk repertoire used in amateur movements shows a number of regularities that are different from those announced above, although these results do not stand in opposition to the most general regularities.

It is a commonly accepted fact that the tendency to shape dance cycles is now maintained mainly by show forms that juxtapose various varieties of dance and zones of tempo (slow–fast). This use of old national and folk dances, which was recorded by Kolberg in the nineteenth century (Kolberg 1857), has survived in transformed versions and in dramatized form in the amateur movement. A consequence of their use is a growth in the size of the form. However, even in the case of the amateur repertoire, cyclic versions consisting of several dances, though practised and demonstrated on various occasions, are not the most popular versions.

The fact that folk material is used in dramatized form directly contributed to the stressing of agogic and dynamic contrasts which are very rare in genuine Polish folk music. This is also connected with the use of repetitions and the spatial extension of form. Never does it assume the character of a structural factor of expression. Moreover, genuine folk material used by amateurs over the past few decades is still close to the original folk pattern, especially with so-called authentic ensembles that make use of the material of traditional regions. This is probably due to the fact that little time has elapsed since the material was taken over from the natural environment and that a still powerful connection with the original region exists. Totally different is the case of the artificially created repertoire, which remains a foreign and unadapted creation.

A different problem is presented when folk material external to a given region is performed by the amateur movement. This contributes not only to its popularization, but also to cross-regional unification, as cultural differences between regions disappear. This is particularly true of sequences of short dance songs and ditties which are performed by ensembles and increasingly lose their regional character. This phenomenon, however, is not evident throughout Poland and is restricted mainly to the dance music of central and southern Poland, where short dance songs or *przyśpiewki* (ditties) are especially popular and seem to be undergoing a process of standardization.

The comparison of conclusions stemming from these two kinds of studies of fairly different material makes it possible to construct a hypothesis concerning developmental tendencies of Polish songs and their historically durable features. The most durable elements include the melodic model on the one hand, which is to a large extent designated by the tonal system and the principles of instrumental performance, and, on the other hand, the rhythmic model determined by the system of versification in the case of songs, and by dancing steps in the case of dance melodies. The durability of these models is evident in comparative diachronic studies and in cross-regional or even international studies, including those of variants of songs among émigrés (Czekanowska 1983).

Entirely different is the problem of form, which is to a large extent variable. As can be seen in the results of these studies, form is largely determined by the circumstances in which it is performed, by the character of presentation, and by the social rank it represents. As historians commonly agree, the form of dance songs, in particular, depends on their social rank. Folk music and folk dance songs from nineteenth- and twentieth-century documentation represent shorter and simplified forms, which are the result of separation from the dance and the transformation of their function. In the rural community, dance songs are limited to a short utterance, an opinion, or a means of conversation. A characteristic feature is not only the shortening of the form of the dance song *przyśpiewka* (ditty), but also the increasing symmetry of the form adjusted to the proportions of the poetic text in favour of the limitation of the means of musical cohesion, in this case presented by limitation of the tendencies to use reprises or repetitive forms (aa'ba or aa'ba'). The general tendency for old dance songs to be shortened, simplified and divorced from dance patterns, and to abandon their own regularities of musical form 'reprise', seems to be accompanied by the democratization of rank and the unification of functions, i.e., their basic function is recreational. This is also connected subsequently to the levelling of the average tempo, with the disappearance of traditional performing styles and with a departure from the principle of cyclic construction. The opposite is the case for folk songs adopted by the amateur movement or adjusted to new functions in the army. In these cases, form is extended and enriched, and expressive values of the folkloristic material are sometimes given prominence owing to a fuller use of contrasts.

At the same time, it is now impossible to state to what extent the character and form of a work is affected by the fact that individuals are isolated from their natural environments, for example because of army service, migration to cities or emigration abroad. In other words, it is hard to determine which factors influence the reductional processes of songs, and which are important in the transformation of properties, and which contribute to their modernization and developmental tendencies. It seems from observations that the problem may present itself differently when various time lapses are taken into account during the study. Despite the intensity of social and cultural changes since the Second World War, transformations detected in relation to historical material (songs from Kolberg's collection) are much more evident. By contrast, the changes observed since the war are mainly limited to signs of reduction and exchangeability of certain elements of the repertoire, while in the case of its adoption by the amateur movement the artificial manners of performing should be noted. It is especially difficult in these circumstances to draw conclusions about natural developmental tendencies. A number of factors seem to indicate that as a result of social transformations and intensive communication among various ethnically and socially different groups, new functions and forms of demand for folk material will develop, which will ensure its lasting character within the new social structures and will make it possible to observe long-term changeability of the repertoire.

One of the most difficult tasks is to arrange in order conclusions drawn from studies of various types of material and at various stages of research, although it could be particularly valuable in a general methodological reflection on studies on the changeability of folk material. The most important thing is to determine durable elements which have a specific influence, modifying the general process of change. A number of features that specify the cultural face of nations, ethnic groups or social classes have not been explained. This is particularly true for performing features which remained undetected for a long time because they were undocumented. As is now known, thanks to studies of both dance (Lange 1975) and music, the nature of the folk and national manner of performing Polish dances depends primarily on the character of tempo and accentuation and above all on a manner of transforming rhythmic and accentuated (dynamic) values within a constant temporal and metric cycle, known as *tempo rubato* (Szachowski 1974), which is a factor of enrichment following the introduction of periodic violations of tempo. What remains unknown is whether *tempo rubato* should be explained by means of musically autonomous factors or, as seems more probable, by means of patterns of behaviour that may be reinterpreted, such as the adoption of a definite tradition from other groups or cultures. Vague ethnopsychological factors seem in this case to play a vital though still not fully explained rôle. The issue of regional conditioning of tempo, however, remains uninterpreted, as is evident in comparisons of variants on the cross-regional and international scales.

2.3.4 The programmes and institutions of regional folkloristic movements: their main concepts and media, and changes

Tradition

Essential feelings of identity generally remain stable, as do basic needs for integration. Skilful manipulation with political and social programmes can penetrate this sensitive domain of human feelings, and it is especially successful when ethnic and regional, or national and regional, factors are applied jointly and instrumentally manœuvred into ideological programmes. As is well known, the development of national feelings clearly stimulated several regional and folkloristic movements during the last two hundred years. Under varied conditions, however, regional and folkloristic activities were shaped differently and adapted to changing needs. After the restoration of the Polish independent state (1918), several new aspects of folk culture partly replaced the national imperatives that dominated previously. At the same time, however, in the early twentieth century the national consciousness of Polish citizens developed and was transformed both politically and socially. In the 1920s, and even more in the 1930s, the interest in folklore was conditioned by certain groups of Polish artists trying to find new inspirations and ideas for modern art (see above, p. 60). It was supported also by the establishment of folk ensembles which developed successfully after World War II. Musical activity, however, came somewhat later than the dance movement and achievements in the decorative arts, and started to develop seriously as late as the end of the 1940s. This was realized by organization of musical festivals, by sound recordings undertaken on a mass scale and by organization of state ensembles of folk music and dance.

The development of centrally supported institutions copying Soviet models and standards encompassed, in the 1940s and 1950s, many areas of Polish life. They were involved in educational programmes and the organization of free time for workers and soldiers, as well as amusement and publicity. Varied types of musical ensembles were concentrated at places of professional activities and at social institutions, often with specific regional emphases. The latter, however, were usually secondary to the central institutions. Amidst different kinds of ensembles which were established, five types seem to be most important. The most common was the ensemble organized at industrial or service enterprises, that is, factories or plants. Quite popular and widely found were the ensembles supported by CEPELIA, *Centrala Przemysłu Ludowego i Artystycznego* (The Centre for Folk and Artistic Industry), the centrally controlled state association which to a certain extent had deep roots in Polish pre-World War II activities and in the attempts to help poor Polish people in the overpopulated villages of that time (see Figure 19). The third type of ensemble was a combination of locally and centrally

Figure 19   The ensemble of CEPELIA in performance

managed activities, organized by a network of local *Domy Kultury* (Houses of Culture) centrally supported by the Ministry of Culture. The degree of independence of these ensembles was clearly conditioned by the power of local culture and the strength of the regional political and artistic structure. Ensembles organized at schools and universities, as well as the state ensembles of Folk and Dance officially infused with propagatory dedication, were also quite active in those days (see Figure 20). The last two categories, however, and the

Figure 20   The State Ensemble Śląsk

university ensembles in particular, did not have many direct links with village activities. Their professional character, especially in the case of state ensembles, was also and still is quite obvious.

The activities of many ensembles have been sharply criticized by Polish intellectuals. The motivations of these institutions were especially criticized, as was the artistic quality of the productions which did not always present the best image of folk art. An objective discussion should consider both the negative and positive trends of these activities. Obviously negative was the tendency towards the unification of programmes and standardization of style, adopting some fashions of the most popular state ensembles. Also negative was the inclusion of artificial elements which either never existed in the folk tradition or had died out many years before. Such was the case, for example, with the 'revival' or 'revitalization' of some instruments known only from literature. A final negative aspect was the use of artificial stage effects to encourage a good response among popular audiences. Some results of the general training system supported and organized by central authorities were also negative, e.g., CPARA, *Centralna Poradnia Ruchu Amatorskiego* (The Central Advisory Centre for Amateur Movement). Nevertheless, the system developed at that time did document and preserve several folk phenomena that were dying out in villages. It also stimulated conscious evaluations of cultures and encouraged local interest in developing feelings of local pride and satisfaction. Participation in regional ensembles also presented additional possibilities of travel and cultural exchange for people inside as well as outside the country, all of which played a significant rôle in Polish contemporary society.

Apart from the activity of all types of ensembles mentioned above, the contributions made by individual musicians and small chamber ensembles as have still been preserved in villages, towns and cities were quite important. These musical activities, though in part officially registered and financially supported by central organizations (Ministry of Culture), presented, and still present, the traditional repertoires of Polish villages, towns, or suburbs. These activities, practised until recently, also preserved the character of a family or guild. The exchange of repertoire and even of services between these kinds of ensembles presents another very interesting area. The city and small town orchestras, with their special styles and repertoires, compete quite successfully with the traditional bands of the villages. This is shown by the engagement of city bands to accompany important village events, even including traditional weddings. It is, however, significant that official recognition by centrally organized support often played a decisive rôle, both in financial support and in cases of conflicts in the legal sense. The officially recognized small ensembles strive hard to preserve their names and repertoires which often offer a unique contribution and are understood as an individual property. Recognition by official authorities also played a decisive rôle in acceptance for local competitions organized at different levels, local, regional, national and even international, which are highly respected by folk performers. Among festivals the one organized every year in Kazimierz has a special importance (see Figures 21a, b and c).

In brief, in the 1950s and 1960s, official support of folk musical activity played a significant rôle, contributing both to the development and to the transformation of the folkloristic legacy. It applied not only to the activity of folk ensembles, but also intervened in the activities of individual musicians, especially in their local recognition and promotion. Many aspects of this policy are today sharply criticized. It is related also to the didactic support organized by central institutions (CPARA), instruction, courses, purchase of musical instruments, as well as the criteria concerning the selection of repertoire and the promotion of individual performers. Several concepts especially promoted and propagated in the 1950s are today forgotten, such as the introduction of folk instruments into school curricula and the performance of folk music in concert halls. Similarly, the concept of recognizing folk performers as national artists, as did Soviet society, was never practically accepted in Poland. Indeed, even the idea of higher retirement pensions or grants for folk performers, though accepted and realized, applied in later years only to limited and rather unpopular cases.

Centrally governed support versus more individual activity

The ten years since 1980 have witnessed rapid social change and transformation of social consciousness in Poland which has been reflected in changes of folk ensembles and in the organization of state institutions supporting folk activity. The centrally organized financial support, which is limited today, does not, however, reflect drastic changes or a decrease in folk productions. Amongst new impulses stimulating the development of the ensemble

Figure 21   (a) Competition in Kazimierz 1980

movement, mention should be made particularly of the productions for tourists and for the Poles abroad. This is especially evident in the regions with strong ethnic background or in the areas of ethnically, religiously or nationally mixed population. Still, modern organizers of folk activity work under different conditions, being compelled to find financial support from various sources while not being able to rely on centrally distributed help.

New technological equipment which is used today also plays a decisive rôle in the transmission of folk culture. Tape- and cassette-recorders in particular contribute to exchanges of repertoire between people in the country and abroad as well as within the country, the region or even the same village. The function of leaflets (*druki ulotne*) and books, still used on certain occasions (for example, funeral ceremonies in some regions) and by certain generations, is today generally taken over by records, tapes and cassettes. The custom of working with impermanent recordings, which were very popular some years ago and distributed on local markets, is today replaced by cassettes distributing the more popular tunes. The fashion of documenting a whole family event, especially a wedding, is also very popular today and contributes to the selection and promotion of some parts of the repertoire. The new media and fashions of popularization are, however, quite distant from traditional forms of transmission and introduce new elements reconstructing the concept of traditional folklore, and its function and position in the framework of society.

In brief, changes of social structure in contemporary Poland, as well as the re-evaluation of many concepts, have had significant consequences and have contributed to the transform-

Figure 21   (b) Competition in Kazimierz 1980

ation of cultural institutions and their social evaluation. The biggest changes are several in number.

First, the need for state support still remains and can only partly be replaced by private sources.

At the same time, however, the centrally organized network of subsidies cannot be managed as in the past. The more individual activities of local or regional groups, in particular, take the initiative and work in different ways.

It may be assumed also that regional and local self-government will grow in the near future and partly take over the activities organized at places of service and production. This kind of activity will probably be especially popular in the regions with strongly developed feelings of ethnic identity and in areas with mixed populations.

The activity of folk ensembles, however good and authentic it may be, cannot replace traditional forms of folk performance either by individuals or groups. For this reason the organization of competitions for folk musicians seems to present the most important element of social intervention. They may be organized at local, regional, national or international level.

The use of sophisticated technical equipment contributes more to the transformation than to the development of traditional culture. At the same time, however, such transmission

Figure 21   (c) Competition in Kazimierz 1980

stimulates more than other factors the interests of the younger generation and helps to preserve folklore in contemporary culture.

Also, the rather unpopular idea of introducing folk music into concert halls is sometimes implemented. This is undertaken mainly by students and the youth movement and does not have much in common with concepts which were popular in the 1950s and the younger generation is currently much more interested in non-European folklore than in the vernacular folk legacy.

Finally, the general trend towards popularization and dissemination of folklore by centrally organized institutions, despite its transformational consequences, did not distort the traditional chains of folk transmission though it did change the nature of folk artifacts. The same may be said of the natural instincts to preserve the legacy of ancestors, despite substantial changes of many structures, including the hierarchy of values. New motivations, developed quite recently, appeal often to the restoration of old family contacts and enforce the prestige of older generations often culturally active in associations for retired people. Old people are today often appreciated for their experience and knowledge of the past.

The transformation of traditional folk culture is unavoidable, but many psychologically motivated factors, and especially those rooted in family structure, religion and the recognition of traditional culture, support the preservation of some rudiments of behavioural patterns which can be identified as genuinely traditional.

3 *Analysis and description*

3.1 Vocal transmission

3.1.1 Functions and genres

Most events in Polish social life traditionally called for songs, the vocal model and structure of accompanying poetic texts being evidently prior to instrumental pieces. Only a limited number of instrumental activities are relatively independent musical inventions, mainly signal melodies performed on wind instruments, particularly trumpets and horns. At the same time, however, Polish musicians do not identify vocal activity as 'music', the term being reserved for instrumental pieces. Songs are considered a manifestation of human and social feelings or responses; they function as a basic communicative medium and not as a phenomenon of artificially created activity. The pertinent folk terminology confirms this fact and reveals primarily the connection of songs with accompanying circumstances, i.e., customs, their episodes, dances, social gatherings or people's professional activities.

The most general division of genres, as seen today by performers, identifies two groups of songs, so-called 'shorter' pieces, such as ditties and dance songs, and 'longer' pieces, such as ballads and lyrics. There are only a few very traditional areas in contemporary Poland, like Kurpie, northern Mazovia or Podhale, where the local terminology is more specific. This applies especially to Podhale and its repertoire (see above, pp. 84–91), and to some categories of Kurpian and north Mazovian lyrics – called *leśne* or *jesienne* (forest and autumn songs).

A more detailed analysis of folk terminology reveals quite a variety of names, many of them used only locally (Stęszewski 1972). These names tend to be especially diversified in the case of 'short' ditties and dance songs, in which the specific names of both dance and song are often mutually exchanged. To be specific, the name *krakowiak* (actually a dance) may be used for a song, and the name *vivat* (actually a song) for a dance.

Rituals and customs: their cycles and songs

The connection of songs with customs, their episodes and situations is a topic in itself and requires special study. In principle it is obvious that its connection with a concrete event or episode determines the character of a song. Still, a difference can be observed between songs evidently connected with concrete activities, e.g., sung *do rozplecin* or *do oczepin* (to unplaiting or to capping), and songs performed only occasionally during social gatherings accompanying these customs. These latter, both 'longer' and 'shorter' songs, are usually more recent and have a substitutive function, although they often receive recognition as high as, for example, some popular religious songs (*Serdeczna Matko*) performed on such occasions. The degree of association with concrete events presents a different subject and may be differently approached in various parts of Poland. As mentioned before, there exists an obvious difference between the repertoires of western and central parts of Poland on the one hand and those of the eastern territories on the other (see above, pp. 29–37). Songs characteristic of central and western Poland are associated with concrete events, especially with weddings, while those typical of eastern Poland are rather unspecified, and one type of melody may even accompany totally different events, such as the wedding and harvest (Moszyński 1939, vol. II, part 2: 1,209), which are related only by some common symbols such as the sun (see Examples 12b and 6).

The ritual repertoire, both annual and that connected with family life, previously determined by solar-lunar cycles, has recently been reduced to a few fragments, clearly transformed by the Christian calendar into its periodical feasts, and also by the church repertoire (e.g., sequences – see above, p. 41). An analysis of the poetic and musical content of ritual songs reveals, however, the existence of deep-rooted Slavonic structures (see pp. 29–37). The poetic aspect of ritual songs has been particularly well investigated (Jakobson 1981) and interpreted in a wider Slavonic perspective, as well as in a multistratal spectrum of context. Thus the significance has been stressed of the principle of negative parallelism as an organizing factor of this kind of structure (Jakobson 1981: 41). The findings also reveal the obvious supremacy of emotive impact over other functions, and demonstrate the significance of musical and metrical patterns. Such patterns obviously operate as systems outside the language and are to a great extent determined, or at least transformed, by accompanying gestures. Finally, it has been made clear that symbolism is a focal point in the repertoire under discussion. This is proved by its organizing rôle in the creation of climactic points of the action, regardless of whether these functions are substitutive or just accessory.

The symbols in the ritual repertoire are always metaphorically projected and clearly metonymic, while metaphoric images and factual descriptions usually exist in parallel. Despite elements of evident dramatism, the main sequence exhibited in the overall code presents a rather flattened stream of moderated waves carried by musical and metrical stereotypes, i.e., formulae and rhythmically repeated sentences. The long time taken by the folk narrator to interpret the main plot, as well as his metaphorically formulated images and the internal nexus of sound and meaning, create the very unique atmosphere of 'old' Slavonic ritual songs, especially well preserved in the repertoire of Poland's eastern border territories.

A more detailed analysis of symbols permits decoding the metonymy of the main actors of the actual drama and the climactic points of the ritual situation. Thus, in the case of wedding songs, there are symbols for the groom, encoded as a falcon or a horse, and for the bride, encoded as a bush, most often a guelder rose; there are symbols, too, for the acts of copulation and impregnation, encoded in archaic texts as *korovai*, dough which is rolled, flooded and finally blossoms (see Example 61). The same applies very much to annual songs with their depiction of watering, sun rising and sun setting or growing up. In both kinds of repertoire (wedding and annual) the complementary function of gesture patterns should not be overlooked either. In annual songs, for example, accompanying jumping gestures indicate the height which the expected crop (linen) should reach the following year. Other gestures include watering and breaking the egg, and also gestures of watering and flooding, practised previously during the *korovai* ceremony.

Example 61   *Korowajowe ciasto*, Czekanowska 1975, p. 246

The significance of metric patterns, their rhythmical arrangements, and formulae coinciding with choruses or invocations in poetry, poses another problem of international interest. This problem has attracted the attention mainly of Irish and Welsh scholars (Watkins 1961), who have discovered similar strata in Celtic and Slavonic poetry, and in the folklore of those nations in particular. This area of enquiry especially deserves attention, for it concerns sentences and vocatives recorded in the earliest sources of Polish literature, as well as in the 'original' Celtic language.

A few songs related to funeral ceremonies and to the birth of a child do not constitute a unified and coherent stratum in Polish folklore. Proper funeral laments obviously fell into disuse many years ago. They are replaced today by religious songs performed by professional singers (female or male), based on the repertoire from books printed in the nineteenth century, and are perceived today as being very traditional and 'old'. Songs associated with the birth of a child as well as with the cultivation of hemp, and pertinent myths, are limited to a few examples only.

Summing up, it should be stressed that the ritual repertoire, consisting of songs obviously declining in modern society, and custom songs preserved and cultivated to a certain extent as traditional strata of social behaviour until today, make two different and coherent groups without numerous references to other types of the Polish repertoire. This is due to their historical disjunction from the legacy of other strata of Polish society, unlike entertainment, professional or other 'common' songs. These, however, were basically recorded in much later periods in which a well-developed written tradition and closer intersocial links were already a widely accepted fact. Finally, it should also be remembered that, unlike the Russian repertoire, Polish ritual songs did not and do not refer to ceremonies and persons of upper social strata (*kniaź, bojary*: knight, nobility); for instance, the focal point of Russian wedding ceremonies is the act of holding a crown over the heads of the groom and bride (cf. Ivanov and Toporov 1974). The dedication of Polish upper classes to western behavioural models might be a decisive factor here.

Dance songs and ditties

The currently prevalent part of folklore is made up of ditties, couplets and different kinds of 'short' songs accompanying dance activities, amusements and social gatherings. They may be considered as a basic axis of social dialogue and correspondence. The substantial function of the dance and its rhythm is revealed by both music and poetry of these songs following the patterns of basic Polish dances (the *krakowiak, oberek, Polski*), not without some non-Polish elements (the pavane, waltz). The rhythmic model determines both the sequence of the verse and the shape of the stanza (Windakiewiczowa 1913) of the repertoire in question. Its musical form is contiguous with the symmetrical stanza and is based upon the principle of musical question and answer. The correspondence of musical phrases based on juxtaposed verses (a and b), creating a musical period of eight bars (4 + 4) is already well elaborated in this kind of song. In poetry, the metaphorically expressed verse (a) relates to the factual description expressed usually by the second verse (b) (see Example 62):

> Ej, wyszły rybki, wyszły
> Jeno karaś został
> Proś Boga dziewczyno,
> Żebym ci się dostał.

> All the fishes left, but the crucian remained
> Pray to Lord in heaven that you catch me, maid. (See Example 62)

Example 62   *Wyszły rybki wyszły*, Czekanowska 1961, no. 172

In music, this pattern is clearly dance-related and evidently plays a unifying role (see Example 63). Dance rhythms are also clearly correlated with certain versification patterns. For

Example 63   *Graboskie chłopaki*, Czekanowska 1956, no. 25

example, the *krakowiak* model coincides with a twelve-syllable verse (6 + 6), the *oberek* (see Example 63) with sixteen syllables (8 + 8), the *Polski* (see Example 64) with ten syllables (6 + 4), the waltz with ten syllables (5 + 5), etc.

The underlying idea of dialogue and correspondence is realized in this repertoire by long sequences functioning as a chain of responses, i.e., questions and answers or corresponding comments, constituting the subject matter of communication between different groups or individuals.

In contrast to other types of repertoire, ditties and dance songs have never attracted any particular scholarly interest. Their communicational function, as well as their being

Example 64   *Dolem, dolem*, Czekanowska 1961, no. 96

conditioned by behavioural patterns and by dance situations in particular, forms an almost unresearched subject, though one worth studying. Mutual relations between this kind of repertoire and other kinds also require special examination. This applies especially to love songs clearly interacting with dance songs (see Bystroń 1934).

Past comparative studies revealed several processes of mutual exchange between folk and non-folk strata within the dance repertoire. This is primarily true of recent transformational trends. They are quite manifest in the reduction of metaphorically projected concepts and images transformed today to more factual descriptions. The process is also accompanied by changes of musical structure involving modifications of the principles of construction. Thus, the fundamental principle of opposition is today implemented by a definite contrast of harmonic functions (DT) instead of the previous oppositions of direction of melody (rising versus falling).

In the repertoire of Polish ditties and dance songs, the repertoire from Podhale is quite specific. It is distinguished by its performance styles and their substantial degree of flexibility, smoothly fluctuating to conform with different types of genre and musical situation. In several examples from Podhale (e.g., the *Góralski* – Highlanders' dance) the influence of a dance rhythm is not so predictable and regular either.

Nevertheless, despite regional differences, Polish ditties and dance songs have common characteristic features. This seems to confirm the existence of a repertoire dating back to a certain period of Poland's history, at the time of the United Polish Commonwealth (fifteenth to eighteenth centuries). Indeed, the Polish repertoire of dances and ditties is still distinguished by a specific set of characteristic features and typically exhibits concrete tonal and melodic models as well as different patterns of verses and stanzas. Uniquely, too, this Polish repertoire reveals emotively motivated interjections and vocatives (*oj, hej, ej*), connected with shouting and fulfilling a structural function of responses in the most direct way. This confirms the social actuality of this repertoire.

Common songs

The so-called 'longer' or common songs – songs not definitely associated with particular circumstances – form a wide spectrum of material of varied descent and often elucidate contradictory trends, being actually the results of recent transformations. Indeed, this kind of repertoire, more than others, has been susceptible to the 'new' impact of popular and current songs including, as of recently, strata transmitted by modern mass media. One can even speak of the phenomenon of folk hits, songs of foreign descent that have achieved special popularity and a relatively long-term existence in the folk legacy. By contrast, several kinds of traditional songs – 'longer' songs, ballads, and lyrics in particular – have been decreasing in number, just as has the number of their performers, basically older women who specialized in this kind of repertoire. 'Longer' songs, previously so typical of north-western, western (ballads) or north-eastern (lyrical songs) Poland, are evidently disappearing.

The identification of genres and appreciation of their status have obviously been subject to change over time. This is particularly true of historical songs, which were highly esteemed in the nineteenth century (see Kurpiński 1820) and interpreted as one of the two substantial categories of the Polish folk repertoire, and were valued at that time much more highly than the other category, dance songs. Another case in point is the improper qualification of the songs documented in literature as *dumy* and interpreted as historical chants. The first correction to this erroneous interpretation was made by Kolberg (1857), who more properly applied the term *dumy* to balladas, ignoring, however, the fact that the term, quite popular already in the seventeenth century, never existed in Polish folk terminology. The terminology and interpretation applied by nineteenth-century scholars revealed clearly an approach dominated by admiration for patriotic and historical topics. Even their best intentions could not, however, change the reality; despite intensive research, epic cycles, so well developed and represented in the east and south Slavonic repertoire, are not to be found among Polish folk songs. It is also clear that songs depicting concrete historical events are not numerous. One can find references only to the Battle of Vienna (1683), to 'tumult' in Toruń (1724), to the Confederation of Bar (1768), and, more recently, to some battles of the nineteenth century (e.g., the Battle of Sadova, 1866; the Russo-Turkish War, 1877; battles fought during Polish uprisings, and also some events of the two World Wars). Indeed, the material in question is limited to more recent periods and constitutes a very small and not too popular part of the narrative repertoire.

In more general terms, Polish 'longer' songs can be divided into two basic groups: narrative songs (see Example 65), obviously in the majority, and lyrical songs (see Example 21). The

A wnie-dzie-le z po - ra - nia, a wniedzie-le z po - ra - nia,

wysz-ła pan - na z ka - za -ₜnia, wysz-ła pan - na z ka - za - nia.

Example 65 *A w niedziele z porania*, Czekanowska 1956, no. 28

former fall into several subcategories such as ballads, and historical, moralizing or hagiographic songs. Among lyrics (dominated by love songs), lullabies, soldier and orphan songs form small, but still evident, types. There are also some other genres, not definitely of narrative or lyrical character, as, for example, satirical, professional or children's songs (see Example 66), which form rather independent strata.

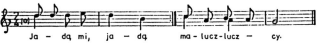

Example 66   *Jadą mi, jadą*, Ligęza and Ryling 1961, no. 86, p. 100

Polish ballads (see Example 48), like ballads in other European countries, have been subject to special attention and scholarly interest. They were chosen for publication in the first academic volume of Kolberg's collection (Kolberg 1857), which featured basic types of Polish ballad in their cross-regional presentation; they figured later in the first volume of Bystroń's series documenting the repertoire of Silesian songs (1927). Finally, the ballad was one of the basic topics systematically analysed by Polish ethnomusicologists of the interwar period, and also in recent years. As a result, the structure of the Polish ballad has been found to contain both narrative and dance elements. This is particularly evident when the musical structure of the ballad is considered, since the narrative sections, transmitting the message in a clearly descending rhythm and with a typical way of phrasing, stand in contrast with the central sections of a definite dance character (aa′ba). The poetic structure, on the other hand, is unequivocally true to the principle of parallelism (:a:) (:b:). The co-existence of these two different types of construction can be explained in historical terms: it indicates the conservatism of the poetic structure and the transformation of the musical structure. The latter took place in Renaissance and Baroque times (see Danckert 1939b: 401). It can also be assumed that the development of the musical form contributed to the extension of the poetic form by the application of repetitions. At the same time, however, it did not transform the structure of the ballad (:a:) (:b:) though it extended its size in a purely quantitative sense. Comparative studies of the poetic structure of the genre under discussion (Bystroń 1920) confirm an evident affinity of the Polish ballad with the west European stock of mediaeval descent and the repertoire developed in England in the thirteenth and fourteenth centuries in particular. The inspiring impact of the very popular source known as *Gesta Romanorum* is hard to question. Such common motifs as Hallewjin (see Example 48), Hero and Leander, King Lear, king and girl, poisoned drink (see Example 67), circulating all over Europe, can easily

Example 67   *Stała się nam nowina*, Kolberg 1857, no. 3t, p. 23

be detected. The affinity of the Polish ballad with the west European legacy is also revealed by morphological features of its poetry and its mediaeval type of verse and stanza, i.e., by the verse of seven syllables (4 + 3) with characteristic repetitions (:7:). The most characteristic features, however, are to be found in the contents of the ballad and its sequence; the description of topical events is unfolded in the central section, while the surrounding phrases have a more narrative and commenting function.

An analysis of the musical structure of the Polish ballad also reveals its closer affinity with western rather than eastern stock. This seems to be true even with regard to very distant

Celtic balladas, known basically from sources, though they preserved more traditional tonality and clearly modal rhythms. A comparison with German material reveals both similarities and differences; the former are to be found in the general projection of the form (cf. aa'ba) while the latter are evident in tempo and rhythm, and especially in the typical German tendency towards the upbeat, which stands in clear contrast with the Polish principle of the downbeat.

In brief, the Polish ballad, in its contents and form, presents a central European derivation of the west European mediaeval legacy. This folk tradition, developed in west Slavonic countries and in Silesia, Pomerania, Moravia and Bohemia in particular, carries a set of specific features which may be identified as typical of the Baroque era. This is especially obvious in most examples recorded in the nineteenth century, constituting a characteristic 'reprise' form (aa'ba).

At the same time, however, many variants of the ballad, especially those recorded in the eastern parts of Poland, and particularly in Kurpie, exhibit a different, and obviously more archaic, structure closer to that of wedding songs (see Example 48). On the other hand, one can also speak about clearly modified ballad songs which can hardly be identified as representative of the traditional legacy of the genre. The modifications have affected both the musical and poetic forms of this legacy. The musical topics are reduced today and complemented only by several repetitions of isolated motifs and sounds, whereas the poetry of recent ballads usually involves presentations of sensational themes. However, characteristic traces of the ballad can still be found even in these transformed strata, such as, first of all, comments and reflections expressing judgements and psychologically explained motivations.

The repertoire of the 'transformed' ballad is very popular and current in suburban areas as well as among newcomers to big cities. Also close to the genre are narrative songs, previously performed by wandering beggars singing and playing the hurdy-gurdy. These traditional singers were not only transmitting historical, military, religious (hagiographic) and moralizing topics, but also preserving some derivations of the legacy of the former upper classes. One has to mention in this connection first of all the case of *Bogurodzica*, the chant of Polish knights of the late Middle Ages (see above, p. 43) as has been transmitted by wandering beggars. Reminiscences of the mediaeval structure, i.e., the so-called litany type, are, in a historical sense, a distinctive feature of some samples of this repertoire, though on the whole it is difficult to speak of their stylistic or morphological consistency. Their moralizing orientation and concentration on historically and humanly significant events may be regarded as a functionally determined characteristic of the genre.

By contrast, the so-called lyrical ballad forms a rather homogeneous stratum, close in its symbols and contents to the wedding repertoire, though evidently transformed with well-established forms of verse and stanza, often including an internal refrain (7, 7, 12, 7; see Example 21).

Pervasive lyricism, so typical of Polish and Slavonic art, and so deeply transforming its expressive qualities, dominates the vocal repertoire of Poland's eastern regions. Its lyrical poetry, usually depicting the beauty of nature and sorrowful sensitivity to the seasonal changes, again refers to generally accepted iconic images (see Example 14). Birds are highly appreciated as the best mediators in a realistic as well as a transcendental sense; similarly, bushes, herbs and trees are recognized as symbolic substitutes. The repertoire pivots round love, loneliness, nostalgia, homesickness. These concepts, metaphorically encoded, are accompanied by somewhat dispassionate comments and judgements regarding human fate. The genre exhibits a variety of styles and subcategories, but what they have in common, their above-mentioned pervasive lyricism, outweighs the internal variation, and so it is difficult to speak of any clear-cut stylistic divisions. The so-called *leśne* (forest; see Example 49) or *jesienne* (autumn) songs from Kurpie or the north Mazovian area may be singled out as the most consistent and characteristic subgroup of Polish lyrics. They are distinguished by their style of performance (see above, p. 96), reminiscences of the 'old' traditional legacy, extended size (many stanzas) and dedication to love and strong emotional expression. At the same time, however, love stories are usually transmitted in a conventional and symbolic way, not without moralizing comments which, too, lack subjective motivation and are expressed in more general terms.

On the other hand, several popular and current lyrical songs, widely distributed all over the country, exhibit features of more recent strata; namely, their type of verse (7 + 6, 8 + 7), the tendency towards the explicit minor mode, the bipartite form and, as far as their poetry is considered, realistically formulated comparisons and concrete conclusions. The repertoire, as can easily be detected, bears reflections both of Russian lyrical songs, so widely distributed in eastern Europe, and of the Polish legacy, well documented in the urban repertoire of the Baroque era (see Badecki 1936). A more detailed analysis will reveal two different strata in the repertoire which may be identified as western and eastern stock, according to the two clearly different cultural impacts indicated above. The dubious folk descent of the western stock seems to be well documented, though it is still often debated.

By contrast, soldiers' songs preserved in eastern Poland have clearly been subject to Russian influence alone, as is the case in many countries of eastern Europe (Lithuania, Finland, eastern Poland, Bulgaria). This is particularly true of the so-called 'recruiting songs' (see Example 14), expressing the homesickness of those conscripted to the army (specifically in the case of the Russian Tsarist Army) for very long terms (twenty years and more) and very far away. These songs, clearly dominated by marching rhythms, depict the loneliness of conscripts which is encoded in symbols, stereotypes and comments typical of folk concepts.

Polish lullabies are also lyrical in mood. This category, however, so evidently connected with female performance, is today scarcely represented and is clearly disappearing. Yet, unlike other Polish lyrics, the category exhibits definitely distinct and quite consistent features, including simplicity of form, limited size, and repetitive character based on short motifs, underlining the importance of the interval of a third and also the prevalence of surrounding refrains which plainly fulfil a 'sleeping' function. The poetry of lullabies – also simple in form like its music – is distinct in character and pivots round wishes and predictions regarding the fate and future of the child. Formulated briefly, these wishes and predictions are expressed in a personal, almost confidential, manner. Polish lullabies, unlike other kinds of Polish lyrics, are devoid of general moralizing ideas and communicate concrete wishes, often formulated in the form of imperatives (see Example 68):

> Uśnij że mi, uśnij,
> Albo mi urośnij,
> Przydasz mi się, przydasz
> W pole gąsek wygnasz.
>
> Fall asleep, asleep,

Example 68 *Uśnij że mi uśnij*, Sobieski 1955, vol. II, no. 72

Or quickly grow big,
Your mum you'll please, will please
Helping raise the geese.

In comparative terms, Polish lullabies, though morphologically clearly transformed, must be regarded as typical representatives of the female genre distributed worldwide. They are short, rhythmic, syllabic, and free of metaphorically transmitted concepts. They should be regarded as songs of labour. Their predominant lyricism is, however, an unquestionable fact.

Children's songs constitute a less consistent category in Poland. They are related to children's games and plays, often associated with customs, especially those pertaining to spring and carnival festivities. The very limited form typical of these songs, resting usually on a number of diatonically ordered sounds, is designed for recitative rather than sung transmission. Nevertheless, the repertoire, which is still in current use, tends to be performed vocally (sung), though its custom-connected contexts of performance have evidently disappeared. The current status of the genre is obviously due to its ideal adaptation to the child's perceptive abilities. Like lullabies, Polish children's songs should be regarded as belonging to the world repertoire of this kind.

The remaining genres, not discussed above, are more easily identified in terms of their function and the contents of their verbal texts than in terms of their musical features. This applies, on the one hand, to labour and professional songs, and so-called 'comic' or satirical songs, on the other. The proper labour repertoire in Poland includes songs and gestures supporting the process of work, its communicative aspects and rhythm, which have essentially a signalling function, and are related to work calls of certain occupations, such as fishermen (see Example 56), shepherds, draftsmen, or market folk (see Example 92). By contrast, so-called professional songs are related to dances and games enacting various events associated with certain occupations and their life. These songs are evidently connected with the tradition of central European dance games (shoemaker, broom-maker). Soldiers' songs, as indicated, as well as songs of miners, can be included in this category, though they seem to be related more properly to the lyrical narrative or even to the repertoire of ditties.

So-called 'comic' or satirical songs, widely distributed in Poland's western regions, are highly inconsistent in their style. A detailed analysis of their poetic texts reveals, however, many interesting elements which may be interpreted as traces of what is known as the 'animal' tale (see Example 69). Religious songs transmitted orally constitute a separate group. They are usually identified by the content of their verbal texts and the functions they fulfil, though morphologically and stylistically they are not uniform. The group called 'songs' in contrast to 'chants' seems to be the closest to the folk tradition (see Bartkowski 1987). The recitative, psalmodic and litany types present obviously different strata. Nevertheless, the religious folk repertoire, even in the category of so-called songs (see Example 70), does not present

Example 69   *Bul ci tu kusy Jan*, Sobieski and Sobolewska 1955, no. 87

Example 70   *Gdy Maryja dawniej*, Bartkowski 1987, no. 186

particular coherence. In this repertoire one finds several examples of the annual ditties cited above, as well as sequences and Christmas songs (*pastorałki*) and the funeral and hagiographic legacy, not excluding those performed previously by wandering beggars (see Example 71). The internal diversity of this repertoire reveals the long process of historical development of this popular tradition. Besides very simple and short forms one also finds complex and developed songs with extended refrains. Analysis of this material confirms both the historical connection with the current repertoire of Polish folk music and its structural distinctness. It is quite obvious that the religious tradition presented and still presents a parallel stream to the current folk tradition, and that integration was never intended. It is also one reason why this legacy is difficult to identify as a folk stratum, though its social acceptance and currency were never in question.

The stylistic identity of this repertoire and establishment of its characteristics is a task needing both historical (source) and anthropological investigation. Ultimately one points,

♩=154

Pro-szę po-słu-chać, pa-no-wie, pa - nie,   czem czwarte,

Bos-kie   jest przy-ka — za - nie: czcij oj - ca,   mat-ke,

ro-dzi-ce swo-je,   przeważnie gdy są   sta-rzy o — bo - je.

Example 71   *Proszę posłuchać panowie*, Bartkowski 1987, no. 299

however, to its simplicity of style and to its suitability for the social needs and musical skills of its performers.

In short, religious songs have played and are still playing a significant rôle in Polish musical culture, and remain both socially popular and historically durable. At the same time, however, they did not develop characteristics as did the authentic folk repertoire, which is clearly dominated by the paradigm of Polish peasant culture.

So-called 'free' vocal forms are evidently not too different from other forms used in calls and refrains added to songs with verbal texts. The main difference lies in that they plainly serve a signal function. Their separation from a verbal text is strictly preserved only in the case of some shepherd calls and love signals, practised by Polish mountain people and known as *wyskanie*, *hukanie* or *łyskanie*. All these signals, hinging on vowels or syllables, present a typical falling slide within the interval of a fifth, extended sometimes by the fourth added below. Precision of intonation may be quite variable and may lead progressively to the phenomenon of glissando. This highly skilled art of communication is obviously different from other signals of a clearly functional character, which are based on repeated intervals of the third, octaves or triads. Function-orientated signals are clearly connected with the process of labour and labour-related communication. Signals of this kind are also distinguished by their semantic qualities, for, unsurprisingly, they operate on the basis of concrete words (e.g., *miotły*, brooms; see Example 92; see Bielawski 1973b: 62). By contrast, signals practised by Polish mountain people are much closer to shouts and, to a certain extent, to the concluding shouts of the ditties of central Poland. Internally, shouts differ first of all with respect to their direction; they have a rising quality in central Poland and a falling quality in the mountains.

3.1.2 The structure

Functional versus historical approaches

Poetry, music and gestures coexist in a deep structural relation which creates a unity of the folk song. In traditional studies the verse of Polish poetry is commonly recognized as a melic structure i.e., penetrated by melody, in German *Melik* (Dłuska 1954: 443), whereas the impact of the gestural activity remains almost unnoticed. This relates also to the correspondence between musical and poetic phrases (Furmanik 1956) and the question of asyllabism that has drawn the attention of scholars for many years (Windakiewiczowa 1913; Dłuska

1947; Łoś 1920; Furmanik 1956), but remains to be explained. Neither has the impact of dance on the regularity of verses and stanzas been taken into consideration. This is quite surprising, considering that the poetic and dance forms, and particularly the division of the form into sections, correspond quite closely. Finally, the structural principles of repetition, contrast and variability, being very much of the same nature in all the types of structure (poetic, musical and dance), are also analysed without reference to gestural patterns of poetry and music.

The mutual relations and the character of the interaction between the structures vary depending on function as well as on context, style and conventions characteristic of particular songs. The obvious differences in the traditions under study, west European based on the Latin and east European based on the Slavonic languages, are here the focal points. And the significance of the social context is also a vital factor.

The traditional systematic of folk poetry and its versification (Windakiewiczowa 1913; Dłuska 1954; Furmanik 1956) is approached historically. It leads to several hypotheses organizing and interpreting the material in a chronological sense. This approach neglects, however, the full context of transmission and, once more to be repeated, does not take into account the rôle of gestures. Thus the new approach should extend the dimensions of interpretation and shift attention towards deeply determined principles of perception and particularly to the rhythmic qualities of behavioural patterns.

Thanks to traditional studies it was possible to discover the simultaneous existence of different types of verse and interpret the material chronologically, and it was also possible to point to the musical determination of the orally transmitted literature, stressing the significance of musical accent. These interpretations, however, could not explain the process of transformation of the stanza with its regularity determined by rhythmically pulsating verses.

In contrast to traditional comparative studies, concentration on the functional purpose of genres and specifically on their methods of transmission (sung, recited, or danced) helps to discover the basic determinants. Thanks to this confrontational procedure (see above, pp. 19–21) it is possible to establish the basic opposition between two main categories: epic and lyric poetry, i.e., between a narrative course with dramatic points in epic, and musically expressed emotional content in the lyric category. The analysis shows also how the manner of performance contributes decisively to the unity of structure, including the function of the gestures exhibited in the ritual acts. Finally, the results of the analysis elucidate different types of transformation of primary or secondary rank. The primary ranks reveal the substantial changes of basic rhythm and its cyclicity when the main function (dance or custom) is progressively released. The secondary changes are limited to the transformation of proportions, to the extension or shortening of certain sections.

The confrontational approach, when applied to historical sources, also makes for better and more comprehensive interpretations. For instance, songs documented in the written seventeenth-century sources (Badecki 1936), though transcribed without musical and dance notation, may help to reconstruct the pattern of transmission and, to a certain extent, to discover the styles in which they were recited and sung. Consequently, it is possible to re-examine the previous context which was not so obviously homogeneous in the social (urban) and national (Polish) sense (see Badecki 1936: 157, 186, 188). The material, as documented in the sources, shows clearly the complexity and heterogeneity of this popular tradition.

As already indicated (see above, p. 40), the total transformation of the traditional Slavonic legacy and the creation of Polish national art took place at the end of the Middle Ages. It is visible in the language, poetry, music and dance re-structured at that time into new qualities with clearly crystallized units of form (motifs) and with well-defined principles of construction organizing those units into 'higher' logical complexes. The internal relations between the basic components were at that time already clear and almost consciously perceived. From this point of view the clear-cut difference between the flexible hemistich of the mediaeval song and the well-organized phrase of the modern structure is quite obvious. The former is susceptible to context while the latter follows an overriding principle, either quantitatively (number of syllables) or qualitatively (character of accent) motivated. The same applies also to the poetic stanza and to the musical period or segmentations of a dance. The 'new' created structures of a 'higher' logic differ obviously from flexible ideas with an undefined shape.

The basic units and principles

The systematic applied in this study has been derived from both historical and functional considerations. This approach helps to show the subject in its historical and contextual dimensions, not disregarding the achievements of previous studies but, at the same time, investigating the phenomena in confrontational terms. It helps also to interpret the contemporary transformations in a more comprehensive way.

The process of stabilization of structure

The structural flexibility of the 'old' mediaeval poetry is a commonly accepted fact. It affects both epic and lyric songs, religious and secular types, as well as songs with clear functions such as those of the more 'common' repertoire. It appears from studies (Windakiewiczowa 1913; Dłuska 1954; Jakobson 1981) that the organization of the song's structure starts with the elaboration of the final formula. In folk songs, this formula is usually connected with the sequence of the last three syllables – Ma-ry-ja; Le-li-ja (see above, p. 22). This ending, evidently 'penetrated' (Dłuska 1954: 449) by music, presents a nucleus of rhythmically organized units, while the so-called 'free' verses are recognized only as the 'sequence-verses' with unidentified units (see Windakiewiczowa 1913). The obvious differences in the nature of syllabism and accentuation, and in the conventions in which the repetitions are applied, revealed the opposite features of the recited and sung poems and their epic or lyric character. Oration remains clearly asyllabic (see Examples 72 and 73), despite its musically well-

A prze-de wro - ty ka - mień zło-ty,   le - li - ja.   Po - bło-gos-ław

że ji   świenty Jó - ze - fie,   z Panem Je-zu-sem   Ma- ry - ja.

Example 72   *A przede wroty*, Czekanowska 1956, no. 20

Example 73   *Pośrataj Boże*, Kolberg 1883, vol. I, no. 167, p. 188

'penetrated' final formulae, whereas the 'freely' performed and usually melismatic, adorned, ritual songs regulate progressively their verses and extend towards a more developed melody with typical repetitions of whole verses ((:7:),7; see Example 61). *Anafora* and *concatenatio*, so typical of prosody, oration and epics, concentrate on the short repetitions of certain verbs, refrains (6+6+5) or phrases (:4:)+3 (see Example 6) whereas the songs, dominated by music, prefer repetitions of the whole verses (:7:)+7. The influence of dance still remains an unresolved subject, especially in the case of mediaeval dances which have almost totally disappeared. It seems, however, to be confirmed by comparative studies of the *korovod* (round) dances (see p. 38) preserved in other (south and east Slavonic) countries, that the songs connected with dances were also in the 'old days' regular and rhythmically pulsating. A detailed analysis of the repetition shows, moreover, the domination of one factor over the other. It consists in the subordination and subjection of the structure to the 'main text' which plays the main rôle. In narrative songs, for example, in which the plot is essential, the music is as a rule repeated according to the demands of the transmitted message, whereas in lyrical songs it is the poetry and its segmentation into sections which have to be repeated according to the expectations and needs of the music. The obvious differences between two opposed traditions, Latin and the original Slavonic, is a well-investigated subject. This applies especially to the discussion indicated above concerning the nature of ending formulae connected with the three-syllable sequence. The generally accepted interpretation of this phenomenon, whose provenance can be traced to Latin patterns, is however in question. What undermines it is its world-wide distribution, which seems to be determined by the basic principle of human perception or by the influence of magic principles (number three). Nevertheless, there is no denying that the cultural impact of Latin sequences played a significant rôle in the transformation of 'old' Slavonic songs and of their formulae in particular.

Briefly speaking, the flexible structures of non-stabilized *stichic* (see Wiora 1952) songs were organized not against the background of definite metric units (feet, bars) but of the so-called hemistichs (see Sokalskij 1888; Neyman 1883) and musical phrases corresponding with their periodicity. These flexible units present raw material for the quantitative (shortening or extending) and qualitative (shifting the accents) penetration which is susceptible to the demands of the accompanying context, including the act of performance itself. The analysis of repetitions presents an excellent introduction to the explanation of these transformational processes, as well as to the interpretation of their structure.

The structure of distichic songs

In contrast to the stichic structures, the distichic complexes (see Bielawski 1973(2)) are already almost syllabic and develop towards forms stabilized in parallel (ab); they also mark some links owing to which both stichos may be bound into one distichic stanza. Nevertheless, the verses of these structures are still not clearly rhythmic and their links are not definite and perfect. These quasi-syllabic verses with 'stops' – compare the term *przestanek* meaning a 'stop' used by Windakiewiczowa (1913) deliberately, and opposed by her to the term caesura as applied to the syllabic verses – are mainly bound together by assonances and imperfect rhymes, while the 'stops' are projected by the musical phrase and not by the poetic foot. The role of repetition, in both its types, i.e., as an *anafora* and as a repetition of the whole verse including the short refrains, also plays a significant rôle in the distichic songs, e.g., (:7:); 8+(:8:); as well as 5+(:3:), 4+(:3:); or 4+(:4:); [(:4+4:) +:3:], as in Example 74:

Example 74   *Koło mego ogródeczka*, Czekanowska 1961, no. 21

Koło mego ogródeczka
Koło mego ogródeczka, raz, dwa, trzy
Koło mego ogródeczka, raz, dwa, trzy

Nearby to the garden of mine
Nearby to the garden of mine, one, two, three
Nearby to the garden of mine, one, two, three

The regular structure of songs connected with dancing

The highly rhythmical verses and stanzas of ditties and other songs connected with dance prevail in the current Polish folk material. The rhythm and regular form of dance songs often explain directly the specific features of some gestures and figures. This happens in the case of the syncopated rhythm, stressing the figure of bowing and kneeling with characteristic shifts and delays (*Polski*); it applies also to the fluent sequences of rotating figures (*oberek* or waltz), to the ruptures of dotted rhythms corresponding with different gestures of stamping (*krakowiak, mazurka, góralski, hołubce, krzesane*), and to the regular course of equal time units expressing walking and processional sections (slow introductions to *Polski* and *kujawiak*). The rich variety of structures still preserved in the repertoire under consideration can be divided easily into subcategories. The most significant difference concerns the size and shape of the stanza, as well as the size of the basic unit (foot, phrase) and, finally, the very principle of construction. This helps to discover the essential difference between the clearly symmetrical short stanza of ditties corresponding with the form of eight bars (see Example 75), and the

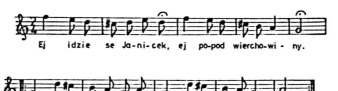

Ej   idzie   se Ja-ni-cek,   ej   po-pod   wiercho-wi - ny.

Gwi - zda   se   i   śpie-wa   po - jad   nie-dzwiedzi - ny

Example 75   *Ej, idzie se Janicek*, Chybiński 1950, no. 2

more developed stanza, sometimes connected with the refrain and usually asymmetric, or metabolic (7, 7, 11, 7 as in Example 21; 10, 10, 7, 7, 5 as in Example 27) corresponding with the musical form with an evident contrast or elements of 'reprise' (aa'bb', aa'ba or aa'bba). Indeed, the last case concerns the more complex forms in which the contrast and evolution are consciously used as basic media projecting the concept of a sequence. The contrast may work as an essential principle opposing the slow and fast sections or the sung and danced sequences (wedding dances) as well as sections of different character, or finally it may shape a sequence of quite different dances often including dances with a different metre (2/4 and 3/8). The opposing of metres may also appear in a striking way as it does in Silesian dances (*trojak*).

In brief, the well-established stanza and clearly rhythmical verse corresponding with stabilized musical units are typical of the majority of Polish folk songs, which were probably developed not earlier than the sixteenth and seventeenth centuries. The connection of these forms with dance is quite obvious, especially in the case of ditties, but it is also a fact with the Polish ballad (Chybiński 1907) and with love songs as well as narrative and moralizing genres. These songs with a more developed stanza, often based on the phrase of three bars (*kujawiak*) or on the phrases contrasting deliberately both sizes (of two and three bars in the 'reprise' form), are usually based on verses of 7, 8, 10, or 12 syllables and present the above-mentioned patterns of metabolic or asymmetric forms (7, 7, 11, 7; 10, 10, 7, 7, 5).

Structures of non-folk origin

This not very numerous group includes songs identified as being of foreign origin. It concerns especially songs with verses evidently copying the patterns of written literature, typical of the legacy of the sixteenth and seventeenth centuries (with syllabic verses of 7+6 and 8+7). These structures, like the unoriginal rhythms, are often connected with imported dances and are rather marginal phenomena, despite the popularity that they enjoyed at some periods and in some societies. Quite different is the case of the waltz, *polka*, and *shot* (écossaise) or *kolomyjka*, which – though also foreign – became integrated into the Polish folk music tradition. The popularity of *polka*, *kolomyjka*, *wiatr* and *szocz* (see Examples 76–8) can be

Example 76 *Laboga chłopacy*, Sobiescy 1973, no. 119, p. 310

Example 77 *Tańcuj wiatra*, Czekanowska 1961, no. 204

easily explained by their unquestionable folk origin; the transformation of the waltz, however, and its integration into the patterns of 5+5 verses, is an interesting example of adaptation, elucidated additionally by local terminology. Indeed, melodies with the characteristic waltz rhythm are identified by local names as *steier* (it means coming from Steiermarkt), or just by the Polish local names (*Majdaniak*, the waltz of Lublin), i.e., places where the dances became popular.

The transformational processes of the folkloristic legacy are much more visible in the examples of patterns developing and changing recently under the pressure of conditions. This applies, on the one hand, to the complex dance structure and to the long sequences consisting of a chain of different dances and, on the other, to the forms of the Polish ballad previously often connected with the reprise form. Both phenomena are undergoing today a process of reduction and standardization which affects both the poetic and musical elements, reducing relentlessly the variety of repetitions, anaforas, and refrains, and putting the whole structure into the rigid 'jacket' of bipartite form, rigorously repeated. It also concerns the interjections and vocatives, which are either completely eliminated or, on the contrary, automatically complemented and added to each verse with a total disregard for the changeable situation in the actual performance. The standardized way of transmission, usually connected with performance at an accelerated tempo, creates a schematically pulsating sequence. The same concerns the gestural structures progressively released from the swinging movements typical of the *tempo rubato* style. This standardized sequence of the musical

Example 78   *Szocz*, Sobiescy 1954, no. 17

and dance rhythms totally dominates the poetic structure, and especially its content and emotional qualities.

Finally, it is to be concluded that neither the musical nor the poetic structure can be autonomous. They are both subordinated to the general course of the dance-music-verbal sequence and to its pulsation. The more independent musical and poetic concepts are usually derivatives adopted from non-folk strata as, for example, in the case of the reprise structure, so typical of Baroque music. The historical existence and the degree of integration of the phenomena indicated is a subject in itself. From a distance, however, these non-folk forms seem to be characteristic only of certain periods.

At some time, however, the structural coexistence of the genuine and adopted legacy has been a fact. Assimilated patterns, though often disappearing sooner than the genuine models, contribute vitally to the creation of the national tradition, including its folk strata. It concerns the Latin models as distributed both by music and by poetry of the religious and secular heritage; it also includes the impact of the west European tradition developed in more modern times and that of the Renaissance and Baroque periods in particular (*pavane*, *saltarello*). Without these adopted elements, so well assimilated and so long preserved in the repertoire of Polish dances and their songs, the creation of a Polish national style would have been impossible. Indeed, though folklore has its own 'language' in the sense of the medium of communication and expressive qualities, and though folkloristic phenomena are always easily identified as different and isolated, folk culture may be interpreted only in close interaction with the culture of other social classes, and especially in relation to that which had deep structural and transformational power.

3.1.3 Peculiarities of performance style

Functions and types of interaction: basic styles

Characteristics of performance style enable even non-folk phenomena to achieve a folk character. The performance features, depending more than others on the context, are deeply embedded in the very function the song has to fulfil.

By including performance characteristics in the analytical procedure, the song is interpreted as a vivid phenomenon stimulated by factors directly perceived (timbre, loudness, tessitura). Concentrating on the analysis of active reciting, singing, playing or dancing, and on the mutual relations between those activities, we are able to discover the structural pattern of a song.

Verbal and nonverbal communications interact in performance with different force according to the demands of the context and to the situational needs. They may push this or that function to a dominating rôle or, on the contrary, pull it back. An analysis of performance, more than anything else, reveals the stylistic diversity of regional or ethnic groups, as well as social and generational differences, and even seasonal and local fashions. Though apparently variable and sensitive to the demands of performance context, it is as a rule subordinated to the deeply rooted traditional conventions and behavioural patterns.

The more detailed analysis elucidates the mechanism of several functions such as acting in the performance when the emotive function of some interjections and vocatives is clearly dominant. This applies especially to those forms of vocatives which act as independent factors and are perceived by the listener as being separate sections of the musical form. This happens in the case of the beginning vocatives, clearly singled out in the songs of Podhale, as well as of the ending shouts which are still in spontaneous use in the ditties and dance songs of central Poland. A communicative function of the performance is directly demonstrated by the introduction of onomatopoeia effects. They are often used in story-telling in such a way that their simulation immediately conveys the intended meaning. This applies also to short refrains and formulae often connected with bundles of nonsense syllables imitating for instance double bass or drum playing (*bum cyk cyk*) or showing the effects of accumulated consonants (*trr, prrr*). Nevertheless, by comparison with the repertoire of other countries, Polish folk songs are rather poor in these effects.

The power of performance media is enhanced by direct impulses acting also in more complex ways. This happens in the handling of some formulae or refrains, including their accompanying gestures, particularly with the formulae of the afore-mentioned repetitions and circling movements connected with customs (see above, p. 38). Performance style itself also determines the very course of the narrative and dance sequences, these being modified by several prolongations, shortenings or suspensions, as well as by shifts and pauses appearing either in the framework of one system (e.g., musical) or as a result of interaction between different systems (musical, poetic, dance). As is well known, dance sequences may vary depending on situational modifications; and they may also be determined by conventional norms. The significance of conventions in dance is clearly determined by somatic and kinetic norms, while their gestural structure influences ways of singing and playing. Indeed, an analysis of performance should start with observations of the singer's or player's attitude during performance, for example whether they perform sitting or standing. Such differences relate to specific genres, for instance the 'shorter' ditties and dance songs are sung standing, but the 'longer' epics and lyrics, sitting. When dancing or work are involved in performance the situation becomes more complex and the patterns of behaviour more complicated. In this analysis, however, we should like to mention only gestures connected with performance styles that have been most investigated. This is above all the *tempo rubato* manner in which the standing singers swing their bodies in a characteristic way, from their shoulders to their legs (see above, p. 82). This is also a characteristic mannerism of seated performers of north Mazovia and is accompanied by a gesture consisting of the hand pressing the head behind the ear. Those particular gestures, made during performance, are not limited to a specific situation or figure, but rather to different sequences punctuating and modifying their fluency.

As regards the preserved tradition, four Polish regions present characteristic and homogeneous performance styles. These are the area of Podhale with its separate culture of shepherds; the region of Kurpie, noted for its vocal genres; central Poland with its richness of ditties accompanied by screaming shouts; and the rather sedate styles of regularly pulsating music of Great Poland. In all of these styles the influence of spoken dialect and its idiomatic and lexical characteristics are quite essential.

The most striking features of Polish vocal performance

The peculiarities of the human voice, and particularly its timbre, remain still largely uninvestigated by Polish ethnomusicologists. Nevertheless, it is already known that the convention of singing in a certain tessitura has been passed down through history. Difference in timbre of the voice and of its tessitura are closely bound to people's feelings of identity and may be compared to the manifestations of a spoken dialect.

Amongst the most characteristic Polish regions the area of Podhale is strikingly different on account of the convention where men and women sing in the same register, so that male voices are highly strained. Very characteristic also is the resounding timbre of Kurpian lyrics, whilst the east Mazovian lyrics are intended for a delicate, well-rounded female timbre. By contrast, the vocal timbres of performance of central or Great Polish ditties are respectively sharp and screaming or marked by a heavy 'breathy' quality. They are evidently influenced by the timbre of the accompanying instrument (bagpipe). Within these overall variations some social differences (professional, generational) are also not without significance, as well as the nature of certain genres (wedding repertoire, lyrics). As has been said, the variety of vocal timbres can be observed above all in the rich repertoire of the 'forest' songs of the Kurpie area as well as in the repertoire of north-eastern Mazovia in which the archaic manner of the so-called *apocope* (Stęszewski 1965a) plays a decisive role. This consists in omitting, or more rarely in singing with a strong diminuendo, the final syllable of the stanza, and has been one of the best investigated and comparatively analysed phenomena of the Polish vocal performance (Stęszewski 1980: 370). It is also well known and has been investigated in other countries (Kodaly 1917; Bartók 1951). According to the results achieved, the *apocope* is totally independent of the semantics of the accompanying verbal text, being correlated instead with the character of the accent on the last word (the tonic one). It is also correlated with the mannerisms of other styles, particularly with the so-called *Flüster Auftakt* (whispered beat), with the 'sliding up to the falsetto' (see Stęszewski 1965a, 1984), and with the glissandi, stuttering and weeping phenomena.

The results of the studies made so far indicate that emotively coloured ways of performance appear at their strongest in paraphrases of human speech and especially in nonverbal communication (vocatives, interjections, signals). These mannerisms transmit messages directly and modify the basic skeleton and course of the narration, while interacting with gestures. The border line between the morphologically designed musical phenomena (motifs, skeletons) and their stylistic 'undulation' is fluid. This is especially visible in the case of melodic adornments and glissandi, as well as in the areas of rhythm and 'agogics' (fermatas, shortened bars).

The peculiarities of performance under discussion are closely correlated with some linguistic phenomena and with the character of the vowels and consonants in particular. It is especially visible in the *Flüster Auftakt* example and in the manner of 'sliding to the falsetto' connected with the vowels *a* and *e* of Example 73. The same can be seen in the difference between the signal forms of *hukanie* or *wyskanie* and the final shouts of central Polish ditties correlating with the vowels *u* (*hukanie*) or *i* (*wyskanie*). These correlations are also clearly connected with the direction of the exclamation and are rising (shouting on *i*) or falling (on *u*). The results achieved so far point to the importance of the linguistic features of the verbal text which constitute raw material for the articulation of contrasting elements. These elements usually appear as essential phonological qualities (the back vowels versus the front ones) and play a structural rôle in some styles of vocal performance. Thus, to a certain extent linguistic phenomena prevail over musical ones, although philologists are inclined to stress the musical character of folkloristic phenomena (Dłuska 1954).

In short, studies in this field point to the evident correlation between some manners of performance and the phonic qualities of the word used. At the same time, they have discovered some negative conclusions. These are the dysjunctions, on the one hand, of definite mannerisms with hierarchically ordered musical values (tonal phenomena, harmonic functions), and, on the other, between semantic units and their systems. The qualities of performance seem to affect the primary elements of musical organization together with the phonic features of the verbal text. The secondary elements of verbal or motivic transmission are not articulated by the variations of performance style.

The mannerism of 'weeping adornment', so characteristic of the eastern regions, is also a manifestation of emotive impact and one of the most significant factors in the genre of Mazovian lyrics and wedding songs. At the same time, however, the mannerism of actually crying or weeping so typical of many Slavonic nations and of their funeral and wedding songs is generally unknown to Polish folk performers, and even when it does appear it does not sound genuine.

Tempi, too, are differentiated regionally (Bielawski 1967) and socially. The basic differences between the slow (north-east) and fast (south-west) tempi are additionally modified by local varieties or by the qualities of particular genres. The most characteristic, however, are the mannerisms shaping patterns of narrative or dance sequences. This applies especially to the slow courses of additional rhythms (3+2; 2+3; 3+2+3; see Example 51) with characteristic fermatas at the end, as well as to the faster and pulsating rhythms such as the so-called giusto syllabic bichronic (see Brailoiu 1948: 26), and finally to the different types of oscillating courses typical of sequences performed in the manner of *tempo rubato*.

The course of sequences may be differently shaped in particular regions and styles. It may consist of extended or shortened phrases according to the demands of different patterns and conventions. The extended phrases can be seen in the introductory section (*ozwodna*) to the *góralski* dance (five bars), while the sections performed in the fast tempo typical of the *krzesanie* sections are already shorter (four bars; see Example 43). Longer phrases are also characteristic of lyric songs, whereas the best example of a balance between shortened and prolonged phrases is demonstrated by performances in the *tempo rubato* style.

The phenomenon of *tempo rubato* should be regarded as a typical mannerism of group co-operation in which several ways of transmission interact mutually. This phenomenon, discussed widely in literature (Kamieński, Sobiescy, Szachowski) and enchantingly stylized in Chopin's mazurkas, is to a certain extent still present in Polish folk performance. The *rubato* mannerisms are additionally modified regionally, while different degrees of their preservation are determined by the functions of songs. Among the regional varieties of *rubato* the most typical and durable has been that of central Poland, which is directly connected with dance. It is different both from the *rubato* style of the highlanders and from that of Great Poland. The regional differences consist, above all, in the character of tempo, and consequently involve the diversity of phrasing that results from the different sizes of the *rubato* phrases. For instance, in the ditties of central Poland, *tempo rubato* operates in the framework of one- or two-bar phrases, whereas in the songs of the highlanders the *rubato* phrases may contain four to five bars. By contrast, in the music of Great Poland, *rubato* is observed within the framework of individual bars.

An analysis of the melodies penetrated by *tempo rubato* reveals not only the transformation of particular phrases but, above all, whole sequences being 'undulated' in this manner. Then, by studying the transformed sequences one has a better understanding of behavioural patterns as being typical of particular regions and their styles; one also sees the interaction between different modes of transmission (vocal, poetic, instrumental, dance). This applies especially to the phenomenon of transaccentuation, which corresponds clearly with some dance figures and with foot stamping. The competition between different groups of performers (male and female), as well as the representatives of different generations (older and younger) or different kinds of transmission (musical, poetic, dance), is exhibited spectacularly in improvised sections performed in this traditional style. Finally, competition between various kinds of repertoire, dances and rhythms, and particularly between the basic rhythm of the *krakowiak* and *oberek*, also play a significant rôle (see above, pp. 82, 93), whereas competition between spontaneous responses and traditionally embedded habits is a focal point in the manner of the *tempo rubato*. This phenomenon can still be observed when one compares the styles of performance in particular regions, although recent changes standardize the courses of sequences and limit the contribution of individual and spontaneous responses.

3.1.4 On the poetics of Polish folk song

'Poetics ... deals with the poetic function not only in poetry, ... but also outside of poetry, when some other function is superimposed upon the poetic function' (Jakobson 1981: 27–8). The poetic function as such, 'focusing on regular reiteration of equivalent units of the time' and 'not concealing its primary essence, just elements of emotive language', as well as 'being based on the basic principle of equivalence from "axis" of selection to the axis of combination' (*ibid.*), functions also in music and dance. This definition applies to many modes of transmission, despite differences which occur amongst them. Whilst the general context of performance and its cyclicity balances and integrates the essence of the idea transmitted, this observation applies especially to the artistic message and to its *differentia specifica*, not limiting the basic function to the delivery of message. Indeed, in a folk song and in the act of performance it is possible to discover the qualities transforming the basic media of transmission into a piece of art. The basic dilemma centres on the question of the nature of artistic transformation. As is well known, in folkloristic transmission concrete objects are often more realistically approached than in classical art. At the same time, however, the folkloristic message still preserves its power to create a quite unique atmosphere directly referring to the instincts and human feelings in which association plays a decisive rôle. The power of folk transmission also articulates its capability of transformation, which simultaneously appeals to the most abstract ideas and to simple human reactions (see above, p. 37).

An evident dysjunction between the semantic and verbally transmitted on the one hand and musical message on the other is a characteristic feature of Polish folk song. It is especially obvious in the dance repertoire, in which verbal and musical texts are almost 'freely' exchanged as long as patterns of verse and stanza correspond with musical and dance rhythms. The same can be said of the 'longer' songs, whose melodies can be 'exchanged' within particular genres. Finally, this applies also to the repertoire connected with customs, which is determined by some rites and the cyclicity of their episodes. Only in the north Mazovian lyrics is the rôle of the verbal text more evident. But even in this case, it is easier to see the correlations of musical message with a particular genre (forest, field or autumn songs) than with the plot and the content of their poetry.

The repetitions also contribute in their variety to the shaping of the sequence and to its cyclicity. Indeed, the returns of well-known situations balanced by the fresh impact of new elements design a typical course of folk narration in which the substantial functions of metaphor and of metonymy play a decisive rôle.

The phenomena of concrete reality are approached differently by several modes of folk transmission, revealing the multiplicity of its aspects. But, at the same time, folk concepts are perceived immediately, owing to their consistency and to the integrational power of the accompanying context. The 'topics' of the message, though selected by external factors such as traditional patterns and functional conventions, are simultaneously 'commented on' and 'combined' by the basic principles of human reactions and by their still mysterious nature. The integrational power of the folk message, which corresponds with the cyclicity of human feelings and with basic ways of thinking, may be considered as a privilege of folk art in general and of Polish folk song in particular.

3.2   Instrumental transmission

Polish instrumental music, unlike vocal music, has been preserved only in some areas and regions. It is linked to traditional forms of performance, to the ways musical ensembles used to be founded, and to the production of 'home-made' instruments. These traditions are still being cultivated in the Carpathian area and the shepherds' community, that with the Walachian background in particular. In the shepherds' community the preservation of folk heritage has to do with strong feelings of identity, and it sustains the social solidarity of the inhabitants. But even in this respect, instrumental activity is limited mainly to certain masters and their families, who are highly respected for their skills and have an outstanding position in society.

A similar phenomenon can be seen in Great Poland, where the tradition of regional instrumental music is still being preserved, though it is decreasing today and no longer has a strong social appeal.

By contrast, music performed on factory-made instruments is still widespread in Poland, although there are again only some areas and regions in which it is still upheld with some vigour (Kieleckie, Lubelskie, Mazovia, Kujavia). Moreover, the degree of authenticity in current performances changes rapidly under present-day circumstances, being additionally affected by all sorts of external support given by institutions and decision-making circles. The most decisive factor seems to be rooted in the psychological motivation of the people concerned, who may simply lose interest in one or another form of the legacy that they have inherited.

The comparison between different sources at our disposal, and the confrontation of historical and ethnographical data in particular, contributes to a better understanding of the basic trends of the Polish folk instrumentarium. It concerns both the isolation of local enclaves and the general process according to which the Polish folk instrumentarium has been changing.

3.2.1 Sources

Instrumental activity on Polish territories goes far back into the past. It is demonstrated by the musical instruments excavated by archaeologists, which date from as early as the Neolithic period (Gabałówna 1960), and by other phenomena recorded in classical iconographic and written documents. The social or even national identification of these early sources is, however, a complicated problem.

According to accepted assumptions, it is difficult to speak about Polish identity before the end of the tenth century, before the official recognition of the Polish State; it is still more difficult to identify some of these ancient documents in their social sense. This applies even to the cultural phenomena of the fifteenth and sixteenth centuries, which remain socially unspecified. Indeed, only the culture of the seventeenth century and its musical instruments in this particular area point to differences between social strata, i.e., they are clearly specified as belonging to court, urban, little town, gentry and village societies. A comparison between the sources of different periods contributes also to a better understanding of the ideological concepts of the people of those times. It is especially evident in the case of the bagpipe, which appears in fourteenth-century documents as an instrument of the angels (Kamiński 1971), then in the sixteenth century as the one played by the biblical shepherds (Banach 1962), but in the seventeenth century as an instrument accompanying a village feast. The very famous woodcut of 1693 (see Figure 7) shows a feast in an inn in which not only instrumentalists but also vocalists are presented, and the bagpipe is exhibited as one of three instruments being played.

The sources documenting Polish instrumental activity should be divided into two basic groups: historical and ethnographic. The former, very different in character, may be divided again into archaeological, classical iconographical (illuminations in the codexes, reliefs, polychromy, copper plates, woodcuts since the sixteenth century, aquafortas, lithographs, etc.), literary (the texts of folk songs, urban and court poetry), and sources in the form of comments by chroniclers, newspapers, etc. By contrast, the ethnographic sources, gathered as late as the nineteenth and twentieth centuries, present more homogeneous and better documented material which provides relatively comprehensive information and gives a more concrete picture of the phenomena under study.

On the basis of the earliest sources it is clear that the majority of instruments had originally fulfilled the function of signals and were intended for noise-making often with a definite magical purpose, or were just meant to 'frighten away the devil'. The first written documents (*Thietmar's Chronicle*) confirm that the music was very noisy and that the pipe and drum were basic instruments accompanying particular events of these 'early' periods. The variety of excavated drums and pipes (Gabałówna 1960; and see Figure 22), as well as different rattles, scrapers and whistles, confirms this assumption. Accessible sources indicate also that Polish musical culture had clearly changed in the fourteenth and fifteenth centuries (see above, p. 43), among other reasons as a result of new (oriental as well as west European) influences adopted from neighbouring or even quite distant cultures. They not only affected artifacts but also contributed to the emergence of new institutions and forms of organization (choirs, ensembles), new techniques of performance and new behavioural patterns (dances).

Figure 22   Drum (from an archaeological source)

Historical sources confirm the existence of some instruments which in time achieved great popularity in the folk practice, though in the late Middle Ages their social status was not quite obvious. This applies especially to the *trummscheidt* (trumpet-marine), to the bagpipe and, to some extent, to the hurdy-gurdy and fiddle, although these were more widespread in society.

A comparative look at the diversity of documented instruments reveals both their geographical distribution and the general trends of their evolution. The bagpipe is an excellent example, having been described in documents as an instrument with many drones (13) (see Banach 1962, nos. 18, 34) and having been recorded as such until the nineteenth century (Karłowicz 1888), whereas it is known today as an instrument with one drone only. The regional diversity of this instrument may be exemplified by the differences between the Carpathian versions blown directly and those of Great Poland and Silesia blown through the bellows. A more detailed analysis confirms once more the great popularity of this instrument documented in several sizes and tunings, and details of construction and decoration, while the ethnographic documentation of more recent times (Gloger 1901) indicates a progressive disappearance of this undoubtedly folk instrument.

By contrast, different kinds of pipes and horns or fiddle, dulcimer and hurdy-gurdy are of varied social or national provenance. The lute and kithar were clearly the instruments of nobility and of urban society, while the hurdy-gurdy was connected with wandering beggars usually of Ukrainian or Byelorussian descent. At the same time the dulcimer and violin were clearly instruments of highly skilled Jewish musicians, well described already in the sixteenth century (Banach 1962, nos. 94–6). They were recognized as masters and played for different strata of Polish and non-Polish society until the Second World War. Quite specific are the membranophones and idiophones which have been popular in different folk ensembles since the Middle Ages, but remain almost unconfirmed by historical sources. Among these instruments the friction drum is a very interesting example, although it has been recorded only since the eighteenth century.

As has been mentioned, a decisive shift in the character of the instrumental ensemble took place at the end of the Middle Ages and was connected with a transition from pipe and drum to an ensemble made up of pipe, bagpipe and fiddle. It may be assumed that this kind of ensemble also accompanied vocal performances (Kamiński 1971). It is also quite possible that the next change took place at the end of the eighteenth century and transformed the ensemble into the forms we find today in conservative regions. Finally, it must also be added that oriental influences, visible especially in the forms of kettle drums and bells (Janissarian bands), should be seen as phenomena of the seventeenth and eighteenth centuries.

The historical survey of Polish instruments reveals a multiplicity of strata and different cultural impacts, whereas the contribution of the instrumentarium of Walachian shepherds, though documented mainly by ethnographic sources, seems to be the most significant. The same sources also confirm North European influences, manifesting themselves in the friction drum, horns and signal trumpet. The diversity of those imports points to the transitional character of the Polish instrumentarium, which was subjected to several cultural streams of different strength at different periods. The most interesting, however, seem to be the isolated cultural enclaves, such as the virgin forest area of Kurpie and the eastern region of the Lublin province (see above, p. 104; Moszyński 1939, vol. II; Chętnik 1983).

The folk material in the nineteenth- and twentieth-century ethnographic sources presents a larger quantity and variety of examples. It includes different kinds of idiophones, such as rattles (*gruchawki, grzechotki*), sistrum (*terkotki*), clappers (*kołatki*), bells, whistles, the friction drum (*burczy bas, huk* or *diabełek*, see Bielawski 1985a; Stęszewski 1980), bull roarer, primitive chordophones, *diable skrzypce* (devil's violin), xylophone and musical bow, although the two latter instruments have only some degree of probability. The variety of instruments includes many kinds of pipes, reed pipes (the bagpipe), horns and trumpets, as well as several forms of fiddle, violin, basses, trumpet-marine, hurdy-gurdy, dulcimer, and, finally, the kettle drums and drums in different sizes and shapes. Ultimately, some manufactured and factory-made instruments should also be listed, such as various types of harmonium, mouth harmonica, clarinets, trumpets and saxophones, as well as the different accessories of jazz and pop music which have become extremely popular in quasi-folk orchestras.

Musical instruments, although diversified and well represented, play only a secondary rôle in Polish folk performance and do it only in some regions where they have achieved an obvious popularity and prominent position. According to the sources, instrumental practice was especially developed in the seventeenth and eighteenth centuries, while at the end of the eighteenth one was already speaking of a decrease in this kind of musical tradition. Thus, we shall limit this study to a survey of musical instruments which are still preserved or known from a recent past. Examples of 'revived' instruments will also be discussed, but only those that have enjoyed a relatively durable position in folk ensembles and had strong social appeal.

3.2.2 Organology: the basic types of Polish folk instruments

Children's toys and simple signal instruments

The most primary instruments to be found are rattles, clappers, whistles and bells accompanying children's games and customs, or directly supporting signal communication. The connections of these instruments with annual festivities are well known and recorded, whereas the connection with family customs has been confirmed only in the case of the wedding ceremony when they used to accompany the announcement of prominent guests (the instrument is called *marszelnik* – bellscepter). The best documented and still partly preserved are the clappers that are used in the annual church ceremonies, and particularly on Thursday and Good Friday in Holy Week, when bells are forbidden in church. Clappers also accompany other customs of the Easter period and specifically *chodzenie po kogutku* (walking with a rooster) (see Seweryn 1928). The clappers used on this occasion are of wood, in the shape of a rooster pushed on a stick by children going round and asking for gifts (*dyngus*). The clappers used in church are of different shapes and types. They may also be pushed by a stick, moved by wheels placed below the vehicle, as well as shaken by hand (*terkotki*).

Folk idiophones are usually instruments of amusement, handmade and often bought at local markets today as children's toys. They are especially popular at festivals of local patrons (*odpust*), or during feasts organized by institutions such as CEPELIA or *Dom Kultury* (see above, p. 121), celebrating, for example, a feast of spring on Palm Sunday. The winter and carnival feasts have their own instruments accompanying the games of that season. Among these instruments the friction drum played an outstanding part, being once used at carnival masquerades or accompanying boys extending greetings and begging for presents on New Year's Eve. As has been indicated, this particular instrument is today being revived as an accessory of regional ensembles.

By contrast, bells, bull roarers (Moszyński 1939, vol. II), horns, trumpets and different kinds of pipes, with or without reeds (Chybiński 1924), and again rattles, have basically signalling functions connected mainly with shepherding. They are used as identity (bells) or calling (pipes, horns, trumpets) tools as well as accessories for hunting, fishing or transportation.

Many of these instruments also have magical connotations usually forgotten or misunderstood today, as in the case of the wedding bellscepter (*marszelnik*) or bells decorating babies' shawls. Likewise, the *diable skrzypce* (devil's violin; see Figure 23) or *diabelek* (friction drum) are dedicated by name directly to the devil. The devil's violin consists of a string attached to two edges of a stick, supported by a resonator of a wooden trunk. This trunk amplifies the

Figure 23   'Devil's violin'

sounds produced by the vibrating string. The sound can change in pitch depending on the tension with which the string is plucked by fingers or by a small piece of wood. Today all these instruments play mainly an entertainment or decorative rôle and are used primarily by children. When used in folk ensembles their function is either decorative, or to produce acoustic effects that will draw the attention of audiences.

The 'revived' instruments are also produced for tourists (friction drum, devil's violin), and are supposed to display authentic 'crude' folk art.

The simple aerophones usually produced by children in the early spring are also closer to toys than to professional instruments. Reeds are used for different kinds of primary clarinet or oboe (*bekace*), and sweet flag is especially popular on Whit Sunday, when it serves as a decoration of houses or as a signal instrument. Finally, children's experiences may also include blades of rye, shells of nuts, or acorns, which like grass, leaves or reeds are stretched with the fingers and put between lips or teeth, using the mouth as a resonator. The folk terminology of these aerophones, as well as of idiophones, stresses their onomatopoeic purpose (*świstawki, gruchawki, terkotki*).

The signal function is also typical of several pipes (*piszczałka, fujarka*) made especially in the early spring of fresh willow or linden branches, cleaned and hollowed out, as well as of pipes and horns twisted from fresh bark. Finally, there are several kinds of whistle (*świstawka*), and ocarinas, usually ceramic or wooden. All these instruments imitate or simulate the natural sounds of birds or of nature (wind) and they, too, function as signals and as simple acoustic experiments popular with boys at some periods of the year. Their direct connection with seasonal entertainment, and their magical connotations, have been practically forgotten, although they still remain in some references and terminology. The transition from the simple signal and ludic functions of instruments to their more 'autonomic' musical forms has been very smooth. This is especially true in the case of the simple flute without holes which may appear a simple children's toy, but in its developed forms tends to become an instrument designed for artistic performance. The same must be said of children's whistles, which may be equipped with elaborate blocks and even have many holes which make them 'real' instruments intended for playing melodies (Kopoczek 1984). Whistles shaped like animals or birds are particularly interesting because of their zoomorphic design.

Melodic and rhythmic instruments

Polish folk aerophones are not as numerous as in other Slavonic countries (Slovakia, Bulgaria, Russia). They may be described in three different groups as flutes, horns or trumpets, and reedpipes.

The first group is especially well developed in the Carpathian area (Chybiński 1924; Moszyński 1939, vol. II; Kopoczek 1984), though the basic type of folk flute with six or seven holes, called *piszczałka* or *fujarka* (see Figure 24 and Example 79), was well known all over the

Figure 24   *Fujarka* (pipe) from Głuchołazy, Silesia

Example 79   Melody of *fujarka*, Sobieska and Sobierajski 1972, no. 100, p. 361

country and may still be found in different areas as an instrument of the older male generation. This instrument is even today quite popular in several markets, especially during the church patrons' festivals. Finally, rich sources indicate that this instrument might have been played in ensembles of different character and adapted to various circumstances.

Organologically, Polish folk flutes should be divided according to such criteria as the position in which the instrument is held during the performance (straight or transverse), the size (from very short, about 28 cm, to those of 170 cm), the number of holes (two to nine, or without holes), the location of the holes (all on the upper side, or one on the back for the thumb), the type of pipe (closed or open, and if closed, then regulated by finger or by special locking), the form of blowing (directly on the edge or through a block), and finally according to the shape of tube (cylindrical or conical). Amidst all these, the shepherd's long straight flute without holes, the straight flute with three holes (Chybiński 1924), the flute with double channel (one for melody, the second for a drone – Chybiński, *ibid.*; Kotoński 1954), and finally the most popular flutes with six or seven holes distributed in both straight and transverse forms, seem to be the most characteristic Polish folk flutes.

The straight flute without holes is usually measured according to the length of the human arm (approximately 40 cm) (Kopoczek 1984). This instrument, still found in western Beskidy has, more than others, retained its shepherding function. It is used to organize a herd and to dignify the chief shepherd, stressing his leading position in the social group. This applies especially to some forms of long pipe (*piszczałka szałaśnikowa*; see Figure 25) which

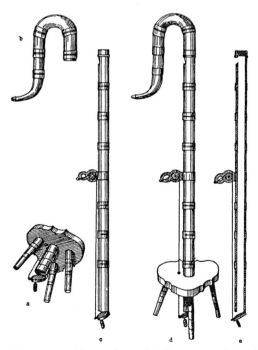

Figure 25   *Piszczałka szałaśnikowa*: a, stolek trójnozny; b, ustnik; c, korpus piszczarka ełożona; e, przekrój korpusu

were appreciated as the attributes of power and social distinction. The folk terminology, as well as the elaborated form of this instrument, were additional evidence of this dedication, such as its larger size (170 cm), its specific and long mouthpiece, shaped like an 'S', and the special supportive table which must be used for performance on the instrument. The pastoral character of the flute is additionally emphasized by the comments of performers and makers, who state that the longer instrument is for cows, and the shorter for sheep.

From an organological point of view, the long flute without holes presents a form with flexible locking (operated by finger or by special locking). It may be played with great mastery and two scales can be played. Indeed, various ways of playing and embouchure (on open and on closed pipe) make possible a scale of nearly two octaves, including some chromatic intervals (see Example 80). Great performers create very intricate ornaments on this instru-

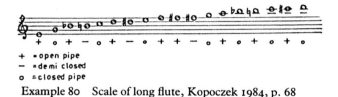

+ = open pipe
− = demi closed
o = closed pipe

Example 80   Scale of long flute, Kopoczek 1984, p. 68

ment, though the range of melodies is not developed and the melodies do not usually reach more than one octave or even a sixth (see Example 81). A comparison of old descriptions of

Example 81   Melody of long flute, Kopoczek 1984, no. 93, p. 270

this instrument (Chybiński 1924) shows how contemporary types have been progressively reduced. It is also clear today that the older forms of flutes blown directly on the edge are replaced by the block forms.

The flute with three holes as described by Chybiński (1924) has now totally disappeared, and it is known only from this old description and from museum pieces. According to all this information, the instrument was quite popular among shepherds and their melodies stressed the basic skeleton of music of the Podhale area (see Example 82).

Flutes with double or even with triple ducts have not been reported by recent researchers. Flutes with four or five holes, still very popular in many east European countries, are not found in Poland. Those that have been preserved are flutes with six, seven, or quite rarely, eight or nine, holes. Amidst the first group, types encrusted with tiny pieces of metal were distributed all over Poland. The ornamentation points to the fact that they were the instruments of professional shepherds of Walachian descent working on large farms and estates in the lowlands. The wide distribution of this type resulted in a variety of standards, as well as of music performed. The tonality and melodics of this music present different variants though they are evidently diatonic in character (see Example 83).

Straight and curved horns are still preserved in the western Beskidy (*trąba szalaśna, trąba owczarska*; see Figure 26). By contrast, in the Podhale area where they are called *trąba pasterska*, one can find only traces of this instrument, though it is still remembered by the older generation. So far as the Polish lowlands are concerned, the instrument disappeared there many years ago. At the same time, however, in northern Mazovia some attempts to revive this instrument (here called *ligawa*) are being spoken of, though this does not apply to the Pomeranian *bazoune*, known to us only from old descriptions and not so far revived. All these instruments have or had a signal function and were connected with shepherding or with the public announcement of news and significant events. They could also be used for purely musical purposes at certain periods of the day. Written sources inform us that in the Beskidy area playing for Angelus was quite popular. It is also confirmed that the long flutes were played at church during Christmas or on Good Friday (P. Dahlig 1985). They could also accompany the ceremonies of the solstice night as well as funerals (mainly in the area of Sanok), and they could be connected with several customs of spring (begging for a *dyngus*) or winter (Advent, Christmas, see Łęga 1961). Unfortunately, the music that has been performed on authentic *bazounes* or *ligawas* is not recorded. By all accounts, it was based on the triad: EGC; CEG (Łęga, *ibid.*).

A comparative study reveals a great diversity of forms. The most prolific type seems to be represented by the long straight horn of the western Beskidy which is relatively close to the *Alphorn* and has a definite shepherding function. This instrument is distinguished by its length, cylindrical tube, and three-piece construction (bell, channel and mouthpiece). Another specific element is the supportive table which helps to steady the instrument during performance. By contrast, Żywiec curved horns are shorter (1.5 m) and do not need extra support. The curved horns do not exist currently as instruments for regular performance, and are produced mainly for festivals and for museums.

By contrast, clarinets, both in the simplest form of reeds fixed to a resonator, and in the more elaborated form of the bagpipe, are quite widely known in Poland. Amidst their variety the transitional form of so-called *siesieńki, sierszeńki* (hornet; Figure 27) or *pęcherzyna* (bladder) is of particular interest. This instrument is clearly reminiscent of the mediaeval *Platterspiel* (cf. Virdung 1511, or Agricola 1545) and is to be found only in Great Poland and specifically in areas where the tradition of bagpipe playing is still preserved. According to J. and M. Sobiescy (1973), this instrument helps in the art of bagpipe playing, and is especially useful for practice in the co-ordination of movements needed to push the bellows and play the melody simultaneously.

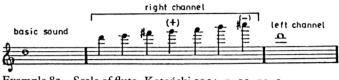

Example 82   Scale of flute, Kotoński 1954, p. 15, no. 1

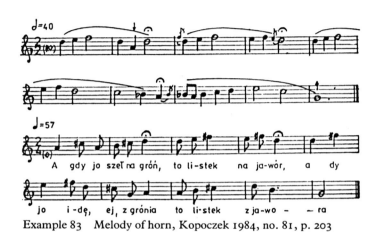

A gdy jo szeł na gróń, to li-stek   na ja-wór,   a   dy

jo   i-dę,   ej, z grónia   to li-stek   z ja-wo -   - ra

Example 83   Melody of horn, Kopoczek 1984, no. 81, p. 203

Figure 26   *Owcarska trąba*

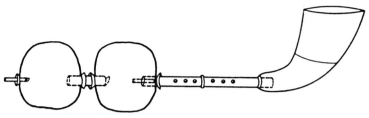

Figure 27 *Sierszeński*

The Polish bagpipe, differentiated regionally, should be divided typologically into three main groups, typical of Podhale (see Figure 12), of Great Poland, and of the western Beskidy (Żywiec area and Silesia). Although the first exists today only as a relic of the recent past, it is the most distinguished. Its chanter has five holes, and there are three channels – for melody, for drone and for direct blowing. The versions of Great Poland, though differentiated internally into several subcategories (Pietruszyńska-(Sobieska) 1936), have many features in common: a drone pipe consisting of two interconnected pieces, which are blown indirectly through the bellows, a chanter with one channel only and with seven holes (six for the fingers and one for the thumb of the left hand). The bagpipe of the western Beskidy is again divided into two main groups, specified even by different terminology (*dudy* in the Żywiec area and *gajdy* in the Silesia area of Cieszyn). Organologically the differences point to the different forms of blowing (directly in the Żywiec area, and indirectly in Silesia) and to the size of drone pipe, which is longer in the version of Żywiec. Finally, there are also some differences in tunings: the Żywiec version has seven holes whereas the Silesian has only six. None of these versions of the Beskidy preserved the chanter with many channels or transform the form of the drone pipe.

A more detailed analysis of all versions points to both their similarities and their differences. The similarities are to be found in the general east European features of the reed (clarinet type), the cylindrical shape of chanter, and recently in the reduction to one drone pipe. The differences concern mainly the structural distinctiveness of the bagpipe of Podhale, and specifically its type of chanter with three channels, which may suggest a predisposition to multipart performance. The other regional differences point either to various tonal adaptations (five, six, seven, or even eight holes, the latter in the case of the *kozioł* of Ziemia Lubuska) or to accommodation to new technical innovations such as indirect blowing or an interconnected type of drone pipe. The most authentic, though practically no longer in use, is a type of bagpipe from Podhale revealing close similarities to the shepherds' instruments of the eastern Carpathian area (an ethnic group called Huculi, see Šuchevyč 1904) and to those of the Balkan area. By contrast, the instruments of Great Poland, which are still the best preserved with seven or eight holes (six for the fingers and one for the thumb), have a diatonic scale and can be distinguished from those of Podhale by their dedication to monophonic or heterophonic (the chanter with one channel only) performance. A detailed analysis of the instruments of Great Poland indicates additionally an obvious difference in tuning and tessitura. As is well documented (Pietruszyńska-(Sobieska) 1936), the tuning of the bagpipe in Great Poland varies regionally, and higher tessitura has been typical for the south-western areas of this province. The organological differences between local versions are clearly manifested by the varied sizes, amongst which the largest and most dignified (called the *kozioł*, which means male goat) come from the western area of Ziemia Lubuska and have the lowest tuning (see Figure 9).

Differences in the scales and tuning of different versions of bagpipe are clearly regional. This applies also to the vocal and instrumental repertoire. At the same time, mutual interchange between vocal and instrumental versions is quite spectacular (see Example 84),

Example 84   Instrumental-vocal interaction, Sobiescy 1973, no. 69, p. 252

especially the influence of instrumental scales and timbres on the human voice, which itself closely resembles the timbre of an instrument.

The comparison of the different versions of the Polish bagpipe reveals a genetic diversity between Walachian imports (versions from the Carpathian area, and Podhale in particular) and European instruments widely distributed in the late Middle Ages. The instruments of the Cieszyn area (Silesia) represent a transitional phase. Indeed, it is quite evident that the long processes of development and transformation limited basic organological differences between structurally different groups.

Analysis of Polish folk aerophones is very helpful in the interpretation of the rudiments of Polish folk music and particularly its tonal background. The principles according to which the folk instruments are constructed also reveal the basic principles of human observation and conceptualization. It is quite clear that the natural sizes and patterns of the human body were of significance for the proportions of musical instruments. For instance, the size of a long pipe was measured by the length of a human arm, and primary techniques of instrumental sound production were derived from vocal concepts. For instance, the manner of overblowing is close to that of overshouting practised by folk singers (see Czekanowska 1985).

Stringed instruments dominate both solo and ensemble folk performance. Their variety presents a rich spectrum from very primitive (devil's violin) to refined, closely modelled on the professional violin (Olędzki 1978: 34–5). Stringed instruments fulfil different musical functions: rhythmic and sonorous (devil's violin) as well as melodic and harmonic (violin, basses). The possibility of creating highly artistic music on the violin and dulcimer contributed to the refinement of these instruments. The manner of stopping the strings, fingering and bowing as practised by contemporary violinists, and their conventions of accompaniment (the so-called *sekund*; see Example 86),[28] evidently transformed contemporary Polish folk music and its traditional patterns and tonal skeletons.

Stringed instruments in the Polish village, and the violin in particular, are today factory-made and bought in stores or – as in the recent past – they are distributed by travelling agents delivering cheap examples of factory-made instruments often signed as 'Stradivari' or 'Guarneri' copies. The generally accepted techniques of folk violin playing, and especially concentration on the two upper strings (E and A), use of three upper fingers interchanging between the open and stopped string, and use of two fingers only (second and third) (see E. Dahlig 1982: 110) transformed, to a certain extent, traditional melodies and their sequences (see Example 38). The latter, previously based on seconds and thirds, have changed into sequences dominated by thirds. At the same time, the technique to avoid the change of position and not to use the fourth finger did not extend the range of the used scale over d^1-c^3 $(e)^3$, though the possibilities of popular violins are much greater $(g-g^4)$. All of these elements contribute to the preservation of certain characteristics of folk melodies in which a vocal model is still traceable.

The contemporary violin does not offer great variety in tuning or performance techniques, especially in view of the technical limitations of musicians, who play *legato* or elements of *staccato*, with very little vibrato and an obvious concentration on keys which are easiest to play (A, G, D).

Performance attitudes, though clearly depending on the individual skills of musicians, are also influenced by regional convention and by the regional manner of ensemble performance, as well as by genre and type of music. The most obvious differences, however, are achieved by the adaptation of several socially or nationally 'foreign' impacts as in the case of the music of the nobility, military styles, church music and above all urban music and that performed previously by Jewish musicians. The Jewish musicians were famous for soft timbres, the art of the 'weeping fiddle' and several innovative developed techniques.

According to both old sources and recent descriptions, the contemporary violin and other representatives of the folk string ensemble have several ancestors going back to the Middle Ages. Many of them are fragmentarily preserved in the folk tradition until this very day.

The great diversity of Polish stringed instruments which are still preserved in folk practice should be divided into two main categories: bowed (including lutes and lyra) and plucked (lute) or struck (zither).

As mentioned, the violin was and still is the most significant for Polish instrumental folk practice. There are many records confirming the great popularity of earlier forms of this violin tradition in the past. Amidst a variety of specific folk versions, the 'smaller' fiddle called *oktawka*, *gęśliki* or *żłobcoki* (see Figure 28) and *mazanki* or *serby* present popular and interesting examples, whilst the instrument called *suka* (bitch) has a rather isolated position.

The instrument called *oktawka*, alias *októwka* or *ochtóbka* (Chybiński 1924; Kotoński 1954), is known from numerous examples documented in several regions of Poland (Chętnik 1983). According to available sources, it was an instrument made from one piece of wood with a raised neck. The tuning pegs were at the side. It could also have a curved head. In principle it was an instrument with an obvious reference to the mediaeval string form, without any

---

[28] 'The sekund plays some sort of double-stop rhythmic/harmonic pattern that accompanies first violin which renders the melody' (Noll 1986: 245–6).

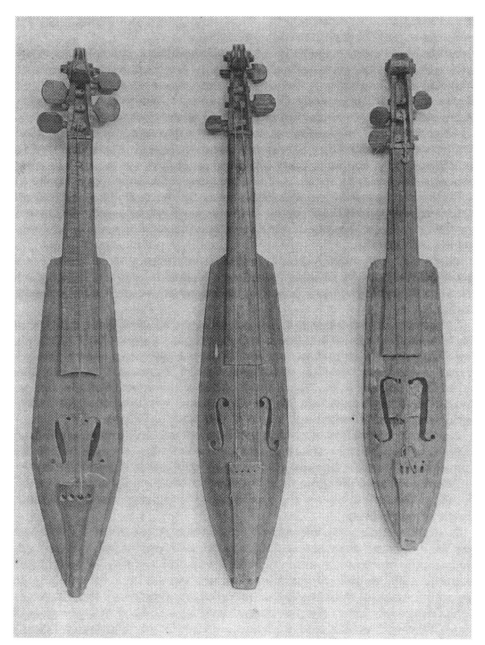

Figure 28   *Gęśliki*

bridge, in which the strings passed from the head over the neck and past the unwaisted bowing space, directly to the holes in the tongue (Noll 1986: 153).

The *mazanki* and *serby*, a local variant of *mazanki*, present probably the closest form to the so-called 'polische Geigen' as mentioned by Martinus Agricola (1545) or to 'kleine polische

Geigen' of Michael Praetorius (1619). The names as indicated point directly to the small size of this instrument whereas its name as known from folk sources points to the technique with which the instrument was played, to the bowing technique and imprecise touching (*mazać* – to smear). Basic information concerning *mazanki* comes from old performers and specifically from Franciszek Szymański, born in Podmokle in Great Poland in 1863, and from Tomasz Sliwa, born in 1892 in Chrośnica in the same province. These data are also complemented by some information from the nineteenth century (Kierski 1861). According to all these data, both *mazanki* and *serby* had only three strings tuned in fifths A, E, B, or G, D, A (Sobiescy 1973: 162) and a single fret in high position which allowed the player to perform in ensemble with the *kozioł doślubny* (*ibid.*). All descriptions at our disposal stress also the octagonal shape of this instrument and the fact that *mazanki* were later (probably in the middle of the nineteenth century) replaced by the regular violin with a cappotasta bound one third up the length of the strings in order to tune it about a fifth higher[29] and be able to compete successfully with the noisy sound of the *kozioł* (see Example 85). Quite recently attempts have been made to revive this historic instrument in the region of Ziemia Lubuska, where it was previously played. Nevertheless, contemporary revivals are with a large *kozioł* and not with a small one (*doślubny*).

The *gęśliki* or *żłób coki* are still the best preserved instruments of the Carpathian area which, after a period of being forgotten, have earned respect and are being played by young people in typical trio ensembles. This instrument was previously connected with solo performance or as an accompanying instrument for the bagpipe. The diversity of known examples includes versions with three or four strings, as well as with different shapes: narrow and spindle-shaped, waisted and basically unwaisted, and even sometimes like the mediaeval rebec. Modern examples have four strings and are tuned like a violin. They are in principle unwaisted and are distinguished by their smaller size and narrower shape. Most characteristic is the way in which the instrument is now played in ensemble. The first violinist holds the instrument at his neck but does not hold it with his chin and usually only uses three fingers. On exceptional occasions he may change to second position.

In contrast, very little is known about the instrument known as *suka* (bitch; Figure 29). Information is limited to a description and a drawing from the nineteenth century (Karłowicz 1888; Gerson 1895).[30] An incomplete instrument was found in the Biłgoraj region, at Kocudza, in 1950. According to accepted information, this instrument was quite popular in eastern Poland in the form of a bowed lute with an unequal bridge (Dahlig 1986) and its four strings were played with fingernails and not fingertips. The researcher's attention is also drawn to the abnormally short and wide neck of this instrument made from the same piece of wood. The same is true of the function of the *suka*, which was apparently connected with the accompaniment of ballads and stories, like the banduras or hurdy-gurdy, usually performed by Byelorussian and Ukrainian musicians playing and singing simultaneously.

The larger bowed lutes which are closer to the contemporary cello usually had the function of rhythmic and harmonic accompaniment in Polish traditional ensembles.

Amidst different versions of these instruments, several have a folk character. This applies

---

[29] The custom of putting a match under the strings and then binding it (*skrzypce podwiązane*) is still practised.
[30] It concerns the watercolour and drawing by Wojciech Gerson, *Suka*. Muzeum Narodowe, Warsaw, Inventory No. 28498.

Example 85   Melody of bagpipe and bound violin, Sobieska and Sobierajski 1972, no. 107, p. 368

Example 85   (cont.)

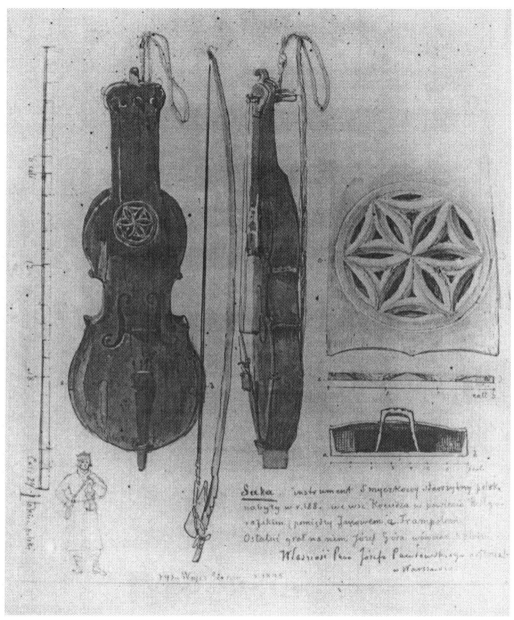

Figure 29   *Suka* after W. Gerson, watercolour and drawing, Muzeum Narodowe, Warsaw.

to the so-called trumpet-marine, similar to the *trummscheidt*, as well as to the *Maryna* or the *basy* and quite recently to the double bass, which still preserves certain regional characteristics.

The trumpet-marine is an instrument bowed like a double bass by the left hand and now fingered with three, previously two, strings. Historically it had an unequal bridge, but now it has bridge legs of equal length, a tongue and a raised neck (Noll 1986). The body is rectangular and unwaisted, with small metallic cymbals attached to the top of the head. The cymbals sound when the instrument is pounded rhythmically on the ground. It also has a wooden spike which is embedded in the bottom of the body. The instrument is bowed or rather touched by the bow. The bow is held by the whole hand and the instrument is turned to the left and to the right, which allows the two strings to be touched.

Other forms of Polish bass instruments are even closer to the orchestral cello. This applies also to the techniques that have been practised, though in all known cases they are limited and stress only the basic harmonic functions (DT). The most authentic form known comes from the Kalisz area and was called *Basy Kaliskie* by the author who discovered this instrument (Lisakowski 1971). It is found in several versions which may have two, three or four strings tuned in fourths, fifths, or fourths and fifths. Its bridge presents both forms, equal and unequal. The earliest form was made from one piece of wood hollowed out with only the top face separated and glued on. The short and wide neck was again made from the same piece of wood. According to Lisakowski, its body was almost rectangular in shape. The cappotasta technique of shortening strings by binding them approximately in the middle of the neck is applied as with the violin (see above). Some details of performance, as well as the body of the instrument and the applied terminology, indicate cultural connections with neighbouring Great Poland. This is confirmed most directly by applying the name of '*dudy*' to this instrument (Lisakowski 1971). It is to be assumed that this bass instrument of the Kalisz region replaced the bagpipe (*dudy*) which was probably used in this area previously.

The basses or *basetla* – the large bowed lutes, not specified by additional names – were once distributed quite widely over the country. Amidst these versions the basses of Great Poland seem to present an elongated model of general Polish type usually called *Maryna* in Central Poland (Mazovia, Kujavia). The difference between the regions points to the unwaisted (central Poland) or waisted (Great Poland) forms, or to the regular or higher (Podhale) bridge.

In brief, bowed lutes, both small and large, often playing together in small chamber ensembles, created a specific idiom of Polish folk instrumental music of the recent past. The instruments could be simple or more elaborate, from one piece of wood or constructed of many parts; they might also be factory made. The more detailed differences point to their forms (unwaisted or waisted), to their bridges (unequal or equal, and higher or regular), and to the differently shaped bodies (rectangular, octagonal, or lute-like). Their development indicates the general trends of transformation of the Polish instrumentarium, which in principle is following world-wide tendencies but at the same time maintains traces of traditional patterns.

The struck and plucked chordophones, though not too popular in Polish folk tradition, are represented by a few types and some subcategories. These are: first and foremost the dulcimer, usually preserved in portable form, of trapezic shape; hurdy-gurdy, bandura, and zither of asymetric type (*cytra gęślowa*) as sketched by Adam Chętnik from Kurpie (1983) and confirmed by some museum pieces (Muzeum Etnograficzne w Toruniu).

The dulcimer has a special position as an instrument which is still preserved in folk practice. Though played today by Polish peasants, it is clearly connected with certain social and national groups, and particularly with Jewish musicians (see Figures 30a and 30b). It has recently been played by Poles, often with a gentry background, and specifically by émigrés

Figure 30   (a) Jewish dulcimer player Guzikow with his ensemble, 1835

from the border regions of the Polish-Lithuanian frontier which were incorporated after World War II into the Soviet Union. Those people brought the instrument to a northern part of contemporary Poland (Mazuria) and are successfully developing this kind of instrumental tradition. The second area of dulcimer tradition is to be found in the Sub-Carpathian region (Rzeszowskie, Nowosądeckie) where it is today clearly a peasant instrument, although previously connected with Jewish as well as gypsy ensembles (especially popular in the areas of Orawa and Spisz). According to source documentation, the dulcimer was popular with folk ensembles as early as the seventeenth century (Bystroń 1960).

The results of modern field research confirm the existence of a portable version of the dulcimer which may have quite different technical standards and various scales reaching even three and a half octaves. Usually, however, the scale does not extend beyond two and a half octaves and has a diatonic character. The instruments modelled after the common patterns have two bridges (one treble and one bass) organizing the scale in three rows (Noll 1986, vol. 1: 207; P. Dahlig 1985: 120).

The number of strings may change: from 12 courses to 26 courses of three strings in each. The instruments under discussion may be struck by two players, which is especially typical for the variants of southern Poland, and accompany only dance music, whilst the instruments of northern Poland might be struck and touched simultaneously (left hand) in the case of instruments accompanying a song. Research in both northern and southern Poland clearly indicates that the dulcimer has been adopted by contemporary peasant society. Some questions, however, remain open, such as the record of its use in a seventeenth century folk ensemble.

In contrast, the other struck or plucked instruments do not have more recent records. This

Figure 30   (b) Jewish violin trio, after a drawing by W. Smokowski, 1840

is so, for instance, in the case of the hurdy-gurdy, which is remembered only by the oldest generation; its best documentation is that of Jan Karłowicz (1888: 434). This presents a typical type of hurdy-gurdy with three strings (one melodic and two for drone) bowed mechanically and equipped with a keyboard for stopping the strings. Very much the same concerns the *bandura*, which is not even documented in written sources but only by oral testimony. It is a type of archlute popularly used for accompanying ballads and stories.

Finally, the so-called *cytra gęślowa* should be mentioned. This instrument, though extremely interesting because of its terminology and of its body pointing directly to other forms of psaltery (box-zither), is unfortunately known to us only from a sketch by Adam Chętnik (1983) documenting a forgotten instrument from the Kurpian virgin forest.

The struck, plucked or mechanically bowed chordophones, in contrast to bowed lutes, preserve a quite isolated position in the Polish folk instrumentarium. Their undoubted 'foreign' descent should explain why they usually accompanied songs and were not exclusively used as an accompaniment to dancing, and did not receive proper popularity in Polish peasant society. They remain only in some areas and regions. As is well known, Polish peasant society prefers instrumental performance which interacts with the sung sections of ditties, and even during the episodes of customs (wedding) performance centres around responsorial exchange between sung and played sequences. At the same time, the custom of singing and playing simultaneously is actually popular in eastern Poland and amidst Polish-Ukrainian groups, being often performed in a mixed language (Polish-Ukrainian).

The membranophones, though still very popular in Polish folk ensembles and well recorded by archaeological and early historical sources (Kostrzewski 1949; Gabałówna 1960), remain almost unnoticed by later sources. There are only some fragments of polychromy confirming the use of the drum, probably a double-headed drum (Kamiński 1971: 68). This poor documentation is to be explained by the ideological concepts of people of that time dismissing drums as instruments 'making noise' and not directly dedicated to serious music. Thus it is to be assumed that many forms of drums have disappeared totally and are unknown today.

The most primary folk form presents a friction drum well confirmed by historical (eighteenth-century) and ethnographic sources. This form, which has actually disappeared today, was revived and included in some folk ensembles. The revived instrument presents a typical example of the northern European friction drum with characteristic indirect friction (so-called *Brummbass* (see Figure 31), *Rummeltopf* or *Rommeltop*; Bielawski 1985a). Its body

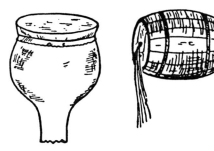

Figure 31   *Rommelpot*

consists of a wooden bucket with a membrane which is stretched over its head, and it is made to vibrate by friction of a cord in contact with a drumhead.

The drums that have been in use until recently are often of the tambourine type. They are usually made of a sieve and are one-headed with additional cymbals or small bells attached to ropes stretched across a frame. The type of double-headed side drums known as *baraban* or simply *bęben* (drum) are also popular. Amidst them the traditional type of mediaeval double-headed drum can be traced (see Kamiński 1971: 62).

The double-headed drums discovered in the area of Kalisz (Lisakowski 1971) are different but still very interesting. They present a distinct form with a characteristic deep body hollowed out of a piece of willow or poplar wood and tensioned by ropes. This type of rope-tensioned drum is also distinguished by the way it is held, in a horizontal position and suspended on a rope from the neck. All of these drums were 'home-made' by craftsmen or barrel-makers. Parts of the instruments and bodies were made either of wood or simply from riddles or slats that would have been used for barrels. Their rims, if used, were simple hemp cords. The skin of the membrane was basically that of a dog or deer. They were, or still are, struck with a stick or with a reed, which could give a ring (*do brzęku*). The rope-tensioned drums were also oil-painted in two or more colours with characteristic square or diamond shapes. It is to be assumed that these instruments were adopted from drums used in military service. Indeed, they indicate clearly the models of drums that were used by the Polish infantry at the beginning of the nineteenth century.

In brief, it seems quite obvious that the drums of Polish folk music did not develop as original forms. They were usually copies of popular models as they now adopt forms of military drums (double-headed side *baraban*) or professional instruments of jazz or pop music. In the recent past, however, they were usually 'home-made' products, and not factory products as is the case today.

Although the drum is used in the majority of Polish folk ensembles, its function is not highly respected. It has basic rhythmic and timbral functions, usually replacing the more traditional functions of drone and ostinato played by instruments such as the bagpipe or basses. Nevertheless, the drum may be played with great mastery, and this is especially true of the eastern regions of modern-day Poland (Lubelskie), where the ensembles of Mazovian style exist in their transformed form. At the same time, the drum is not welcome in the society of lesser gentry (especially in eastern Mazovia), where it is not accepted and is considered a 'vulgar' instrument.

Historical survey points to the changeable position of the drum in Polish folk society. Highly appreciated in the Middle Ages thanks to its magical power, it started to be disregarded in modern times especially among certain social groups and strata and is regarded mostly as a military instrument. At the same time, it is the drum which dominates the folk ensemble and especially the bands performing entertainment music in which it is needed as a basic instrument of rhythmic support, doubtless with a ludic function.

3.2.3 Instrumental folk ensembles

The small traditional folk ensembles called in the folk terminology *muzyka*, and the much bigger bands with numerous non-folk instruments (*orkiestra*), are still quite active and socially needed in Polish society. They usually accompany local or family events and only quite exceptionally perform just to be listened to (*do słuchu*). The diversity of these bands is great and they may be found in different groups and societies of villages, small towns, or even large cities (street orchestras). Their social and professional status may be different, as are their repertoires and artistic levels. In very general terms, folk instrumental ensembles are more developed in the south than in the north of Poland, though the numerous bands of the Sub-Carpathian area (Rzeszowskie), and those of Silesia in particular, do not often have too much in common with the traditional folk ensemble. The basic development that has taken place in folk ensembles is in the expansion of harmonic thinking. Taught in special classes and courses or by occasional teachers, this technique replaces progressively the previous convention to play drone or ostinato. The process as described is directly connected with the exchange of traditional basses (see above, p. 171), played with open strings by basses close to the cello, or by double bass stopped with fingers. The change also includes the technique of playing *sekund* by the second violin. These techniques, well developed in southern Poland (see Example 86; Noll 1986: 252), introduce certain elements of harmony, i.e., the simplest forms of playing in double stops based on triads with occasional fifths and sevenths. The

Example 86   *Sekund* technique, Noll 1986, no. 19

techniques of playing *sekund* may demonstrate varied levels of skill. In general, however, the Carpathian and Sub-Carpathian regions present a much higher level of collective playing, introducing some inversions as well as suspensions of chords. By contrast, this technique is totally unknown to the musicians of central and northern Poland except in some areas with specific local traditions (Biłgorajskie in the area of Lublin) in which the *sekund* has developed quite independent versions. In central Poland, indeed, the most evident difference depends on the genres and circumstances of performed music. The music accompanying the episodes of a wedding has a vocal character and is actually transcribing vocal patterns. Dance music, in contrast, is more independent in presenting an accompaniment to the dance. Central Polish ensembles still lead their instrumental parts monophonically or heterophonically (Great Poland), following the main melody in the same register (see Example 85). The main accompaniment is performed in these cases by a drum, quite exceptionally by the basses (*Maryna*) or by a drone in the case of playing with the bagpipe. The instrumental ensembles of Żywiec represent a transitional form of collective playing, in which the violin accompanying the bagpipe only roughs out the main harmonic functions. It is quite possible that this way of playing was previously much more popular.

   Today, the technique of collective playing is evidently influenced by several 'imported' patterns, such as those of military or other professional groups – orchestras of firemen, miners (see Figure 32) or railway workers. As already discussed (p. 171), the influence of other

Figure 32   The miners' ensemble 1955, after a woodcut by S. Wójtowicz

national groups is, or at least was, an important factor in the recent past. Perhaps in this way it would be possible to explain the phenomenon of the higher development of instrumental music in some areas. This applies, for instance, to the local music of Biłgorajskie, which is probably influenced by the music of gypsy musicians who have been very active in this area for many years as traditional sieve producers.

Traditional folk ensembles are at present preserved only in some isolated areas, first and foremost in the Podhale area (see p. 167) with its highly skilled string trios; it applies also to modest ensembles of the Żywieckie area, consisting of bagpipe and violin; and to the even more different styles and tunings of the ensembles of Great Poland, which have been the basis of different types of bagpipe and violin or 'bound' violin (see Example 85). This applies also to the ensembles of the Cieszyn area (bagpipe and violin); finally, to certain ensembles of central Poland specializing either in the *oberek* style (violin and drum, with eventually harmonium added, typical of Mazovia and Kujavia) or in the *polka* repertoire (Małopolska and the Sub-Carpathian area). The last type of orchestra already includes several non-folk instruments; besides the dulcimer and violin it also has the clarinet, trumpet and others.

There are non-folk instruments which are transforming performed music. This process, however, starting in the nineteenth century, is slow, but it develops progressively, penetrating the specific turns of melodies, changing the ways in which the parts are introduced and replacing the traditional formulae by standard sequences of quasi-functional harmony (see Figure 33). These new techniques completely annihilate the heterophonic model of thinking in which every instrument, following the same model, presents its characteristic skills and possibilities. The transformation also attacks the way of phrasing promoted by the rather

Figure 33   Musician of an urban area, after a drawing by W. Pruszkowski, 1880

rigid conventions of collective performance. It limits the possibilities of flexible *tempo rubato* and tends towards greater standardization of repetitions. Ultimately it also concerns performance attitudes, following today's fashionable styles of pop music with its loudness, very fast tempi, and schematic repetitions.

The changes described lead to the almost total transformation, if not annihilation, of substantial patterns of Polish folk music and of its traditions of collective performance. It is the main reason why individually performed music, such as that of violinists and flautists, still presents more authentic forms and often higher artistic standards. But even this cannot change reality, for this transformed quasi-folk music is mostly popular and in real demand.

Despite all transformations, a comparative survey still reveals differences between distinct regions. An appreciation for tradition and a tendency to follow modern trends often coexist side by side. At the same time, however, differences between the habits and mentality of

Figure 34   The street musician from Warsaw, 'The Foreigner', after a drawing by H. Pilatti

people are especially marked in certain areas, and particularly between those of western and eastern Poland. The people of the western Polish provinces, such as Silesia, Pomerania and Great Poland, have for long been accustomed to work collectively, whilst the people of central and eastern Poland are motivated much more individually. It is also quite obvious that the people of southern Poland, and particularly of the Carpathian area, are rooted in the deep structure of nomadic society. These facts have had and still have a strong influence on the nature of music ensembles, as well as on the character of the repertoires performed.

The differences in the character of ensembles are visible when we compare the guild-like organization of the performers of the bagpipe of Great Poland with the structure of the ensembles of central and eastern Polish musicians. At the same time, differences of repertoire are obvious even within one region.

The organization of teaching procedures also reveals obvious regional differences, though this has changed quite rapidly over the last few years. During the 1930s and 1940s, music lessons in Mazovia, even in the neighbouring area of Warsaw, were still paid for in natural products, and the duties of a teacher included not only musical performance but also the construction of an instrument (violin). The situation was totally different in western Poland.

Differences in standards of civilization contributed to the diversification of the folk tradition. On the one hand, knowledge of musical notation as well as the inclusion of technically more advanced instruments modified traditional patterns of folk music. On the other hand, the highly civilized regions were often better prepared to preserve these traditions and the inhabitants of those areas were more able to understand the integrational power of the traditional legacy. Subsequently, the inclusion of factory-made instruments, usually adopted from military bands (E flat clarinet, trumpet), did not distort the traditional ensemble in these highly developed regions (Great Poland). At the same time, however, some very traditional and not advanced provinces of Central Poland (Kieleckie), cultivating simple performance styles, preserved their artistic sensitivity and admiration for traditional patterns in the best sense.

Performance practice as developed in the resettled areas introduces a separate issue. Ensembles were organized by official institutions (e.g., factories) as well as created more individually, often on the basis of quasi-regional or local initiatives. In these ensembles, the 'newcomers' had a very diversified background but co-operated with some groups of local inhabitants (Opole, Silesia). This applied especially to the areas resettled in the late 1940s in western and northern Poland, where the 'newcomers' evidently dominate the original inhabitants. The co-existence of mixed populations may also have several consequences for the transformation of musical techniques. The collectivity of new ensembles may be supported additionally by feelings of national identity that are particularly visible amongst Ukrainian and Lithuanian groups. Non-Polish musicians (Ukrainian, Lithuanian) usually have a decisive influence on the music performed by ensembles. It is clear that instrumental activity is stronger as an area of innovation than vocal performance. Instrumental performance is often additionally supported by the revival of forgotten instruments, such as the friction drum (*burczy bas*).

3.2.4 Theoretical concepts and non-verbal media of Polish folk performers

Folk terminology often provides the key to the interpretation of several concepts and aspects of musical performance. This applies especially to expressive qualities as well as to the creative motivation and objectives behind a performance, concentrating on the rôle of music and situational context of performance. The investigation of terminology reveals basic concepts and theoretical assumptions that are crystallized in the performer's mind.

According to current opinion, music of an instrumental character is particularly dedicated to accompanying dances and social gatherings. The motivation just 'to make a noise' and 'to frighten away the devil' has totally disappeared. Nevertheless, some instruments, and specifically the violin, though an instrument of relatively recent origin, preserved their obvious magical connotations. The dedication to the devil is in this case quite well confirmed by several stories which have been current amongst violinists. This applies above all to the magical power of the instrument understood often as a vehicle used, for example, to cross a river. It reminds one clearly of the world-wide legends about stringed instruments, for example in Siberian shamanistic beliefs. In the first place, however, these stories describe competitions among violinists, pointing to the secret power of the devil helping or distorting the efforts of performers by exchanging the strings.

The most current and popular stories are those about a violin which was playing while hanging on a wall without being touched by the performer. Such stories stress also the corpomorphic aspects of the violin's body, and specifically the names of its parts (head, neck, sides, back, etc.). Much more interesting, however, seem to be the corpomorphic names that have been given to the musical sections of musical form, especially the name of the basic section known as *kolano* (knee; see Examples 87, 88a and 88b). This term as applied to

Example 87 *Chłop świętokrzyski*, E. Dahlig 1982, no. 19

Example 88a   *Chłopski (Paur Thantcz)*, Chybiński 1948, no. 27

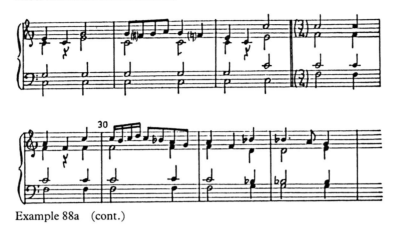

Example 88a   (cont.)

instrumental music, and particularly to that performed on the violin, achieved special significance in folk reflections on musical form (P. Dahlig 1983). All these facts indicate clearly that in the case of the violin we have an instrument with developed magical connotations revealing the concepts of magical thinking. At the same time, it is also clear that in this case the basic concepts are quite universal in character and not specific to Poland. Very much the same applies also to the idiophones and aerophones understood simply as substitutes for the voices of animals, birds and nature.

The mixture of different traditions can also be traced in some general concepts of musical pieces which obviously are not verbally expressed, such as concepts which are memorized by fingering or other non-verbal indications. This kind of communication is, above all, popular amongst instrumentalists playing an accompaniment on the double bass or on a keyboard instrument (chamber organ). It may also be helpful to singers and to those with experience of singing in church choirs and memorizing according to the fingering of the player (keyboard instrument). These observations and non-verbal procedures help musicians to memorize and to recognize the basic skeletons of popular songs known and current within a particular group. The fingering works usually as a mnemotechnic means beside references to well-known verbal texts identified by their *incipits* or indications of function and situation (e.g., called *do czepka* – to a capping; *do rozplecin* – to unplaiting; or *do wianka* – to the wreath) or even *za krowami* (behind the cows). It may also be substituted by the widely accepted practices of tapping the rhythmical patterns, or repeating the syllables (double bass players). The analysis of these non-verbal indications reveals that there are several concepts and conventions which are only partially known, but basically intuitively felt. The most substantial concepts concentrate, however, on the possibility of distinguishing a basic contextual determination (dance, custom) and of obtaining or examining the sphere of an intuitively felt melodic model in its basic entity. In other words, the musical concept known as *kolano* (knee) corresponds usually with a basic musical phrase. This may later be varied or complemented.

The analysis of folk terminology and of non-verbal concepts and methods of communication (fingering, knocking, tapping) reveals once more the complex nature of contemporary folk tradition in Poland in which the past and the present exist side by side.

Example 88b   Jan z Lublina 1964, 218 v., p. 491

3.2.5 On the concept of performance style

The basic problem is the assessment of individual creativity in all types of folk instrumental performances. The second problem is the extent to which instrumental performances transmit directly what has been handed down, since the transmission of instrumental performance is less direct than that of vocal performance. On the other hand, instrumental performances are usually much more institutionalized and connected with several forms of social and political activities and their programmes.

The best and most authentic instrumental performances, similarly to the vocal ones, are to be found in the original 'home-productions' which are only occasionally shown today on the stage during regional competitions (see Figures 21a, b and c). This applies especially to some instrumental performances of central and eastern Poland, which present a highly artistic level of playing, with delicate ornamentation. This is true of many violin and flute solo pieces and of shepherds' melodies played solo, e.g., *za krowami* (behind the cows), or of violin pieces accompanying the touching episodes of a wedding, and particularly the melodies dedicated to the bride as an orphan. The ornamented melodies could also be performed on the bagpipe (*dudy* or *koziol*) accompanying these sentimental events. Finally, ornamented sections are also spectacularly exhibited in the introductions to the dance *góralski (ozwodna)*. In all these situations the melodies are more instinctively created than learned. The creative need of performers is not limited to the area of ornamentation. It is also heard in phrasing and articulation, though in instrumental performance it is more controlled than in vocal practice. The ways to play *legato* or *staccato*, and degrees of loudness, tempo and tessitura, may all be interpreted in regional terms, depending on the genre and function of the music. Some mannerisms of articulation as performed by the bagpipe also have an evidently regional character, for example the *staccato* (see Example 89) (so-called *pukanie*, knocking) or

Example 89   Bagpipe (knocking), Sobiescy 1973, no. 36, p. 217

preferences to play in a higher register, or to play with special vocal timbre. These mannerisms may be additionally stressed by the terminology applied, as was the case of the so-called 'sour' fiddle playing in the high register (Lusatia). In contrast, the violin in eastern Poland very often has a soft timbre which corresponds to the lyric atmosphere of poetic songs and the richness of their symbols and diminutives. The 'sour' music of western provinces and the soft and delicate music of eastern Poland clearly point to obvious differences of taste, temperament and aesthetics which vary regionally.

The emotional climate of the music performed is clearly connected with certain notions of trance as being typical for specific dance situations in certain areas. A preference for trance develops quite differently, according to the various temperaments and psychological predispositions of individuals and groups, and it follows only to a certain degree traditional patterns of behaviour and conventions. In central Poland, the violinist often plays with his eyes closed, as also the drum-player who, in certain sections, breaks away from the standardized limits and creates an unusual whirling dance in a very fast tempo with uncontrolled repetitions. In contrast, there are dances where a regularly pulsating rotating dance (*vivat*) still preserves a certain balance, and although the dances of mountain people (*góralski*) are full of rage and fury, the dances do not develop the elements of trance. Indeed, in the *góralski* dance, and even in its fast section (*krzesane*), performers still remain sensitive to the context and its changeable stimuli.

The instrumental activity also seems to be very important in the professional and social organization, especially in the shepherds' and in some agricultural societies. In the lowlands the agricultural calendar dictates the dates of weddings and other feasts. In spring young boys were especially excited by seasonal games stimulating their sensitivity towards acoustic and artistic exercises demonstrated in these cases by the production of musical instruments. It was also typical of winter time and the carnival that musical instruments were demanded for certain masquerades and games.

As already discussed, the instruments were and partly still are approached and evaluated differently by several authorities. They could be banned or, on the contrary, played as a privilege on certain days or periods. This is often puzzling. It is, for instance, difficult to understand why folk instruments could be played in church on a day of official mourning while professional instruments were forbidden. This question is difficult to answer since these privileged instruments are not limited to modest clappers or rattles but also include flutes and horns. Biblical guidance and church rules on the one hand and folk concepts on the other often overlap. It seems obvious that the presence of instruments at annual customs is motivated by the entertainment function of these events, whilst more significant and more serious family customs are dedicated to vocal performance, which is considered a deeper and more authentic medium.

Contemporary movements with social or political involvement (see below) neglect neither musical instruments nor their ensembles. The spectacular qualities of instrumental music are highly regarded. To a certain extent, the social aspects of instrumental practice are emphasized, because of the more evident need to rehearse collectively. At the same time, however, the motives that contribute most to the cohesion of the group are derived from the conviction that the vocal repertoire presents the mainstream and most natural vehicle of the tradition.

3.3   Musical structure

Musical structure is shaped by systems which come to some extent from outside the music itself. This applies especially to the metric and rhythmic patterns that are clearly penetrated by the systems of language and by basic behavioural rhythms and gestural structures. By contrast, the tonal structure shows an independence based on harmonic principles related directly to human perceptual attitudes. In the most general sense, the organization of musical form is interpreted as a coexistence of two basic systems, those of pitch and time, modified additionally by some other factors. The rudiments of those particular systems are, however, dependent on principles which may be interpreted in a very abstract sense as symmetry, proportions and cyclicity, revealing in the best way the basic ideas of human thinking and behavioural articulation.

The history of music shows that the different states of balance between tonal, rhythmic and formal factors are of structural significance for musical phenomena. In the case of folk art, the links with basic situational needs and functions are much stronger than in classic art. In folk art the dominance of socially accepted conventions is evident. This social factor shapes and standardizes the models which are preserved in folk tradition for many years. At the same time, however, the very nature of musical transmission modifies and individualizes the content of the artistic message. To find a proper balance between the more universally and the individually created phenomena and to identify them in more concrete social, national, regional and artistic terms is a complex, though gratifying, task.

3.3.1 Pitch organization: tonal structures

On the modal aspects of Polish folk music structure

Vocal and instrumental patterns can be easily recognized in the tonal organization of Polish folk music. They vary in particular regions, of course, but the vocal model is fundamental in both of them and better preserved.

The traditional tonal patterns seem to be rooted in the basic structures of tetra- or pentachord often complementing each other in a form of hepta- or octotonic structure:

The indicated skeleton is significant for both vocal and instrumental Polish folk music (E. Dahlig 1982: 98), whilst the non-Polish counterparts of these skeletons of other east European cultures are well known and recorded (Bartók 1925: 62; Sokalskij 1888). The skeleton's varieties depend on the nature of basic structures (tetra- or pentachord) and they either preserve the modal character or, on the contrary, are already affected by modern tonality. The structure of skeletons is usually recognizable: by the obvious concentration on the frame of the fourth, or fifth; by the interval structure (seconds and thirds); and, in some cases, by the articulation of special melodic turns. So far, however, melodic formulae of this kind, it must be said, are more typical of special genres than of tonal modes (Czekanowska 1972: 61). By contrast, tonally transformed melodies concentrate on the articulation of obvious harmonic functions and centre around their zones (see Example 38).

The essential difference between modal and modern tonal organizations resides in their integrational consistency, i.e., in their mono- or polycentric tendencies which either bind the skeleton into one structure (heptatonic) or preserve its tonal lability according to which the scale consists of two elements (tetra- or pentachords) orientated towards two different central tones (see Example 72). In this connection, one might recall the well-known statement by the Russian scholar Peter Sokalskij (1888) describing the concept of Slavonic modality as a manifestation of polycentric, equivocally balanced orientation. The basic imperative of this structure is formulated as the necessity 'to find unity in heterogeneity'. 'In order to define a tonic and its position it is necessary to find unity in heterogeneity, which can be effected in several different ways, derived from melody, rhythm and the content of an accompanying text. The above-mentioned factors can function both jointly and dysjointly and their unification is dependent not only on basic necessity, but also on the need for beauty' (Sokalskij 1888: 3).

The modal approach as formulated by Sokalskij helps to interpret several phenomena of Polish folk music in a relatively comprehensive way. It reveals, for instance, the complex nature of many melodies and shows their elements functioning often as isolated tonal structures (the so-called narrow-range melodies, Czekanowska 1972) of diatonic or anhemitonic nature (see Example 61) (Wiora 1951, 1957), or, on the contrary, as different forms of coexistence of tetrachords or tetra- and pentachords. The modal approach as formulated by students of Indian music (Jairazbhoy 1971) is perhaps even more helpful in explaining the dynamic profiles of Polish folk melodies. According to this suggestion, modal concepts determine the basic principles of tonal centralization, which results in different kinds of interval structure and in the specific shapes of melodic turns. This approach is especially helpful in the explanation of complex interrelations of tonal structures in the case of transitions from one state of relative balance into another (Jairazbhoy 1971: 38–9), and it also contributes to the interpretation of modes of modification in a structure under study. This interpretation concerns both the alternation of steps and the principles of their omission (Czekanowska 1981a: 516). Consequently, this analysis explains not only the direction of the melodic line (rising or falling) and its shape (simple or inflected), resulting from the different location of leading tones, but also the hierarchy and preferences stressing the functions of particular degrees. Moreover, it also explains the varying intensity and modes of transition from one structure (tetra- or pentachord) to another, as well as the presence or absence of some extra-scale intervals (Jairazbhoy 1971). This analytical approach seems to be much more helpful than the interpretation of a scale according to its superficial specifics (formulae), stating the accumulation of certain tonal elements, the products of processes of tonal centralization. At the same time, however, the presence of some scales such as pentatonics or heptatonics and the Major/Minor system are in Polish folk music an obvious fact, while the influence of performance attitudes is also very significant. The latter can be seen especially in the instrumental music and in its specific scales.

In the traditional literature, the systematization of basic skeletons of Polish folk music is approached historically, with much attention being paid to the evolution and transformation of basic tonal ideas, interpreted from the angle of the history of music and of its cultural differentiation. This is especially visible in the fascination with the pentatonic scale which was so typical of European continental ethnomusicology in the 1920s and 1930s (Riemann 1916; Bartók 1925; Windakiewiczowa 1933). The Lydian Mode was treated with equal interest, as the scale typical of the Polish Carpathians (Chybiński 1924; Kresanek 1951; Kotoński 1953). Finally, the so-called narrow-range melodies popular in Polish eastern territories (Kvitka 1926, 1928; Wiora 1951, 1957; Reinhard 1958; Bartók 1951; Czekanowska 1972) also became the subject of extensive scholarly discussions. All these phenomena, though represented statistically at a very low percentage in contemporary Polish folk music, obviously contributed to the creation of the Polish musical idiom, and to its regional characteristics in particular. They also influenced the character of instrumental scales, which, though not very numerous and varied, were not without significance for the creation of Polish national and folkloristic styles (for example by K. Szymanowski). All these elements form a contrast with the present Polish tonal system dominated by the modern Major scale. Nevertheless, the preservation of those traditional elements adds a special colour to music and makes even the contemporary melodies sound authentic and fresh (Bartók 1925: 63).

The basic skeletons and general trends of tonal transformation

The coexistence of different tonal systems is a typical feature of Polish folk music (see above pp. 188–9). This applies especially to the preservation of penta- or tetratonic, and penta- or tetrachordal melodies (see Wiora 1957), as well as to the characteristic formulae within the already transformed tunes. The most significant, however, seem to be the aforementioned general modal principles of tonal centralization, based on the concept of a drone or ostinato.

The phenomenon of pentatonics discussed extensively in the Polish musicological literature (Windakiewiczowa 1933; Sobieski 1953) appears in some traditional folk music, particularly in melodies of the wedding ceremony (the bride's farewell to her maids, capping ceremony; see Example 27), in the solstice night music (Example 2b), or in some ballads (Example 48) and lyrics (Example 21) documented especially in certain regions (Kurpie). Although pentatonic elements are at present disappearing, they can still be heard in a wide range of varieties, which show how very popular they used to be and how widespread they were all over Poland in the past. This also finds confirmation in the variety of their forms (di- and anhemitonic) and in the preservation of some pentatonic turns. At the same time, however, it should not be forgotten that the devices of a pentatonic system are limited to these melodic turns which stress the absence of some degrees, i.e. to the so-called 'gaps' typical for pentatonics, whilst examples of complete pentatonic melodies have almost disappeared today (see Bartók 1925: 20 for remarks on Hungarian melodies with pentatonic background). Nevertheless, the common features of pentatonic melodic types and their correlations with some genres and particular regions, so well described if not properly valued in the literature, prove the significance of this tonal system.

The phenomenon of the Lydian Mode is a special case in Polish folk music, since it appears only among the Tatra highlanders (see Example 75). Their music can be regarded from both the ethnographic and the purely musical point of view. First, the music was connected with the people's shepherding activities, and secondly, its very form was determined by the instruments used (flutes, horns), which need intense blowing. Thus they achieved a musical culture of very distinct features which remained isolated until the twentieth century. At the same time, the tonality of this music is related to pastoral traditions of other countries, while being influenced by the very nature of the shepherds' signal instruments (Wiora 1949–51; Danckert 1939a: 117).

From the historical point of view, the noticeably different music of the Tatra highlanders had fascinated Polish society at least since the end of the eighteenth century. It found its expression in the opera by Jan Stefani (1794) entitled *Krakowiacy i Górale* (The Krakóvians and Highlanders). Consequently, the folk music of that region contributed to the creation of a folkloristic style rooted in the Lydian Mode, as well as in the whole context of its performance, in which the essence of the music is determined by its collective performance and its tendency to improvisation. It is also connected with a characteristic predisposition for multipart singing and playing, actually projecting the skeleton of the tonal-melodic thinking. The character of the music is also articulated by the direction of melodic movement (falling) and by typical skeletons fixed within the framework of the tetrachord. Finally, the articulation of some intervals (semitone in the upper tetrachord and rising fourth in the lower) and the characteristic stress of the raised fourth as the final formula, seem to be the most significant features.

This wide range of very specific features suggests an alien origin for this particular shepherds' culture in which the intensely blown horns and flutes played a significant rôle. The social structure of this professional group, as well as an obvious dedication to collective performance, were undoubtedly decisive factors in this case.

A separate topic was formed round melodies with rising fourths made up of patterns of figuration typical of the music of the Polish central regions and of Mazovia in particular. These melodic turns were made popular through Chopin's stylizations (Windakiewiczowa 1926). The reference to the Lydian Mode, suggested by some Polish authors, is still problematic. The instrumental arrangement of some vocal models (Noll 1986), or perhaps the natural tendency towards figuration which is also apparent in vocal folk melodies (Czekanowska 1961), probably inspired these very successful stylizations. Yet, it is difficult to be sure that Chopin knew the music of the Polish highlanders.

The use of instrumental scales is particularly evident in the case of the melodic formulae typical of some instrumental playing. This also concerns the changeable intonation of particular degrees precipitated occasionally for technical reasons. In more general terms, however, the influence of instrumental music is expressed in a tendency for transformation and in the creation of regional or even individual ideas. As has been mentioned above, the idiom of some instrumental scales, and of those of the Carpathian regions in particular, played an important part in artistic stylization. This stylization, however, mainly enhances general properties and postures of performance, and tonal elements have only a secondary influence.

The so-called narrow range melodies present again a totally different and heterogeneous material having only this tendency in common, to be limited to the nuclei of tonal scales (Reinhard 1958). The literature on the subject has described the phenomena of the narrow range quite comprehensively, pointing to the existence of their diatonic or anhemitonic forms. The interesting correlations of these melodies with certain groups of the traditional repertoire of wedding and harvest customs of eastern territories are also widely discussed, as well as the problem of their affiliations to their non-Polish counterparts. This concerns, above all, affiliations of the anhemitonic versions of 'narrow structure' to the north Ukrainian and Byelorussian counterparts whereas the diatonic versions are evidently affiliated to the south Ukrainian and south Slavonic counterparts (Czekanowska 1972). The studies carried out so far have confirmed the existence of basic structural properties in this tonal type described as the principle of rotation around the central tone with evident domination of some intervals such as the second and the fourth (Bielawski 1973b). In brief, the phenomena of narrow range are interpreted as a relic of the 'old' Slavonic strata which became isolated and restricted to some areas in the present-day repertoire of Polish folk music, although it is also clear that without considering this structure it would be impossible to establish the characteristic features of Polish folk music.

We find completely different material in the melodies of children's songs and games (see

Examples 35 and 66), relating often to spring and sometimes to winter customs. This particular repertoire, distributed more in western than in eastern Poland, is evidently of diatonic character and though also limited in range (pentachords or tetrachords) reminds us rather of fragments of heptatonic scales than of independent structures with their own tonal character. The most striking feature in this case is the use of recitation, which seems to be a general characteristic of European children's songs. The signals, call melodies, and refrains, although apparently diatonic, again present different systems clearly determined by their functions (Bielawski, 1985b).

The influence of the Major-Minor system is well documented in Polish folk music. It concerns above all the instrumental repertoire performed on factory-made instruments (clarinet, trumpet, harmonium). The impact of this music is obviously stronger in the south-western than in the north-eastern Polish provinces. This modern impact has contributed to the progressive transformation of traditional tonality, modifying the conventional formulae that have recently been changed to sequences of short and oft-repeated motifs, stressing their basic harmonic functions. This is especially typical of the music performed by ensembles who play according to the principle of *sekund*, and of modern bands of wind instruments who refer only occasionally to the traditional patterns and repertoire, but identify their ensembles as being 'folk'.

Thus, in some traditional regions, only the harmonic model of accompaniment remains faithful today to traditional principles (Podhale), while in other conservative regions the music is limited to the monophonic model, in which particular instruments play the same melody, this being related to the drone (Great Poland) or to the ostinato (some parts of Mazovia).

The differences in the use of Major and Minor scales vary according to regions; the Minor is more popular in the eastern than in the western Polish provinces. Statistically it is the Major that prevails, while the Minor is limited to the recent songs of the lyric repertoire. The modal melodies with the minor or changeable third are, by contrast, quite well represented and have created the image of the Polish folk song, especially the folk ballads and lyrical songs. They also often have a changeable sixth and seventh, and can consequently be regarded as Aeolian or Dorian Modes (see Examples 52, 63 and 65), not too remote from melodies with a major third and changeable sixth (Mixolydian) or with a minor second (Phrygian). All these phenomena are easily explained as being structures of 'equivocal balance', which may be additionally enriched by 'apparent chromatics' (Windakiewiczowa 1926) and 'orientalism' (augmented second). The coexistence of so many elements creates a rich variety of expressive qualities which contribute to the creation of an idiom of typical Polish folk song, changeable in its emotional moods. More detailed analysis shows that many formulae and stereotypes have been inherited from non-folk sources (plain chant melodies, sequences); whereas at the same time some elements of folk song can also be detected in the music of other social strata (church music).

The strong influence of modern tonality has not significantly transformed traditional concepts. This is confirmed by a comparison with the music of west European countries, and with the music of Poland's neighbours to the west (Germans, Czechs) in particular. The main difference appears in the concentration on the two basic functions (Tonic and Dominant) which is regarded as a typical feature of Polish folk music. By contrast, the music of Poland's western neighbours is more advanced in harmonic terms and stresses also the functions of the

Subdominant – as well as modulations to parallel keys. According to Mersmann (1922, 1924), who attempted to chronologize the German folk material according to the character of harmonic functions, melodies concentrated on the Tonic and Dominant are typical of seventeenth- and eighteenth-century German music, while the nineteenth-century music used already to stress the functions of the Subdominant and parallel keys. Discussion of the modal background of Polish Minor and Major melodies should not exclude the elements of quasi-Major skeletons either, as they have been embedded in traditional strata and show a clearly modal character. The tendency to be presented in 'plagal' form, i.e., finishing on a fifth, and balancing between two basic functions (Tonic and Dominant; see Example 38) seems to be the most characteristic feature of this melodic type (Bartók 1925: 63).

On the creative impact of the performing act

The tonal skeleton and its melodic 'undulation' create in the best cases an organic unity and confirm the existence of a still-vivid and developing musical tradition. This can be seen in the areas where the vernacular strata still preserve some creative power. In these cases also, the impact of performance style plays a significant rôle, especially through the ornaments which modify the character of tonal patterns. The richness of melodic ornamentation is manifested in different types of acciaccatura preparing and following the basic tones, as well as by lower and upper shakes, mordents, double mordents, and by appoggiaturas and trills. All are found in both the instrumental and the vocal repertoire, and lead often to the changeability of some degrees, and especially to the afore-mentioned phenomenon of 'apparent chromatics'. The strong impact of performance style is shown to perfection in Chopin's stylizations with their accomplished manner of handling the melodic and harmonic aspects of figuration. It must be said, however, that the creative contribution of the performance media is also balanced by structural factors in which the behavioural adjustment (accompanying gestures) play a significant rôle and inspire musical ideas.

To sum up, the history of the Polish tonal systems reveals the significance of the vocal legacy and of its skeletons which are deeply rooted in mediaeval modality. By contrast, the instrumental impact seems to be better adjusted and more sensitive to 'modern' trends of transformation. The instrumental tradition seems to be very important in the creation of Polish national and folkloristic styles. Also very significant are the basic models of social interaction, deeply rooted in conventional patterns of tonal organization and in the articulation of basic ideas of hierarchy (poly- and monocentric models). They create some types of melodic movement (oscillating), some essential kinds of interval structure (seconds and fourths), and they generate the basic principles of tonal organization. Although the structural function of performance style cannot be easily evaluated, it seems that it does play an intrinsic rôle, being determined by the basic patterns of human behaviour.

3.3.2 Temporal organization: rhythmic structures

Spoken and dance patterns

Thanks to the studies of Polish linguists (M. Dłuska, I. Furmanik), musical structures have now been analysed in relation to language and its patterns (Bielawski 1970). The basic features of Polish language and of the Polish folk music structure can be summarized as follows:

Polish folk music structure has a definite downbeat and a falling sequence of rhythmic phrase which distinguishes it from west and central European structures. At the same time, the typical initial accent has changed in many regions progressively into a paroxytonic one.

Unlike west European languages, the Polish language does not stress differences between accented and non-accented syllables, and is governed by a strong syllabism. A correspondence between the sequence of syllables and their time units is strictly preserved.

In the final result, the system has a more quantitative than qualitative character; and the rhythmic motifs are structurally fixed in the frame of the bars, starting on the strong beats and finishing on the weak. Most characteristic, however, is the tendency to divide the narration into equal time units while groups of language accents preserve a similar time quantity (Dłuska 1954). The last tendency goes together with the principle of not contrasting long and short syllables.

The dominant trend towards the falling rhythm is closely related to the principle of initial accent which determines the whole pattern of narration as well as the endings. The principle of preserving equal time units coincides with a tendency to isolate some fragments perceived sooner as independent sections (verses – stichos) than as parts of the construction. Finally, the relative negligence of verbal accent, so typical of Polish folk song, is also one of the basic factors making for the independence of the metrical, musical and verbal courses of narration which act independently.

The rhythmic phenomena determined by the features of the Polish language, and particularly by its spoken forms, underwent transformations through history. The latest of these resulted from the development of new behavioural patterns in more recent times which, according to some writers (Stęszewscy 1963), has to do with the development of modern dances. This transformation coincides with the characteristic shift of the initial accent (Bielawski 1985b) to the weak beat, with the creation of a characteristic syncope. The latter transformation of the fifteenth to seventeenth centuries has been generally considered the most typical feature of Polish rhythm, whereas the acceleration of tempo, which is evident in historical perspective, contributed to the evident annihilation of some specifics of these dance rhythms.

The most characteristic features of Polish national dances do not exclude the existence of other rhythmical phenomena typical both of versification and of musical sequences. Nor do they exclude regional varieties which are different in both agogic and rhythmical senses.

The characteristic features of Polish rhythm in the past related on the one hand to patterns of asyllabic verses, and on the other to the complicated rhythmic figures of particular dances. Asyllabic verses, though not numerous, are regarded as typical of the weak, irregularly pulsating poetry of mediaeval origin, and are often connected with the elements of musical 'free' rhythm so well described in Slavonic and especially Russian literature (Lvov 1858). Classical examples of asyllabic verses are not easily found in Polish folk music, being replaced today by phenomena in a transitional stage, and when they do appear it is in orations (see Example 72) or in wedding songs in Polish eastern territories.

A regional survey shows a great variety of rhythmic patterns often connected with some dances and their characteristic dotted rhythms (góralski dance); or, by contrast, they are

Da-na, mo-ja da-na,   nie pój-de za pa-na,

pój-de za   ta-kie-go,   ja - ko   i   ja   sa-ma.

Example 90   *Dana moja dana*, Bielawski 1970, no. 53, p. 128

found in slow monotonous sequences, probably typical of the walking and round dances that have recently disappeared (north-eastern Poland; see Example 90).

Differences in tempo are also regional in character and contribute to the articulation of specific features. This applies again to the slow tempo of the north-eastern regions (Kurpie) and to their additional rhythms or, by contrast, to the very fast tempo and some ambivalent rhythms of the Great Poland area.

An analysis of dance structures is an additional procedure by which one can interpret properly the nature of some rhythms, and especially of some forms of shifted accents, syncopes and dotted patterns, as well as different forms of their articulation. This analysis should not, however, be limited to an investigation of some motifs that are thought to be movement-based, but should extend to the whole rhythmic sequence, clearly differentiated and conceived in accordance with the general ideas of a dance.

The basic patterns and characteristics of Polish dances

The predominance of triple and duple metre in Polish folk music is an obvious fact, though other forms of complex, mixed, additional, ambivalent or oscillating rhythmic patterns are also well represented. One can find examples of four, six, five, eight or, exceptionally, seven beats (see Examples 53, 35, 51 and 90 respectively). Examples of four and six beats usually go with a complex metre, examples of five and eight with an additional rhythm, while those of seven are usually a result of specific forms of articulation. The very characteristic oscillating rhythms are connected mostly with the *tempo rubato* styles, while the ambivalent rhythms (see Example 26) of Great Poland are also the effect of a specific manner of performance and articulation. Finally, the examples of mixed metre should be described as totally different structures, mostly of foreign origin, and are usually connected with some dances of the Baroque period and their sequences. The last of the indicated metrical patterns must also be considered separately from the changeable metre typical of the structures in a process of stabilization.

No other factor can better articulate regional variations than rhythm, directly reflecting differences in temperament and style. This diversity is closely related to the character of the tempo, being additionally articulated by the genre and functional motivations. The wide range of rhythmic varieties to be found in Polish folk music expresses a flow of feelings and reactions to different sorts of situations. These may be spontaneous, and yet they are usually controlled by behavioural conventions. It has been well recorded in history that it was just the Polish rhythms and Polish dances that used to draw the attention of foreign observers fascinated by the music and movements of Polish dances. Their impressions and observations expressed themselves in a description of the Polish way of dancing 'nach Ahrt der Pohlen' (Neumark 1652). The strong domination of dances in triple rhythm in Polish folk music is the result of a major transformation which took place in Polish music in the Renaissance and Baroque periods. It led to the creation of many dances such as the walking dance (*Polski*, transformed later into the polonaise), mazurka, *kujawiak*, and *oberek* so well preserved in Polish folk music until recently. The articulation of the basic rhythmic figure usually called the mazurka rhythm ♪ ♪ ♩ ♩ is connected with the shift of accent to the weak beat and has been described by some writers as having been correlated with the crystallization of the paroxytonic accent in the Polish language. Depending on the character of the dance and on its tempo, this mazurka figure may be articulated variously. It may appear as a steadily repeated short motif of a whirl dance (*oberek*) in very fast tempo (MM. ♩=180-220); as an oscillating figure with capriciously shifted accents in a fairly vivid tempo (mazurka, MM. ♩=160-180); as a pattern with longer phrases and with a characteristic change of tempo in particular sections (*kujawiak*, MM. ♩.=120-140); and finally as the stately walking dance, full of dignity and fantasy, accompanied by various gestures of bowing (*polonaise*, MM. ♩=100-120).

A comprehensive study of Polish dances reveals their great variety. We can see a transition from walking dances to those running in pairs and following the leader (*krakowiak*, mazurka), and finally the whirl dances (*oberek*). Those transformations were connected with the articulation of visible metric and agogic contrasts as well as with other forms contrasting the character of the dance (sleeping and hunting in *kujawiak*) or showing different forms of transmission (sung and danced in wedding dances).

In trying to answer the basic question of the class origin of the main Polish dances and their rhythms, we must accept as a fact their cross-social functions. Yet at the same time it should also be said that the complex dance sequences, adopted probably from the upper classes, did not find a lasting response among the peasants. Indeed, the complex sequences were relatively short standing and have disappeared, while the simple forms, limited to the basic figures, still remain alive and popular (*oberek*).

Beside the most popular dances in triple metre, dances in duple rhythm should also be considered. This applies especially to the *krakowiak* and to its rhythm. The *krakowiak* sequence, so characteristic of dance movements of the Renaissance, concentrates also on the syncope which may be articulated as ♪ ♩ ♪ or ♪ ♩. , with the characteristic appearance of this figure at the end of the basic two bar phrase as ♫ ♫ | ♪ ♩. (Kolberg 1871: iii–vi). In spite of the long-standing rivalry between those two most popular dances, *krakowiak* and *oberek*, what is very important in both of them is the syncope and the performance in *tempo rubato*. It shows how much in common they have, despite their different metres. In trying to establish the folk identity of Polish national dances, notable characteristics are their shortness and simplicity, the vocal character of the patterns, and their being fashioned by the context and character of their performance style (*tempo rubato*).

Dances of an evidently national character and with well-recorded history are no longer very popular now, yet in some regions those with their characteristic rhythms continue to be well known. By contrast, the distinctly regional character has retained the dances of the Polish highlanders, and among them the so-called *góralski* and *zbójnicki* in particular. These regional dances still preserve their extended sequences of different movement patterns and are noted for their characteristic dotted notes, stressing the beat at the weak part of the bar:

♪ ♩ ♪ ♩ . This rhythmic figure is evidently different and much sharper than the Polish syncope ♪ ♩ ♩ , being clearly reminiscent of the rhythmical patterns of Poland's south Carpathian neighbours (Slovakian and Hungarian). The same can be said of the regional character of the *kolomyjka* dance, widespread in the south Carpathian area, which has strong affiliations to the music of the east Carpathian nations (Ruthenian groups and Roumanian). Of much more locally limited character is the *vivat* dance of Great Poland, showing no foreign affiliations. By contrast, the dances of the Kurpian area present a separate phenomenon, and are regarded as a relic of a completely different (Baltic) tradition that was prior to and original in the culture of that area.

The modern whirl dances, performed in pairs (*polka*, waltz, *szocz*, szot, écossaise; see Examples 76, 64 and 78 respectively) are clearly different from the dances with a regional or national background. The character of these dances consists in the monotonous sequence of repeated motifs, not variable and no longer sensitive to the basic contextual conditioning. This, however, does not concern the whirling *oberek* which, though danced in pairs, does remain open to movement variation (stamping, kneeling) and still keeps its improvisational character by exchanging inspiration between the music and dance ideas.

Despite historical changes, the Polish rhythm remains relatively stable and has kept the basic idea of downbeat, while shaping patterns as a succession from *thesis* to *ars*, i.e., in the opposite direction than is the case in west European music (from *ars* to *thesis*) (Bielawski 1970).

The significance of the performance context

The impact of performance style results from the feelings and expressions that the performers wish to convey, frequently by way of direct association.

The basic rhythmic patterns are often transformed during performance into quite new qualities. This is especially apparent in the examples of *tempo rubato* and triplets (see Example 91), as well as in the cases of the agogic 'undulation' which enriches the regular flow of the

Oj, si-wy koń, si - wy   koń   da,   pod-kó-weczke · zgu - biť,

oj, ja ma - jq-tek stra - ciť da, com pa - nien-ki. lu - biť

Example 91   Triplet, Kolberg 1857, no. 368

narration or dance phrases with all sorts of details such as *diminuendo* or *ritardando*. The rhythmic peculiarities of performance media may be compared to some traits of a spoken dialect, and their main function is to paraphrase the way of transmission. They can be compared to various repetitions of some syllables, as well as in the syllabization of consonants and in the swallowing of syllables, i.e., in various media modifying both the vocal timbre and the rhythmic course.

3.3.3 The principles of musical form

The independence of folk musical structure: does it really exist?

A glance at musical form shows that its independence is rather limited. The flow of musical narration is obviously determined by the functions music has to fulfil.

The characteristic shapes of form depend mainly on the kind of repertoire, on its genre and historic characteristics. It has also been established that foreign influences and adoptions are more apparent in the projection of form than in other musical characteristics. This applies especially to the repertoire of urban or noble origin in which the autonomy of musical form is relatively high. Musical independence obviously becomes greater in modern material and in genres not directly determined by poetic or dance structure (ballad, lyric poems). The autonomy of form depends on its maturity and has to do especially with conscious manipulation of musical contrast and its quality of opposition to repetition. The maturity of form is also connected with the equalization of time units. In brief, an independent musical structure is complex in its make-up and is no longer regarded as a sequence of juxtaposed sections, repeated faithfully or with small variations.

By contrast, the traditional stichic structures consist of single phrases connected to single verses, and the margin of their independence does not go beyond the addition of vocatives, interjections or interruptions, i.e., being an intervention of performance styles which penetrate the main course of musical narration. The structures of distichic form and many dance songs and ditties are a transitional phenomenon dominated by a poetic or dance structure in which, however, the idea of parallelism connects single elements (musical counterparts of the verses) into elementary wholes.

The structural differences between traditional and modern forms reflect differences in thinking and associations typical of the mentality of people belonging to different historical periods and ethnic strata. They may also be influenced by various types of functional determination and present different degrees of internal autonomy. The most archaic forms are evidently conditioned by concrete functions and symbols, while the modern ones show no obvious contextual determination.

In the eighteenth century, the musical forms of Polish folk music achieved relative independence, but lost at the same time their openness and sensitivity to the creative impact of the performance context. As a result, the musical form became standardized.

The basic types of musical form

Musical form has been traditionally linked to the structure of versification (see above, pp. 137–44), and both vocal and instrumental music have been interpreted as derivatives of the vocal repertoire. This approach is especially popular with students of east European music and has been adopted by Filaret Kolessa (1906) and Béla Bartók (1925), though as an analytical proposition it has not been accepted by west and central European ethnomusicology and its representatives, who tend to analyse form in purely musical terms (Mersmann, 1922/1924). As already mentioned, the east European approach stresses the dependence of the musical structure on verse patterns, but at the same time it neglects the dance structures with which musical thought is concerned.

The relatively conservative forms in a process of stabilization appear in several types and show the prevalence of either poetic or musical factors. As has been said, that internal dependence can be seen in the repetitions and in the ways they are applied (Czekanowska 1961). It is, for instance, obvious that in structures dominated by poetry (orations), repetitions are governed by the demands of the verbal text, and musical motifs are repeated according to the demands of poetic structure (see Example 72). By contrast, in the forms dominated by music, the situation is reversed and any additions of words and syllables are subordinated to the requirements of musical ideas.

Totally different structures, including signals or calls, arise from the requirements of particular situations and the tasks that songs have to fulfil. It can be seen in the very character of the basic intervals displaying signal qualities (fifth, octave; see Examples 92 and 93) and in

Mio - tły, mio - tły...

Example 92   *Miotły miotły*, Bielawski 1973b, no. 1, p. 62

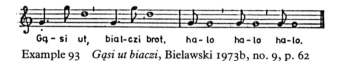

Gą - si ut,   biał-czi brot,   ha - lo   ha - lo   ha - lo.

Example 93   *Gąsi ut biaczi*, Bielawski 1973b, no. 9, p. 62

the shape of short rising or falling motives which are regularly repeated. This functionally determined material is quite varied. The signals are distinct according to their context of performance, i.e., to their accoustic conditioning and their cultural background. The calls, and especially the dialogue forms, are as a rule characterized by longer phrases and a different way of articulation. Elements of direct illustration and even of onomatopoeia are also to be found among these forms.

The structures of children's songs and games are limited to the repetition of phrases performed usually in the duple rhythm (see Example 35; Bielawski 1973b). The same can be said of the form of ditties, and especially those ditties of the mountain area that are developing against a repeated phrase of four bars (see Example 75). By contrast, the ditties of central Polish areas include periods of eight bars bound by the corresponding relations of cadences or by the elements of contrast displayed by the opposing melodic lines, falling and rising (see Example 37 and above, p. 81). Very much the same concerns the construction of the distichic forms, which are additionally enriched by the repetition of the sections of verse 4+(:3:) or just of the whole verse (:7)+7 = aa'b (see Examples 6 and 61). The transitional phenomena deserve special study, whilst investigations of this type might contribute to a better explanation of the different factors which, acting jointly, determine the structural properties. It is, for instance, quite obvious that the apparent asymmetry of form with a repeated verse (aa'b) is at the same time balanced by the equalization of the time units. It results in the prolongation of the last phrase (b), which balances the fast repeated two former phrases: (aa' takes eight seconds while b takes seven seconds). In this one can see a typical feature of the Polish mediaeval structure, with its trend towards the equalization of time units.

The relatively independent forms of modern songs are clearly based on the principle of contrast. It appears in the rhythm and metre as well as in the tempo of the reprise structures. The degree of contrast in the reprise and refrain forms may, however, be quite different. The strongest contrasts appear in the forms with a characteristic mixed metre (the so-called 'Zwietache' typical of central European dances (Hoerburger 1956). A combination of these two principles, i.e., of the addition of refrain and of reprise, can be seen in the classical customary songs with a characteristic stanza of five verses (aa'bba'; see Example 27). In this form, the different (b) refrain is crowned by the repetition of the second phrase (a'), which plays the rôle of the final formula. By contrast, the typical forms with an internal refrain (aaba) are not endowed with specific features, while the refrain section is more evident in the verbal (often nonsense syllables) than in the musical sense, and plays the rôle of an extended interjection. The forms with a surrounding refrain are not connected with a specific stanza. They are typical of recitation in which the last section of a verse refers to the initial section of the next verse, thus creating a sort of chain construction, binding and 'adding' the separate musical sections. So it is a basically stichic form.

Polish folk instrumental music is more developed, spacious and extended than the vocal, although it has been created against the same background of the vocal model. The extension of its form is achieved through bigger phrases (four bars instead of two or three bars), and through a lavish use of repetitions.

The instrumental short and 'open' forms can be found only in signal pieces, performed on primitive horns (see Example 83), and so have not developed into clear structures. Also popular are short and changeable melodies in instrumental pieces based on vocal patterns.

The instrumental forms, despite their regional variety, have many features in common. This applies above all to their segmentation into phrases and motifs, which appears more clearly in the instrumental than the vocal repertoire. The same must be said of the articulation of their structure, which consists of repetitions and contrasts.

The greatest musical 'autonomy' can be seen in the initial, final or 'interluding' formulae in the music for several instruments, especially in that for violin (see Example 94), flute and bagpipe (see Example 95). These formulae reveal the piece's tonal organization and the

Example 94   Formulae for violin, E. Dahlig 1982, p. 92

Example 95   Formulae for bagpipe, Sobiescy 1973, no. 34, p. 216

specific turns characteristic of particular instruments. They also reveal the features of a multipart structure (drone, ostinato) and some acoustic phenomena (overblow) which may be achieved on certain instruments (see Example 25). In such pieces one can find the individual contribution of performers as well as some conventional stereotypes typical of this sort of repertoire, for example melodies dedicated to special occasions. They assume an elaborate form in those regions (central Poland) where the wedding ceremony has still a major social function, and where such episodes as the entrance of the wedding's main actors is accompanied by specific marches.

Regional differences result from the character of particular areas, with their power of inspiration and invention. A special case in this respect is the instrumental music of Polish Tatra highlanders, a music with long sequences of corresponding phrases shaped with striking fantasy and flexibility (see Example 42), articulated by both the melodies and their harmonic accompaniment. The music of the Great Poland area, usually played by a bagpipe ensemble, is also open to some invention, although basically it sticks to a single tune which may be articulated in different ways. In both those cases (in the music of the Tatra Mountains and of Great Poland) there is a continuity of ancient regional styles which have withstood drastic changes. The instrumental music of central Poland, apart from its introductory marches and formulae, is basically given to repetition which in some cases assumes something like an obsessional character. This does not mean, however, that this music has not developed its own ideas expressed, for instance, in rich embellishments (see Example 96). Polish

Example 96   Melodic adornment, Chorosiński 1949, no. 16, p. 45

contemporary instrumental music of central and southern Poland has been strongly influenced by modern band music. In some of these areas players clearly differentiate between traditional and 'imported' repertoires, and this may even be confirmed by the consciously applied terminology, as in the Kieleckie region, where different musical forms of *oberek* have been given special names, such as *śpiewany* (vocal) – typical for traditional versions – and *techniczny* (technical) for more elaborated versions (E. Dahlig 1982). Characteristic names have also been given to two basic phrases of the *oberek*, i.e., *kolano* (knee) and *powtór* (repetition) (E. Dahlig 1982). Analysis of the musical content shows that this second phrase is not limited to repetition, and is often based on an answer or complement of the main 'knee' (p. 181).

A general look at instrumental forms reveals many features which make it possible to present them in chronological order. Polish folk instrumental music, apart from some instances of instrumental signals, seems to have developed between the sixteenth and nineteenth centuries. This instrumental repertoire performed by bands made up of a bagpipe and violin and later of violin and basses (Noll 1986) is considered the most significant for the articulation of the Polish folk style.

4 Towards a concept of Polish folk music: Polish and non-Polish music in Poland

4.1 The function of folk culture in contemporary Poland: ethnic and national identity

In order to identify the idiom of Polish folk music, we must find the integrational power unifying the diversity of cultural impacts. It is not so much a matter of pointing to Polish characteristics as of discovering the underlying motivations that lead people to recognize some phenomena as being 'ours' or at least of the same legacy.

The coexistence of different cultural and ethnic groups is limited in present-day Poland to some border areas and enclaves, while non-Polish inhabitants make up no more than 3.5 per cent of the population. This national homogeneity has created a situation that is totally different from that of historical Poland, which used to be a commonwealth of nations and traditions. In contemporary Poland one can find only traces of the previous ethnic, national, religious, social and cultural diversity, which led both to conflicts and to a cultural fertility stimulated by previously different and often contradictory trends.

From a historical point of view, there is a basic dilemma about the identity of Polish culture in the eastern territories. That culture, though transmitted in the Polish language, is closer to the cultures of the eastern neighbours (Ukrainians, Byelorussians) and has evolved against the same background of the 'Old' Slavonic legacy. Though it was deeply transformed in the later periods under the impact of a definitely Polish culture, it does preserve some traces of the previous background. A parallel situation also affects the culture in many western provinces (Pomerania, Silesia) since it is based on the west Slavonic and 'Old' Polish legacy but was transformed by the influences of west and central European cultures. And so it is the culture of the central areas with a homogeneous west Slavonic and Polish background, reinterpreted by the creative power of the 'Old' Polish culture flourishing in this territory for many centuries, that has preserved the most integrated and representative tradition of Polish folk music.

The results of long historical processes spreading cultural phenomena from strong radiating centres to their peripheries and the effects of particular political programmes typical of shorter periods often overlap. Nevertheless, short-term trends, typical of modern times, often have the power of rearticulating deeply rooted habits, as well as of re-establishing the forgotten past, finding in them new possibilities of restoration and identity. This goes both for peoples living in a historical territory and for those in immigrant enclaves, although the sense of identity can now be felt differently than it used to be in the past. Indeed, the awareness of a common history and the possession of the same legacy is often used by various national and nationalistic programmes as an effective instrument of identity and integration.

Strong feelings of ethnic identity are found mainly among the highlanders of the Podhale (Tatra) area. This is due to the fact that this particular group has until recently preserved the awareness of their cultural separateness from their neighbours, although their national (Polish) identification is also a fact. Cultural separateness can be sooner observed among other ethnic groups in Poland in a national rather than in an ethnic sense. This applies especially to the east Slavonic or Lithuanian inhabitants of Poland, whereas religious identity in their case plays a secondary though still significant rôle.

Except for the Podhale highlanders, and to some extent some people of Silesia, ethnicity in Polish society does not play a decisive rôle, and the tendency towards the preservation of the traditional legacy either has a more instinctive character and is understood as an imperative to preserve the legacy of former generations, or, on the contrary, is consciously cultivated and concentrates on the elaboration of ideas of national culture and style which is rather a recent phenomenon stimulated by intellectuals. By contrast, in the non-Polish societies the legacy is instinctively felt and consciously recognized, whereas their ethnonational significance is often an instrument of direct manipulation. The power of ethnic impact is much stronger in these cases and more deeply rooted in the 'old' magical and belief systems; this is most evident among the east Slavonic and Lithuanian groups.

Despite some differences, most significant for all the groups under discussion seems to be the possibility of transforming these values of traditional culture into qualities that may be needed and demanded by contemporary people. In the Polish case, however, the traditional legacy is more transformed and includes many elements of cross-social character, while the contribution of other social strata and even of other nations has also been historically quite significant. As is well known, Polish culture has never been isolationist in its character, whereas the cultures of Poland's neighbours to the east (Ukrainian, Byelorussian, Russian and Lithuanian) have been more concerned with their ethnic legacy and its uniqueness.

4.2 The musical culture of non-Polish groups in modern Poland

Non-Polish communities reside for the most part in Poland's border territories. They are to be found in the south-eastern (Ukrainians), eastern (Byelorussians), north-eastern (Lithuanians) and south-western (Germans) border areas (Pudło 1984–5). Apart from these communities, there are also small enclaves of the Russian Old Believers in north-eastern regions of Poland, and gypsies dispersed all over the country, but rather in southern than northern Poland and especially in the Carpathian and Sub-Carpathian areas.

Migrational movements after World War II contributed seriously to the dislocation of many national groups, especially Jews fleeing the Nazis, the German population resettled in Germany, Polish people of the eastern territories resettled in the west after the incorporation of their homeland into the Soviet Union, and Ukrainians resettled forcibly as a consequence of the dramatic conflicts inspired by German policy.

The Ukrainians form the largest and most homogeneous non-Polish group (some 300,000) confessing the Greek Catholic or the Orthodox Rite (Pudło, 1987: 7). The Byelorussian group (some 280,000) is divided more evidently in respect of their religion into Greek Catholics and Orthodox. In many cases, however, the borderline between these two religious and national groups is fluid, especially in the Podlasie area. A small but distinctly different group are the Polish Lithuanians (10,000) with strong national feelings. By contrast, the groups identifying themselves as being German do not possess an ethnic identity (Pudło 1984–5) owing to the fact that their culture and awareness are of national and not of ethnic character. All of these non-Polish traditions have an evident musical character.

The gypsy tradition is limited to musical instrumental forms and was never so well developed as in Hungary, Romania, Russia, Ukraine and Czechoslovakia (Kovalcsik 1985, 1987). It is still practised by some street ensembles playing in big cities. As mentioned, this music contributed to the popularity of the dulcimer (see p. 173) and played a part in the articulation of some tonal phenomena. It also popularized some more advanced techniques of playing together (*sekund* technique) and stimulated the use of more complicated rhythmic patterns performed on drums.

A totally different problem is the musical culture of the Jews, recorded historically but at the present time almost non-existent. The old Jewish tradition is thoroughly documented, and although mainly of urban character it had developed some peculiarities of performance style that can be detected even in the folk tradition. These related especially to dulcimer playing and to some kinds of violin music. In 1988, there are about 2,000 Orthodox Jews concentrated around some active synagogues and practising Jewish religious music. This number is evidently increasing.

The folk music of Poland's Ukrainian inhabitants has not been investigated in our time, though it was studied quite comprehensively by Ukrainian scholars of the first half of the twentieth century, in the then multinational Poland. Ukrainian music, though identified today more in a national (Kwilecki 1961) than in an ethnic sense, along with the prevailing national literature and history, has very strong ethnic roots which are still instinctively felt. Ukrainian folk culture in Poland is differentiated ethnically (Łemki, Bojki, Volhynian and Galician Ruthenians, Sub-Carpathian Ruthenians), but it can boast a rich and quite homogeneous folk repertoire. It includes wedding, Christmas (*koljadki*, *ščedriwki*), solstice and hay-gathering songs, as well as many lyrics and ditties, connected with dance (*kołomyjka*). This very popular repertoire also includes songs of non-folk origin intended usually for multipart performance. Among them are lyrics with patriotic and didactic content which play a significant rôle of national identification. They often recall the heroes of the distant steppes (Kozaks), symbolizing the idea of freedom in the recent past. There is also talk in this popular repertoire of the need for education.

By contrast, the Byelorussian minority presents not only a different repertoire but also different interests and predispositions in its national programme. This seems to be motivated by the different political situation of this national group, which is not dispersed over the whole country but concentrated in a single territory and co-operating more closely with its neighbours in the Soviet Byelorussian Republic. Members of this group, and especially the Greek Orthodox, are deeply engaged in religious musical activity, organizing several festivals and competitions dedicated to the Orthodox religious repertoire (at Hajnówka). Folk music and dance are also quite popular with them and contribute to the restoration of a forgotten tradition. Nevertheless, the number of traditional tunes sung by the Polish Byelorussians is rather limited. The famous Byelorussian harvest songs, for instance, described so extensively in the literature, as well as their performances in the heterophonic style, are unknown to inhabitants in the Polish territory. The present Polish Byelorussian repertoire consists of modern dances and lyrical songs which are usually a mixture of the Polish, Byelorussian and Ukrainian traditions.

Both these east Slavonic nations should be regarded as the main successors and inheritors of the 'Old' Slavonic culture, that of historical Volhynia and Galicia in particular. A comparison between Byelorussian, Ukrainian and eastern Polish cultures reveals some evident similarities, although the languages and the ways of performance remain different. History, and the fact of belonging to different religions in particular, reshaped this traditional culture with a common background in different ways. And yet vestiges of the ancient roots as well as evidence of subsequent contacts, can still be seen in the culture of that transitional territory. The common background is especially apparent in the customs and rituals, mostly in those connected with agriculture and family life. Traces of the 'old' ritual of the *korovai* can be found in all these cultures (see Examples 97 and 61). Participation in various historical

Example 97   *Radujsia matinoňko*, Rozdolskij and Ljudkevyč 1906, no. 3

processes, contacts, and the pressure of different cultural influences contributed on the one hand to the creation of separate features, and on the other to the blurring of border lines.

To the east Slavonic culture belong also the Russian Old Believers who have been dispersed in the Polish north-eastern and northern territories. The representatives of this group are descendants of the émigrés who left Russia following the religious persecutions they suffered in the seventeenth and eighteenth centuries. Among the countries which accepted them were Poland and Germany, as well as the lands which are now again within the Polish State, particularly Mazuria. In accordance with their strong religious prohibitions, the Old Believers are not supposed to have families and children and are expected to concentrate on their religious rites within the framework of their religious group, i.e., being independent of other hierarchies and church structures. For that reason their liturgical music remains totally secret and not accessible to 'others' who are not members of that religious sect. In practice, however, the contemporary Old Believers are more liberal and cultivate family and secular life. Nevertheless, their family customs have not developed a respective repertoire so far. The same must be said of musical instruments, which are hardly available with the Old Believers. The historical isolation from the home has not entailed in their case a lack of contacts and cultural exchanges. Contemporary Russian songs, and especially lyrical songs and ditties, are quite popular today in the Polish Old Believers' community.

The Lithuanian minority in Poland are a special case, as their ethnic separateness is determined by a clear national awareness. Indeed, the Lithuanian group living in eleven villages and centred around three parishes (Puńsk, Szypiliszki and Sejny) is integrated by a common national programme. This makes for a coherence which was achieved against an alien ethnic background when their ancestors migrated in the sixteenth to eighteenth centuries from different parts of Lithuania. Nevertheless, they are divided internally into two basic groups known as *Djuki* and *Aukstota*, with different folk repertoires. At the same time their integration is achieved by a selection of songs accepted by the whole community and commonly recognized as being 'purely' Lithuanian. This repertoire consists of rather recent lyrical and patriotic songs, although the most popular ones, the *sutartinas*, are regarded as the most 'archaic' and connected with a cult of the sun. Like many other songs, *sutartinas* are designed for multipart performance and appear in both vocal and instrumental versions. Having achieved a privileged position in the Lithuanian programme, these particular songs now help to integrate large groups of performers (singers or flautists). The performance itself consists of each person playing or singing isolated or short motifs in the fashion of a canon, a hocket or other simple polyphonic styles. This way of playing has met with great international success, and although not restricted to a folk repertoire it has its roots in a folk tradition.

Elements of the *Djuki* culture are more evident in language than in music, although comparative studies of the repertoire of customs confirm a cultural presence of this stratum as well. The creation of the Lithuanian national programme is due to the efforts of some individuals and also the effect of close co-operation with the society of friends of the Lithuanian Republic (see Figure 35). Their neighbours often visit Poland to give concerts and exhibit traditional musical instruments completely unknown to Polish inhabitants. The activities of cultural Lithuanian institutions in Poland, and especially of music ensembles (there are eleven of them), already have a long tradition and concentrate on the reconstruction of Lithuanian history, ancient habits and customs. Cultivation of the *sutartinas* tradition and their professional forms have been sustained by international exchanges and numerous concerts given in major concert halls. These may be regarded as the most striking expression of Polish Lithuanians' cultural activities (see Examples 98a and 98b).

So far, however, their exchanges and mutual relations with Polish folk culture are rather poor. This may be attributed to the difference of the language and to their performances being more institutionalized and concentrating on group and collective forms, and to the multipart texture of these songs. It may be assumed, however, that historically, cultural contacts between Polish and Lithuanian societies used to be much stronger. There are many vestiges of similar background on the one hand, and records of mutual influences on the other. The former relate particularly to the common elements of Polish, Byelorussian and *Djuki* (see Example 99) folk culture, whereas the latter are evident in the exchanges of the repertoire of songs. Indeed, there are many indications that Polish and Lithuanian national programmes were much closer to each other in the past than they are today (see Examples 21 and 100–2).

The cultural activity of Polish Lithuanians, concentrating on history and folklore, has been influenced by the cultural policy of the Lithuanian Republic (see Figure 35). It has contributed to the unification of their diverse ethnic background.

The small national minorities living in contemporary Poland and their musical cultures show common trends both in articulating their own identity and in coexisting and interacting with other groups. The forms and ways in which these activities are carried out are again quite different. More detailed studies could explain the similarities and differences, since they may be motivated historically, socially or psychologically. The specific conditions of life in Poland – that is, the concentration or dispersion of a given group, its connection with one or more religions, and finally friendly or hostile relations with neighbouring groups – can modify the character of a culture as well as influence the prospects for its development in the future.

Figure 35   Ensemble of Lithuanians visiting Poland

4.3   Polish folk music in the resettled areas and abroad

To deal with culture in the resettled areas one has to approach this problem in a broad sense. Leaving aside Polish external migrations, let us turn first to the geographical areas incorporated into Poland after World War II. They are Poland's historical territories, which had undergone a thorough Germanicization in the course of centuries. They are inhabited to some extent by the autochthonous population, representatives of the historical Silesians, Mazurians, Warmians and others, while the majority of the population are newcomers resettled from the Polish eastern territories incorporated into the Soviet Union, and by other groups of Polish people from different areas coming there to improve their living standards. Other nationalities living in these territories include above all the Ukrainians, Germans and some quotas of Greeks and Yugoslavians and others. This national complexity has created a conglomeration of very different standards of civilization and of various social habits. Consequently, the culture that has developed in these territories owes its diversity not so much to its background as to recent circumstances.

Every region of these territories is culturally unlike the others, being inhabited by different

Example 98a   *Sutartine*, Slaviunas 1972, p. 13

Example 98b   *Sutartine*, Slaviunas 1972, p. 12

Example 99   *Vaikštinejo*, Cetkanškaite 1949, no. 8

Example 100   *Motule mano*, Cetkanškaite 1949, no. 67

Example 101   *Znaj matulu znaj*, J. Stęszewski 1955a, p. 44

people and often governed by different rules. The most integrated is the area of Opolskie (Opole Silesia), where the percentage of the original inhabitants is still relatively high. Warmia and Mazuria, having preserved by now very few autochthonous inhabitants, are in a different situation, while their marked diversity does not exclude a tendency for continuity. This may be explained by the fact that the newcomers arrived here from not very distant, and often even neighbouring, territories. By contrast, the situation in Western Pomerania is very

Example 102   *Anan šoni ažero*, Cetkanškaite 1949, no. 64

different, as the population there consists almost exclusively of newcomers from very distant territories. In each of these regions the local culture has a separate character, in which tendencies towards integration and absorption of different streams, and isolationist trends, coexist to a greater or smaller degree. The latter depend on local circumstances and on general policy which changes with cyclical regularity. The character of many political programmes is often determined by ideas elaborated outside a province and may appeal to the Polish as well as to the non-Polish heritage, articulating the Polish or non-Polish character of a local culture. This applies, for instance, to the policy of the Roman Catholic Church, stressing the definitely Polish character of Silesia; this applies also to some Polish emigration programmes, exaggerating even some historical aspects of this culture. But it applies even more emphatically to non-Polish programmes stressing the German legacy or expressing nationalistic aspirations of other nations, especially of the Ukrainian groups. Polish official programmes tend usually towards the unification and integration of different strata, but the changeability of politics creates this cyclicity, so that at some times they support the re-establishment of regionally or locally articulated traditions. This supports the feelings of identity which express themselves in the repertoire and in stylistic attitudes. Trends towards the restoration and articulation of ethnonational sympathies are usually connected with institutional decisions to support and stabilize those tendencies. The variety of political decisions results in a diversity of forms, programmes and institutions. This is particularly apparent in the diversity of ensembles that are formed. They differ from each other according to whether they are nationally mixed or are purely national groups (Ukrainian, Lithuanian).

Polish folk or quasi-folk institutions and ensembles abroad are also a separate case. However diverse their standards and background, it must be said once more that the most authentic and pure ethnic character is possessed only by the ensembles of the Polish Podhale highlanders. They come together and co-operate abroad as they usually do in Poland after emigrating to cities and industrial centres. Other emigrant groups do not show this degree of spontaneity. Nevertheless, such natural responses also appear among other emigrant groups who are trying to preserve the legacy of their parents and grandparents. In their case the repertoire is made up of remembered dances (*polka*), songs and customs which produce a medley hardly representative of the tradition they wish to transmit. Despite its obvious limitations, this form of transmission is an attempt at direct cultural continuity and is therefore more appreciated and highly regarded than the activities of many institutional ensembles.

The ensembles with socio-political or commercial aims have developed completely different forms and institutions. The character of their productions depends on prior motivation, and they tend in their performances either to demonstrate the most popular and easily perceived repertoire or, on the contrary, to revert to the quasi-'rustic' or 'exotic' elements. A concentration on technical accomplishments and acrobatic skills is usually the most characteristic feature of these entertainments. It should be stressed also that the institutionalized ensembles are usually in regular touch with the home country and import from it costumes and instruments, or co-operate with its instructors. There is always the possibility of participating in Polish local competitions and festivals. Indeed, it is quite exceptional for a group to give up direct contacts in selecting a programme. When this does happen, it is with ambitious ensembles usually founded by intellectuals. Their repertoire is dominated as a rule by elaborate ideas of national stylization, often reminiscent of ideas current in the 1930s (see above, p. 61).

Ensembles that have no direct links with the surrounding community, or disregard the character of that community, are of less significance than those that maintain direct and natural continuity. It has been shown that natural continuity protects their social perceptions much better, even though the artistic results may be rather poor.

Thus, the basic factors motivating the preservation of the folk legacy may be found: – in the instinctively felt needs and demands for an authentic folk tradition characteristic especially of communities with strong feelings of identity and a well-preserved folk art; – in the urge for creativity, expressed in the need for continuity of tradition; – in the necessity for creating national programmes in which folkloristic elements may be reinterpreted.

These three kinds of national motivation are differently distributed among Polish communities abroad according to the regional character of their culture, as well as the social structure, living standards and circumstances of each particular group. When one looks at them in historical perspective one cannot fail to notice changeability of these processes in which some fashions rise and fall, including even a lack of interest in folklore at all.

Examining these very numerous and different Polish groups, one comes to the conclusion that their activities are rather limited, unlike those of many non-Polish émigré societies (Ukrainians, Lithuanians), both in Poland and in other countries. It seems to have to do with a different function of folklore in Polish society and with its entertainment character. The substrata of 'old' customs and beliefs which are still present, demanded and being revived in east Slavonic and Lithuanian societies no longer play any active rôle in Polish society, having been shifted to the margin of social awareness. The function of folklore in Polish circumstances is linked to the habit of dancing and so has much in common with various forms of social behaviour. The patterns of melodic and rhythmical phrases, as well as the changeability of moods rooted in tonal ideas and their sequences, clearly articulate the ways Polish people feel, think, and behave. The reinterpretations of these folk patterns, which have been taking place during the last two centuries under the impact of the romantic and post-romantic programmes, increased the significance of folk art across the whole society and created a background for this kind of tradition. At the same time, however, the national programmes contributed to the transformation of the folk tradition and often changed the hierarchy of its values. The substantial values, however, remain relatively stable.

A comparison of the Polish situation with that of other countries and of Poland's neighbours to the east in particular, reveals at once the limited interest of Polish society in folk music, whereas the natural links with the authentic background are still preserved. Polish interest in the 'earliest' strata is limited, though they are still cultivated by the eastern Slavs. Only folk dance music and songs remain fairly popular in Polish society, especially in the central areas and in the Sub-Carpathian regions, as well as among many Polish communities abroad. Appealing to all social strata and not without some elements of other nations' music, it is also appreciated internationally. This repertoire owes its vitality and capacity of transformation to the fact that it is constantly examined, verified and influenced by social demands, control and appreciation. This is also the reason why the distinctive music of the Podhale area, which has so strongly and successfully inspired the creators of the national or folkloristic style (Karol Szymanowski), seems to lack this socially wide and international appeal. So the Podhale music, for all its power of ethnic identity, cannot compare in social perception with the music of Polish dances and with the latter's function in creating a background of national identification.

Finally it must be said that, within the framework of big states and conurbations with all their annihilating processes, people often organize their activities around local and regional centres, trying through them to articulate their own identity and cultural uniqueness. They do it both in their home country and while living abroad as emigrants. International contacts and people's mobility are often counterbalanced by these trends and by the concentration on small areas, while the motivations behind such activities are of ethnic or regional character. The rôle of folk music in them, although rather problematic, not unlike other phenomena of contemporary culture, seems to be motivated basically by psychological, and even by therapeutic, factors. This kind of demand is especially strong among those living as émigrés inside their own country as inhabitants of big cities and as factory workers in particular. In their case the preservation of the folk tradition usually acts as an instrument of relaxation and helps in adaptation to conditions. Preservation of the folk repertoire, and of its music in particular, is a substitute for the authentic environment of people's former lives. The simple form and directness of the musical message seem to be well suited for the kind of therapy that people need, especially those who live in big conurbations.

Polish folk music has been considered in this study in the full variety of its forms, variants and regional characteristics. It has been examined as it is at home and as it is cultivated abroad, stressing the homogeneity of its background and its integrational power. Also significant are the influences and creative impact of other cultures on it. It has been undergoing various processes of selection, so that it has retained from the past only those elements that are currently demanded by people. From the historical point of view, three strata of the folk music legacy seem to be significant.

There are the remnants of 'old' Slavonic culture that are still found in the most traditional repertoires of certain areas, which though limited to relics, contributed to the articulation of basic psychological attitudes perceived instinctively as Slavonic.

The second, and most significant, stratum is that of the culture of what was once the Polish Commonwealth, with its behaviourally articulated patterns, especially the rhythms of speech and dance.

Finally, the third stratum consists of the trends of the romantic nineteenth- and twentieth-century programmes, reinterpreting folkloristic elements in new forms and transmitting those elements with a new energy.

At the same time, it is impossible to neglect the recent phenomena of selection and filtration from the resources of the traditional legacy in response to the demands of contemporary societies and of groups of people living in totally new conditions.

The presence and significance of all these strata are quite evident in the preserved folk culture. From the musicological point of view it is possible not only to indicate the characteristics of particular strata, but also to point to the historical aspects of some musical features and to their significance for historical interpretation. The structural properties of the 'old' Slavonic culture are, for instance, most apparent in the basic tonal concepts, as well as in the main principles of spoken rhythm, and in expressive qualities. These properties may be compared with the ideas and symbols conditioning the thinking and associations of people of that time. The culture of the Polish Commonwealth is still best articulated by behavioural patterns, and specifically by dance rhythms, while the influence of modern culture and its transformations go together with the growing autonomy of musical forms and with less concern for the accompanying context.

The transformational trends are also accompanied by different processes of revival, retransmission or reinterpretation of traditional culture, although they are quite distant from the original folk music that, reinterpreted, still preserves its function and appeal in society. Indeed, this re-examined folk music is addressed to basic social attitudes which seem to have functioned in Poland in both the past and the present.

A comparison of Polish folk culture with its counterparts in other countries, and with the culture of Poland's neighbours in particular, reveals fundamental differences not only in the morphological and stylistic features but in the different social functions and motivations of particular societies. These differences are related not so much to diversity of historical backgrounds as to differences of political situation and social structures. This applies to the deeply transformed cultures of Poland's western neighbours and to the more traditional cultural phenomena rooted in ethnicity, of Poland's neighbours to the east. It also applies to the more stratified social systems of the western nations and the more egalitarian societies of the east.

The object of this study has been an examination of Polish folk music in all its diversity, its aspects, functions and intrinsic values. The subject still remains quite open, however, with many unanswered questions. These have little to do with a scholar's approach but are due to the variable nature of Polish folk music. And yet it may be assumed that by means of a thorough selection, based on historical and social facts, it is possible to identify relatively stable and confirmed features which can be regarded as truly representative of Polish folk music.

Discography

Grajcie dudy, grajcie basy I
Folk Music from Mazowsze, Kurpie, Ziemia Mazurska i Warmińska, Ziemia Lubuska i Wielko-
polska, Kaszuby
Muza SX 1125 ed. J. Sobieska

Grajcie dudy, grajcie basy II
Folk Music from Opoczyńskie, Śląsk Opolski, Beskid Śląski, Podhale, Biłgorajskie, Rzeszowskie,
Sądeckie
Muza SX 1126 ed. J. Sobieska

Polska Muzyka Ludowa dla Dzieci (Polish Folk Music for Children)
Folk Music from Lubelskie, Podlasie, Kieleckie, Kaliskie, Kujawy, Wielkopolska, Podhale, Śląsk
Cieszyński, Krakowskie, Orawa, Kurpie, Kaszuby
Muza SX 1770 ed. P. Dahlig

Polski Folklor Muzyczny
Folk Music from Rzeszowskie, Piątkowa, Sowa-Family-Ensemble: polonezy, polki, krakowiaki,
wolne, do oczepin, chodzone, sztajerki, walczyki
Muza SX 2348–2349 ed. J. Sobieska

Polski Folklor Muzyczny
Music Ensembles from Rzeszowskie Region: Bachórze, Piątkowa, Trzciana, Wysoka Strzy-
żowska, Siedleczka, Krosno, Bobowa, Roztoki
Muza X 0876 ed. A. Szałaśna

Podhale śpiewa (Podhale sings)
Ensemble from Zakopané, Maśniaki, Kościelisko, Podhale from Biały Dunajec
Muza XL 0337

Polska Muzyka Ludowa
Maśniaki Ensemble from Zakopane, 'Bacówka'
Muza SX 1716–1717

Polski Folklor Muzyczny
Kurpianka Ensemble
Wedding, Chants a. Dances
Muza SXL 0683 ed. J. Stęszewski

Polski Folklor Muzyczny
Lachy Ensemble from Sądeckie Region
Muza SX 1032 ed. A. Szurmiak-Bogucka

Podhale 1
Wierchowe, ozwodne, krzesane, drobne, zielone, pytackie, weselne, wychodne, polki i marsze
Veriton s x v-728

Podhale 2
Sabałowe, wierchowe, ozwodne, krzesane, drobne, baciarskie, zielone, pytackie
Veriton s x v-729

Podhale 3
Sabałowe, wierchowe, ozwodne, krzesane, zielone, drobne, pytackie, słowacka, do zbójnickiego
Conductor Tadeusz Sztromayer
Veriton s x v-730

Bibliography

Agricola, M. 1545 *Musica Instrumentalis Deudsch*. 4th edition, Wittemberg
(Vladikina)-Bačinskaja, N. 1969 'Muzykalnyj stil russkich khorowodnych pesen'. Unpublished PhD thesis, Moscow
Badecki, K. 1936 *Literatura mieszczańska w Polsce, pieśni, tańce, padwany*. Lvov
Banach, J. 1962 *Tematy muzyczne w plastyce polskiej (Grafika, Rysunek)*. Cracow
Bartkowski, X. B. 1987 *Polskie śpiewy religijne w żywej tradycji: style i formy*. Cracow
Bartmiński, J. 1979 *Język folkloru*. Wrocław
    1985 'Dwie wersje tekstu pieśni ludowej: meliczna i recytacyjna'. Lublin, typescript
Bartók, B. 1925 *Das Ungarische Volkslied*. Berlin. English translation, Cambridge 1931
Bartók, B. and A. Lord 1951 *Serbo-Croatian Folk Songs*. New York
Baudouin de Courtenay-Ehrenkreutzowa, C. 1927 'Obrzędy weselne ludu polskiego jako forma dramatyczna', *Ilgi Zjazd Słowiańskich Etnografów i Geografów we Polsce*, section 6. Vilnius
Berghe, P. L. van den 1978 'Race and ethnicity: a sociobiological perspective', *Ethnic and Racial Studies*, 1, 401–11
Bielawski, L. 1967 'Wartość rytmiczna a tempo w zapisach melodii ludowych'. In Z. Lissa (ed.), *Studia Hieronymo Feicht Septuagenario Dedicata*, pp. 64–76. Cracow
    1970 *Rytmika polskich pieśni ludowych*. Cracow
    1973a 'Folklor Muzyczny Pomorza'. In Z. Chechlińska (ed.), *Ogólnopolska Konferencja Muzykologiczna*, pp. 7–16. Gdańsk
    1973b 'Polnische Volksgesänge ohne Strophenbau und primitive Strophenformen'. In D. Stockmann and J. Stęszewski (eds.), *Analyse und Klassifikation von Volksmelodien*. Cracow
    1985a 'Brummtopf und Brummbass in deutscher und polnischer Volkstradition'. In E. Stockmann (ed.), *Studia instrumentorum musicae popularis*, vol. VIII, pp. 108–11. Stockholm
    1985b *Rhythm and Rhythmic Systems in the Baltic Area*. Twenty-eighth Conference of ICTM. Helsinki
Bobrowska, J. 1981 *Pieśni ludowe regionu żywieckiego*. Cracow
Borowski, H. and E. Lukač 1931 *Masurische Volkslieder*. Königsberg
Brailoiu, C. 1948 'Le giusto syllabique: Un système rhythmique propre à la musique populaire romaine', *Polyphonie*, 2
Brückner, A. 1895 *Kazania Średniowieczne*, Rozprawy AU, Wydziatu Filologii, vol. XXIV. Cracow
    1918 *Mitologia Słowiańska*. Cracow
Brzeg 1880 F. Sulimierski, B. Chlebowski and W. Walewski (eds.). In *Słownik Geograficzny Ziem Polskich*, vol. I, pp. 396–7. Warsaw
Bystroń, J. S. 1916 *Zwyczaje żniwiarskie w Polsce*. Cracow
    1920 *Polska Pieśń Ludowa*. Cracow
    1927 *Pieśni Ludowe z Polskiego Śląska*, I, part 1, *Pieśni Balladowe*. Cracow
    1934 *Pieśni Ludowe z Polskiego Śląska*, I, part 2, *Pieśni o zalotach i miłości*. Cracow
    1960 *Dzieje obyczajów w dawnej Polsce, wiek XVI–XVII*. Warsaw
Četkauskaite, G. 1974 *Dzuku Dainos*, records, Nos. 033839–46. Vilnius
Chętnik, A. 1983 *Instrumenty muzyczne na Kurpiach i Mazurach*. Cracow
Chopin, F. 1961 *Mazurkas*, Paderewski's Edition, vol X. Cracow
Chorosiński, J. 1949 *Melodie taneczne Powiśla*. Cracow
Chybiński, A. 1907 'O metodach zbierania i porządkowania melodyi ludowych', *Lud* 13, 171–201
    1924 'Instrumenty muzyczne ludu polskiego na Podhalu'. In *Prace i Materiały Antropologiczno-Archeologiczno-Etnograficzne, Polska Akademia Nauk*, vol. III, pp. 45–142. Cracow
    1926 'O muzyce górali tatrzańskich', *Muzyka*, 11/12, 35–40
    1948 '36 tańców z tabulatury Jana z Lublina'. *Wydawnictwo Dawnej Muzyki Polskiej*, 20. Cracow

1950, 1951 *Od Tatr do Bałtyku*, vol. I, *Spiewnik Krajoznawczy*, Cracow, vol. II, *Lud polski gra.* Cracow

1959 *W czasach Straussa i Tetmajera.* Cracow

Cowell, H. G. 1950 'Music of the Ukraine', *Ethnic Folkways*, L P 443. New York

Czekanowska, A. 1954 *Pieśń Ludowa Warmii i Mazur*, Konferencja Pomorzoznawcza P A N. Gdańsk

1956 *Pieśń Ludowa Opoczyńskiego na tle problematyki etnograficznej*, Studia Muzykologiczne, vol. v, pp. 450–560. Cracow

1958 'Badania nad muzyką ludową w ostatnim dziesię-cioleciu (1945–1955)', *Lud*, 43, 122–56

1961 'Pieśni Biłgorajskie: Przyczynek do interpretacji polskiego południowo-wschodniego pogranicza'. In *Prace i Materiały Etnograficzne*, vol. XVIII, part 2. Wrocław

1964 'Les anciennes mélodies de noce en Pologne', *VI Congrés Intern. des Sciences Anthropologiques et Ethnologiques, Paris (1960)*, vol. II, pp. 97–101

1971 *Etnografia Muzyczna: Metodologia-Metodyka.* Warsaw

1972 *Ludowe Melodie wąskiego zakresu w krajach słowiańskich.* Cracow

1975a 'Muzyka ludowa z perspektywy uwarunkowań i oddziaływań społecznych', *Muzyka*, 3, 38–48

1975b 'The importance of Eastern Religions'. Calendars for rhythm of annual folk songs in Slavic countries'. In *Baessler Archiv. N F*, vol. XXIII, pp. 239–55

1977 'On the theory and definition of melodic type', *Yearbook of International Folk Music Council*, vol. VIII, pp. 108–16. Ottawa

1978a 'The influence of investigated material on the concept of popular and folk music', *Proceedings of 20th Congress Sareza Udružena Folklorista Yugoslavije (1973)*, pp. 553–8. Novi Sad

1978b 'Dotychczasowe wyniki badań nad cechami starosłowiańskimi muzyki ludowej: Próba chronologizacji', *Studia Etnomuzykologiczne*, 21–48. Wrocław

1981a 'Theory of modality in Slavonic musicological literature'. In R. Pečman (ed.) *Hudba Slovanských Národů*, pp. 511–17. Brno

1981b Discussion in Panel 'East European Folk and Art Music', *Report of the Twelfth I M S Congress, Berkeley 1977*, pp. 51–2

1982 'New approaches to the problem of national style and ethnic identity in music'. In *II Milletlerarasi Türk Folklor Kongresi Bildirileri*, pp. 75–81. Ankara

1983 *Główne Kierunki i Orientacje Etnomuzykologii Współczesnej: Refleksje Metodologiczne.* Warsaw

1986 'The application of Polish statistical methods to the classification of folk melodies', *Polish Musicological Studies*, 2, 94–110

In press. 'Signal vs. Aesthetic Functions', *Proceedings of the Symposium 'From Idea to Sound', Nieborów 1985.* Bydgoszcz

Czekanowski, J. 1957 *Wstęp do Historii Słowian.* Poznań

1969 'Slavs', in *Encyclopedia Britannica*, vol. XX

Dąbrowska, G. 1980 *Taniec ludowy na Mazowszu.* Cracow

Dahlig, E. 1982 'Z zagadnień ludowej gry skrzypcowej', M A Thesis, University of Warsaw

1986 'W sprawie suki biłgorajskiej', *Muzyka*, 31, no. 2, 91–3

Dahlig, P. 1983 'Swiadomość muzyczna wykonawców ludowych w Polsce', PhD Thesis, University of Warsaw

1985 'Zródła do dziejów ligawki mazowiecko-podlaskiej', *Muzyka*, 30, no. 2, 89–120

1986 'Das Hackbrett im Nordosten Polens'. In E. Stockmann (ed.), *Studia instrumentatorum musicae popularis*, vol. VIII, pp. 118–21. Stockholm

Danckert, W. 1939a *Grundriss der Volksliedkunde.* Berlin

1939b *Das Europäische Volkslied*, vol. II. Berlin

Davies, N. 1981 *God's playground: history of Poland.* Oxford, 2 vols.

Demo, O. 1969 *O. Hrabalova, Żatevne a dožinkove pisne.* Bratislava

Dileckij, N. 1979 *Ideja Grammatiki Musikijskoj*, Moscow 1679, ed. W. Protopopov. Moscow

Dlugossi, J. 1964 *Annales Seu Chronicae incliti Reghi Poloniae 1366*, ed. in 2 vols. Warsaw

Dłuska, M. 1947 *Prozodia języka polskiego.* Cracow

1954 'Wiersz ludowy – Wiersz meliczny', *Pamiętnik Literacki*, 2, 443–502. Warsaw

Dygacz, A. 1956 *Spiewnik pieśni górniczych.* Stalinogród (Katowice)

Dygacz, A. and J. Ligęza 1954 *Pieśni Ludowe Śląska Opolskiego.* Cracow

Elschekova, A. 1966 'Methods of Classifying of Folk Tunes', *Journal of IFMC*, 18, 56–76
Ewald, Z. 1979 *Pesni belorusskogo Polesja*, Moscow
Feicht, H. 1962 'Polen'. In *MGG Enzyklopädie*, vol. x, pp. 1,385–400. Kassel
    1975 'Polska Pieśń Średniowieczna'. In Z. Lissa (ed.), *Studia nad muzyką polskiego średniowiecza*. Cracow
Feicht, H., E. Ostrowska and J. Woronczak 1962 *Bogurodzica*. Wrocław
Francis, E. K. 1978 *Interethnic relations*. New York
Frasunkiewicz, D. 1985 'Charakter repertuaru pieśni świeckich staro-obrzędowców zamieszkałych na terenie Polski', *Muzyka*, 1, 59–70
Furmanik, S. 1956 *Z zagadnień wersyfikacji polskiej*, Warsaw
Gabałówna, L. 'Zagadnienie bębnów glinianych na Kujawach'. In *Prace i Materiały Muzeum Archeologicznego w Łodzi, Seria Archeologiczna*, 5. Łódź
Gajek, J. 1947 *Polski Atlas Etnograficzny*. Lublin
Galicia 1984. In *Micropedia: Ready References Index to Encyclopedia Britannica*
Galli Anonymi Cronicae et gesta ducum sive principum Polonorum 1952 C. Maleczyński (ed.). Cracow
Gasparini, E. 1974 'Slavic religion'. In *Encyclopedia Britannica*, 15th edition, vol. xxvi, pp. 874–8
Geertz, C. 1973 *Interpretation of Cultures*. New York
Gloger, Z. 1900–3 *Encyklopedia Staropolska*, 4 vols. Warsaw, new edition 1972
Goldberg, J. 1985 *Jewish Privileges in the Polish Commonwealth. Charters of Rights granted to Jewish communities in Poland-Lithuania in the 16th to 18th Centuries*, Jerusalem
Gomółka, M. 1580 *Melodie na psalterz polski*. Cracow
Grajewska-Harasiuk, A. 1974 'Przemiany stylistyczne tradycyjnego folkloru opoczyńskiego w procesie popularyzacji', *Muzyka*, 3, 34–48
Hoerburger, F. 1956 *Die Zwiefachen, Gestaltung und Umgestaltung der Tanzmelodien in nördlichen Alt-Bayern*. Berlin
Ivanov, W. W. and W. N. Toporov 1974 *Issledovanija v oblasti slovjanskich drevnostej*. Moscow
Jairazbhoy, N. A. 1971 *The rags of north Indian music: their structure and evolution*. London
Jakobson, R. 1981 'Poetics and Linguistics'. In *Selected works*, vol. iii. The Hague
Jan z Lublina, *Tabulatura Organowa* (*c.* 1543), facsimile ed. by K. Chomińska (Wilkowska). Cracow 1964
Kamieński, Ł. 1918–19 'Tempo-rubato', *Archiv f. Musikwissenschaft*, 1
Kamiński, W. 1963 'Frühmittelalterliche Musikinstrumente auf polnischem Gebiet'. In *The Book of the first Congress devoted to the Work of Chopin, Warsaw 1960*, pp. 551–8
    1971 *Instrumenty muzyczne na ziemiach polskich*. Cracow
Karłowicz, J. 1888 'Narzędzia muzyczne na wystawie', *Wisła*, 2, 434–5. Warsaw
Kaufman, N. 1959 *Nijakoi obšti čerty meždu narodnata pesen na bulgarskite i iztočnite Slovjan*. Sofia
Keyes, C. F. (ed.) 1981 *Ethnic Change*. Seattle, London
Kierski, E. 1861 'Zwyczaje, zabobony i obrzędy ludu w niektórych okolicach Wielkiego Księstwa Poznańskiego', *Tygodnik Ilustrowany*, 109, 158–61
Kleczyński, J. 1888 *Melodie zakopiańskie i podhalańskie*, Pamiętnik Towarzystwa Tatrzańskiego, vol. xxii. Cracow
Kodaly, Z. 1917 *Oftoku Hangsor a Magyar nepzeneben*, *Zenei Szewmle*. Budapest
Kolberg, O. 1942 *Pieśni Ludu Polskiego*. Poznań
    1857–1907 *Dzieła Wszystkie – Opera Omnia*, 63 vols., new edition 1961–7. Cracow-Poznań
    1857 Vol. i, *Pieśni Ludu Polskiego*. Warsaw. New edition, 1961
    1865 Vol. ii, *Lud, jego zwyczaje, sposób życia, mowa, podania, przysłowia, bbrzędy, gusła, zabawy, pieśni, muzyka i tańce*, Sandomierskie. Warsaw. New edition, 1961
    1867 Vol. iii, *Lud . . . Kujawy*, part 1. Warsaw. New edition, 1961
    1871 Vol. v, *Lud . . . Krakowskie*, part 1. Cracow. New edition, 1962
    1886 Vol. xxv, *Mazowsze – Obraz Etnograficzny*, part 2. Cracow. New edition, 1963
    1887a Vol. xxvi, *Mazowsze – Obraz Etnograficzny*, part 3. Cracow. New edition, 1963
    1887b Vol. xx, *Lud . . . Radomskie*, part 1. Cracow. New edition, 1963
    1888 Vol. xxi, *Lud . . . Radomskie*, part 2. Cracow. New edition, 1963
    1965a Vol. xxxix, *Pomorze*. Cracow
    1965b Vol. xliii, *Śląsk*. Cracow
    1965c Vol. lxiii, *Korespondencja*, vol. i. Cracow-Poznań

1968 Vol. LII, *Białoruś-Polesie*. Cracow

Kołessa, F. 1906, 1907 *Rytmika ukrainskych narodnych pisen, Zapysky Towarystwa im. T. Szewczenka*, vols. 69–74, 75–6. Lvov

1916 'Introduction to "Melodji ukraińskych narodnich piseń z Podila, Pidlasia, Chołmščyny"'. In *Materijały do Ukraińśkoji Etnolohji*, ed. L. Płosajkewyč and J. Sienčyk. Lvov

1923 *Narodni pisni z Piwdennoho Pidkarpatija*, Użhorod

1929 *Narodni pisni z hałyćkoji Łemkivščyny*, Etnohrafičnyj Zbirnyk, vols. XXXIX–XL. Lvov

Końskie 1883. In *Słownik Geograficzny . . .*, vol III

Kopoczek, A. 1984 *Instrumenty muzyczne Beskidu Śląskiego i Żywieckiego*. Bielsko-Biała

Kostrzewski, J. 1949 *Pradzieje Polski*. Poznań

Kotoński, W. 1953 'Uwagi o muzyce ludowej Podhala', *Muzyka*, 5/6, pp. 3–25; 7/8, pp. 43–58; 11/12, pp. 25–45 (1953); and 1/2, pp. 3–15 (1954)

1956 *Góralski i Zbójnicki*. Cracow

Kovalcsik, K. 1985 *Vlas Gypsy Folk Song in Slovakia*. Budapest

1987 'Popular dance music elements in the folk music of gypsies in Hungary'. In *Popular Music*, 6, no. 1, pp. 45–65

Kresanek, J. 1951 *Slovenska ludova piesen so stanoviska hudobneho*. Bratislava

Krzyżaniak, B., A. Pawlak and J. Lisakowski 1975 'Kujawy'. In *Polska pieśń i muzyka ludowa, Źródła i Materiały*, vol. I, parts 1 and 2. Cracow

Kuraszkiewicz, W. 1932 'Przegląd gwar województwa lubelskiego'. In J. Czuma (ed.), *Monografia Statystyczno-Gospodarcza Województwa Lubelskiego*, pp. 215–324. Lublin

Kurpiński, K. 1820 'O pieśniach w ogólności', *Tygodnik Muzyczny*, 6, pp. 21–2; 8, pp. 29–30; 9, pp. 33–4; 10, pp. 40–1. Warsaw

Kuryłowicz, J. 1966 'Accent and quantity as elements of rhythm'. In *Poetics*, vol. II, pp. 163–72. Warsaw

Kvitka, K. 1926 'Pervisni tonorjady'. In *Pervitne Hromadjanstvo ta joho pereżytki na Ukrajini*, vol. III, pp. 29–84. Kiev

1928 'Anhemitonični prymityvy i teoria Sokalskoho', *Etnohrafičnyj Visnyk, Ukraińska Akademia Nauk*, vol. VI, pp. 67–84. Kiev

Kwilecki, A. 1961 'Grupa Łemków na Ziemiach Zachodnich: Szkic Socjologiczny', *Ziemie Zachodnie*, 5, 233–99

Labuda, G. 1969 'Slavs'. In *Encyclopedia Britannica*, vol. XX

Lange, R. 1975 *The Nature of Dance*. London

1978 *Taniec Tradycyjny w Polsce*. London

Leach, E. R. 1976 *Culture and Communication*. Cambridge

Ligęza J. and S. M. Stoiński 1938 *Pieśni Ludowe z Polskiego Śląska*, vol. II, part 1, *Pieśni Balladowe*. Cracow

Ligęza, J. and F. Ryling, 1961 *Pieśni ludowe ze Śląska*, vol. III, part 2. Katowice

Lippman, E. A. 1965 'Stil'. In *MGG Enzyklopädie*, vol. XII, pp. 1,302–30. Kassel

Lisakowski, J. 1971 *Pieśni Kaliskie*. Cracow

1966 'Folk elements in Polish music from the Middle Ages up to the 18th century', *Proceedings of Conference – Musica Antiqua Europae Orientalis 1966*, pp. 354–82. Warsaw

Lissa, Z. 1958 'Über den nationalen Stil von F. Chopin: Kriterien und Wesenbestimmung', *Bericht d. Internationalen Musikwissenschaftlichen Kongress, Wien (1956)*, pp. 355–64. Cologne

Luhmann, N. 1971 *Soziologische Aufklärung*. Opladen

Lvov, A. 1858 *O svobodnom ili nesimetričnom ritme*. St Petersburg

Łęga, X. W. 1961 *Ziemia Chełmińska*. Wrocław

Łoś, J. 1920 *Wiersze polski w ich dziejowym rozwoju*. Warsaw-Lublin-Łódź-Cracow

Łowmiański, H. 1979 *Religia Słowian i jej upadek*. Warsaw

Marcinkowa, J. and K. Łobozińska 1975 *Pieśni, Taniec i Obrzędy Górnego Śląska*. Warsaw

Mersmann, H. 1922–4 'Grundlagen einer musikalischen Volksliedforschung', *Archiv f. Musikwissenschaft*, 4, pp. 141–54, 289–321; 5, pp. 81–135; 6, pp. 127–64

Mickiewicz, A. 1834 *Pan Tadeusz*, first edn Paris

Mierczyński, S. 1930 *Muzyka Podhala*. Lvov-Warsaw, reprinted many times, e.g., Cracow 1949, 1973

1935 *Pieśni Podhala na 2 i 3 różne głosy*. Warsaw

Moszyński, K. 1968 *Kultura Ludowa Słowian*, 2 vols. Cracow 1929, 1934, 1939; reprinted Warsaw 1968

1957 'Pierwotny zasiąg języka prasłowiańskiego', *Prace Językoznawcze PAN*, 16. Wrocław

Możejko, Z. 1971 *Pesennaja Kultura belorusskogo Polesja*. Mińsk

1985 *Kalendarno-pesennaja kultura Belorussiji*. Mińsk

Müller-Blattau, J. and A. Jeziorowski 1934 *Masurische Volkslieder*. Berlin

Neumark, G. 1652 *Poetisch und Musikalish Lustwäldlein*, Hamburg

Neyman, C. 1883 'Kupletnyje formy narodnoj jużno-russkoj pesni', *Kievskaja Starina*, 6. Kiev

Noll, W. 1986 'Peasant music ensembles in Poland: A culture history', PhD Thesis, University of Washington, Seattle

Olędzki, S. 1978 *Polskie instrumenty ludowe*. Cracow

Ottich, M. 1958 'Chopins Klavierornamentik', *Annales Chopin*, vol. III, pp. 8–62

Pascall, R. J. 1980 'Style'. In S. Sadie (ed.), *New Grove Dictionary of Music and Musicians*, vol. XVIII, pp. 316–20. London

Perz, M. 1981 *Mikołaj Gomółka*, 2nd edition, 2 vols. Cracow

Pietruszyńska-(Sobieska), J. 1936 *Dudy Wielkopolskie*. Poznań. Reprinted in *Muzyka ludowa i jej problemy*, ed. L. Bielawski, Cracow 1973

Pikulik, J. 1973 'Stan badań nad muzyką religijną w kulturze polskiej'. In *Monodia liturgiczna w średniowiecznej Polsce*. Warsaw

Pokshishevsky, V. V. 1975 'On the Soviet concept of economic regionalization: a review of the geographical research in the USSR on the problems of economic regionalization, *Progress in Geography*, 7. London

Popova, T. 1962, 1964 *Russkoe narodnoe muzykalnoe tvorčestvo*, 2 vols. Moscow

Potkański, K. 1922, 1924 *Pisma Pośmiertne*, 2 vols. Cracow

Praetorius, M. 1619 *Syntagma Musicum (De Organographia)*. Wolfenbüttel

Przerembski, Z. 1979 'Preferencje muzyczne górali podhalańskich', MA Thesis, University of Warsaw

Pudło, K. 1987 *Lemkowie, Proces wrastania w środowisko Dolnego Śląska 1947–1985*. Wrocław

1984/5 'O ludności niemieckiej bez mitów 1945–1985' *Kultura Dolnośląska*, 1–4, 39–40

Reinhard, K. 1958 'On the problem of pre-pentatonic scales: particularly, on the third-second nucleus', *Journal of IFMC*, 10, 15–18

Riemann, H. 1916 *Folkloristische Tonalitätsstudien*. Leipzig

Rogowska, E. 1974 'Ballada ludowa na Warmii i Mazurach', MA Thesis, University of Warsaw

Ross, H. 1974 'Poland'. In *Encyclopedia Britannica*, 15th edition, vol. XIV, pp. 634–8

Rozdolskij, J. and S. Ljudkewyč 1906 'Hałyćko – ruśki narodnyje melodji', *Etnohraficznyj Zbirnyk*, 21. Lvov

Rudneva, A. 1957 *Narodni Pesni Kurskoj Oblasti*. Moscow

Sankiewicz-Frąckowska, M. 1978 'Polskie Pieśni żołnierskie z okresu i wojny światowej', *Studia Etnomuzykologiczne*, pp. 49–142. Wrocław

Schmitt, K. 1950 *Der Nomos der Erde*. Cologne

Seweryn, T. 1928 'Z żywym kurkiem po dyngusie', *Materiały Komisji Etnograficznej PAN*, 6. Cracow

Shaper, E. 1969 'The concept of style: the sociologist's key to art?', *British Journal of Aesthetics*, 9, 246–325

Shapiro, M. A. 1956 'Style'. In A. L. Kroeber (ed.), *Anthropology Today*, 2nd edition, pp. 287–312. Chicago

Sikorska (Jankowska), K. 1986 'Maniery wykonawcze w pieśni kurpiowskiej', MA Thesis, University of Warsaw

Skierkowski, X. W. 1929, 1934 *Puszcza Kurpiowska w Pieśni*, 2 vols. Płock

Slaviunas, Z. 1972 *Sutartines*. Leningrad

Sobiescy, J. and M. 1954 *Szlákiem kozła Lubuskiego*. Cracow

1963 'Das Tempo Rubato bei Chopin und in polnischer Volksmusik'. In *The Book of the First International Congress devoted to the Work of F. Chopin, Warsaw 1960*, pp. 271–94

1973 *Pieśń ludowa i jej problemy*, ed. L. Bielawski. Cracow

Sobieska, J. 1976 'Grajcie dudy, grajcie basy', *Muza SX 1125, 1126*

Sobieska, J. and Z. Sobierajski 1972 *Ze studiów nad folklorem muzycznym Wielkopolski*. Cracow

Sobieski, M. 1955 'Oblicze tonalne polskiej muzyki ludowej', *Studia Muzykologiczne*, 1, 308–32. Cracow

Sobieski, M. and M. Sobolewska, 1955 *Pieśni ludowe Warmii i Mazur*. Cracow

Sobolevskij, A. 1888 *Pamiatnik drevne-russkoj literatury posjaščennye Vladimiru sv. Čtenija v letopisnom obščestve Nestora letopisca*, folio 2, line 2. Kiev

Sokalskij, P. 1888 *Russkaja narodnaja muzyka (velikorusskaja i małorusskaja) w jeji melodičeskom i ritmičeskom strojeniji*. Charkov

Stęszewscy, Z. and J. 1963 'Zur Genese und Chronologie des Mazurka-Rhythmus in Polen'. In *The Book of the First International Congress devoted to the work of F. Chopin, Warsaw 1960*, pp. 624–7

Stęszewska, Z. 1962, 1966 *Tańce Polskie Tabulatur Lutniowych*, 2 vols. Cracow
   1977 'Polonika w źródłach muzycznych pochodzenia niemieckiego i w twórczości kompozytorów niemieckich od XVI do początku XVIII w.', *Muzyka*, 3, 83–9
   1979 'Z zagadnień kształtowania się stylu narodowego w muzyce polskiej XVI do XVIII w.', *Muzyka*, 4, 77–82

Stęszewski, J. 1955a *Piosenki z Lubelskiego*. Cracow
   1955b *Piosenki z Kurpiów*. Cracow
   1965a 'Chmiel, Szkic problematyki etnomuzycznej wątku', *Muzyka*, 3, 3–33
   1965b 'Problematyka historyczn a pieśni kurpiowskich', PhD Thesis, Institute of Art of Polish Academy of Science, Warsaw
   1972 'Sachen, Bewusstsein und Benennungen in ethnomusikalischen Untersuchungen. Am Beispiel der polnischen Folklore', *Jahrbuch f. Volksliedforschung*, 17, 131–70. Berlin
   1980 'Poland (Folk Music)'. In S. Sadie (ed.), *New Grove Dictionary of Music and Musicians*, vol. XV, pp. 29–39
   1984 'Szeptany Przedtakt (Flüster Auftakt) w polskiej musyce ludowej na tle problematyki porównawczej'. In I. Poniatowka (ed.), *Dzieło muzyczne: téoria, historia, interpretacja, dedicated to J. M. Chominski*, pp. 95–107, Cracow

Stoïn, U. 1931 *Narodni pesni ot sredna severna Byłgarija*. Sofia

Stoiński, S. 1964 *Pieśni żywieckie*. Cracow

Strassoldo, R. In press. 'Boundaries in sociological theory: a reassessment'. In A. Kukliński and J. Lambooy (eds.), *Societies, Regions, Boundaries*. Karlsruhe

Strumiłło, T. 1954 *Szkice z polskiego życia muzycznego XIX wieku*. Cracow
   1956 *Źródła i początki romantyzmu w Polsce*. Cracow

Sušil, F. 1860 *Moravske narodne pisne*. Prague

Svitova, K. 1966 *Narodnyje pesni brjanskoj oblasti*. Moscow

Sydow, B. 1955 *Korespondeńcja Chopina*, 2 vols. Cracow

Szachowski, T. 1974 'Próba pomiaru maniery tempo-rubato', *Muzyka*, 3, 63–75

Šuchevyč, U. 1899–1904 *Huculščyna*, vols. 1–4. In *Materijały do ukraińśko-ruśkoï etnolohiji*, vols. 2, 4, 5, 7/8. Lvov

Szweykowski, Z. 1966 'Some Problems of Baroque Music in Poland'. In *Acta Scientifica Congressus: Musica Antiqua Europae Orientalis*, pp. 294–310. Warsaw
   1977 'Concertato style in Polish vocal-instrumental music of the 17th century', *Polish Musicological Studies*, 1, 155–66. Cracow
   1964 (ed.) *Muzyka w dawnym Krakowie*. Cracow

Szymanowski, K. 1982 *Korespondencja*, vol. 1. Cracow
   1984 *Pisma muzyczne*. Cracow

Świeży, J. 1952 'Strój Krzczonowski'. In *Atlas Polskich Strojów Ludowych*, vol. VII. Lublin

Thietmar's Chronicle 1953 ed. Z. Jedlicki. Poznań

Virdung, S. 1511 'Musica getuscht und ausgezogen'. In *Publikation älterer praktischer und theoretischer Musikwerke*, vol. I. Basle

Volhynia in Micropedia: Ready References Index to Encyclopedia Britannica 1984, p. 486

Watkins, C. 1961 'Indo-European origins of a celtic metre'. In *Poetics*, pp. 99–117. Warsaw

White, J. R. 1964–6 (ed.) *The Tablature of Johannes of Lublin*, vol. VI, parts 1–3, *Corpus of Early Keyboard Music*. Rome
   1963 'The tablature of Johannes of Lublin', *Musica Disciplina*, 17. Rome

Wilden, A. 1972 *System and Structure*. London

Windakiewiczowa, H. 1897 'Rytmika ludowa muzyki polskiej', *Wisła*, 11
   1913 'Studya nad wierszem i zwrotką w poezyi polskiej ludowej'. *Rozprawy Akademii Umiejętności Wydział Filologiczny*, 52, 175–269. Cracow

1926 'Wzory polskiej muzyki ludowej w mazurkach Chopina', *Rozprawy Wydziału Filologicznego, Polska Akademia Umiejętności*, series 3, vol. 16, 3–50. Cracow

1930 'Ze Studiów nad formą pieśni ludowej (Okres kolisty)'. In *Księga Pamiątkowa ku czci Profesora A. Chybińskiego*, pp. 115–24. Cracow

1933 'Pentatonika w muzyce polskiej ludowej', *Kwartalnik Muzyczny*, 17/18, 1–27. Warsaw

Wiora, W. 1949/1951 'Alpenmusik'. In *Musik in Geschichte und Gegenwart*, vol. 1, pp. 359–70

1951 'Der tonale Logos', *Musikforschung*, 4, 1–153: 154–86

1952 *Europäischer Volksgesang: Gemeinsame Formen in charakteristischen Abwandlungen*. Cologne

1957 'Älter als die Pentatonik'. In *Studia Memoriae Belá Bartók Sacra*. Budapest

Wójcicki, K. 1836 *Pieśni ludu Białochrobatów, Mazurów i Rusi znad Bugu*. Warsaw

Wójcik-Keuprulian, B. 1930 'O trioli w mazurkach Chopina'. In *Księga Pamiątkowa ku czci Adolfa Chybińskiego*, pp. 3–8. Lvov

Woronczak, J., E. Ostrowska and H. Feicht 1962 *Bogurodzica*. Wrocław

Wróbel, A. 1965 *Projęcie regionu ekonomicznego a teoria geografii*. Warsaw

Wyczański, A. 1976 *Społeczeństwo staropolskie*. Warsaw

Żadrożyńska, A. 1983 *Homo Faber – Homo Ludens*. Warsaw

Zaleski (z Oleska), W. 1833 *Pieśni polskie i ruskie ludu galicyjskiego, z Muzyką Karola Lipińskiego*. Lvov

Zemcovskij, I. 1975 *Melodika Kalendarnych pesen*. Leningrad

Zientara, B. 1985 *Świt narodów europejskich*. Warsaw

Żerańska-Kominek, S. 1986 *Symbolika struktur modalnych*. Warsaw

Index

LaVergne, TN USA
22 July 2010
190401LV00003B/6/A